The New York Times GUIDE TO BUSINESS AND FINANCE

The New York Times

GUIDE TO BUSINESS AND FINANCE

THE AMERICAN ECONOMY AND HOW IT WORKS

By ALBERT L. KRAUS

HARPER & ROW, PUBLISHERS

NEW YORK, EVANSTON, SAN FRANCISCO, LONDON

1817

To Pat

STANDARD BOOK NUMBER: 06-012462-8

LIBRARY OF CONGRESS CATALOG CARD NUMBER: 70-138745

Contents

Preface

One of the privileges of writing for a daily newspaper is the possibility of amendment. Events may be permitted to unfold in their own way and at their own pace; if the last word isn't immediately forthcoming, there is always tomorrow. There is no need to pretend omniscience or to resort to that contrivance of publications with longer lead times, the oracular imperative: "Do this," "Check Washington for that," "Watch for these coming developments." There is even room for genuine surprise as when a President who has resisted most kinds of direct governmental economic coercion reverses abruptly to embrace wage and price controls.

When a newspaperman turns to writing a book, he finds his privilege of amendment vanished. Like an astronaut committing himself to the forces of moon and earth gravity, he must chart a course that, hopefully, will put him where he wants to be when he gets there. Under ordinary circumstances, this may present no special problem, but in writing now about the structure of American business and finance— their institutions and their organization—it does. Seldom has change been greater or more pervasive. Industry is finding its traditional ways of doing things challenged, its whole reason for being under fire. Washington is in the midst of a tremendous new debate between those who would give the government control over private decision making and those who would resist growing governmental control. The securities markets are experiencing a major change in the nature of their demand compounded by technological innovation greater than any seen in 100 years. And, it is generally agreed, the international monetary order that emerged from World War II is now dead and its successor has not yet been born.

This book was begun three years ago when things were more comfortable and the future seemed more certain. If what was to come had been known, the book might never have been started. The effort was assigned to me by Thomas E. Mullaney, financial and business editor of the *New York Times,* who responded to a suggestion by Ivan Veit, executive vice president. Mr. Veit wanted a volume to explain the business scene to readers with no previous acquaintance with it. The writing was done chiefly on vacations, weekends and hours off, but it could not have been accomplished without Mr. Mullaney's generous assistance in helping me fit the book into my working schedule and in relieving me of certain chores. What was included and what was left out was largely my own decision, but I was aided immeasurably by Harvey Segal, my principal editor at Harper & Row, whose help in structuring the book was also invaluable. I am indebted additionally to Nahum Waxman, who has also served as my editor at Harper & Row, and whose encouragement and suggestions were greatly appreciated. My sources, some of whom extended themselves greatly with no promise of reward other than gratitude, are too numerous to be catalogued separately. My critics, whom I imposed upon to read parts of the uncompleted manuscript, are several. I would like to acknowledge particularly the constructive suggestions of John J. Abele, my associate in producing the *Times* Sunday financial section, and of Daniel Rosen of the Federal Reserve Bank of New York. Mrs. Barbara Bennett, a *Times* news researcher, helped greatly in tracking down statistical information. Edward Meehan of the *Times* art department helped with the charts.

ALBERT L. KRAUS

Cranford, N.J.
September 1971

1. Business Is Small: Garment Making

Business is big and business is small, but many more businesses are small than big. At last count there were almost 12 million businesses in the United States, including 1.5 million corporations, almost 1 million partnerships, and 9 million proprietorships of unincorporated businesses.

A tally by the Census Bureau showed that there were more than 3.5 million business enterprises—manufacturing, mining, trade, and service establishments—with their own places of business. Of these, concerns employing fewer than fifty persons accounted for almost 95 percent of the total, while those employing five hundred or more accounted for only 0.3 percent. In terms of sales and receipts, three dollars out of every five of the total were chalked up by companies with fewer than five hundred employees, and half of this by those with fewer than twenty. Contrary to some notions, then, small business in the United States is far from dead.

The range of small business is wide, including, among others, farmers, builders, store owners, truckers, lawyers, doctors, insurance agents, and real estate brokers. It is also much more important at the retail level than at the wholesale or manufacturing levels. Of the 3 million enterprises enumerated by the Bureau of the Census, well over half were retail stores and five of six were either retailers or service establishments—barber and beauty shops, automobile repair shops, service stations and garages, hotels and motels, laundries and dry cleaning establishments, and motion picture theaters. More than 97 percent of all such enterprises employed fewer than twenty employees and only an insignificant percentage more than five hundred. It is interesting nonetheless that retailers with more than five hundred employees accounted for twenty-five cents of every dollar of retail sales.

At the wholesale level the companies were found to be somewhat bigger. Wholesalers with fewer than twenty employees accounted for only 89 percent of all wholesalers, while those with twenty to five hundred employees accounted for more than 10 percent and those with more than five hundred less than 0.1 percent. The largest wholesalers, however, enjoyed a smaller share of total sales than the biggest retailers. Wholesalers with more than five hundred employees accounted for only 6.8 cents of every dollar of wholesale sales.

In manufacturing, small business has given the greatest ground. At this level companies with fewer than twenty employees accounted for only 72 percent of all enterprises; those with twenty to five hundred employees, 26 percent; and those with more than five hundred employees, 1.2 percent. While these figures may suggest that even in manufacturing small business remains supreme, factory sales are dominated by the big companies. Of total factory sales, seventy-one cents of every dollar is enjoyed by companies with five hundred or more workers, including fifty-one cents by those with five thousand or more.

In many manufacturing industries—aluminum, automobiles, rubber, steel, chemicals, processed foods, industrial textiles, and others—the biggest concerns enjoy half the industry's sales or considerably more. The Bureau of the Census regularly updates the share of the market accounted for by the four biggest concerns in each of about 420 industries. Here is a sampling of the findings: locomotives, 97 percent; crude coal-tar chemicals, 95; electric lamps, 91; chewing gum, 86; linoleum, 89; steam turbines, 88; batteries, 85; sewing machines, 81; gypsum, 80; processed cereal, 88; and television tubes, 84. In the primary aluminum industry, the first eight companies enjoyed 100 percent of the market.

These findings are less surprising perhaps than the fact that concentration in manufacturing has changed little since World War II and may have declined since 1900. The Council of Economic Advisers reported that the average share of the market for the four largest concerns was between 41 and 42 percent in both 1947 and 1966. Rough estimates, it added, indicated that on the average concentration in manufacturing industries had probably not increased and may even have decreased since the turn of the century. This is in contrast to overall concentration—the percentage of total industrial activity accounted for by the 100 or 200 largest concerns—which has risen.

Even more interesting is the fact that several industries have remained little touched by concentration. Printing and publishing is one, home building another, light metalworking a third. Perhaps no industry, however, is more lacking in concentration than the manufacture of apparel, particularly women's wear. In only four of twenty-four apparel categories listed by the Bureau of the Census did the four largest concerns enjoy 30 percent of the market, and in only eight others did the first four enjoy 20 percent of the market.

For a manufacturing industry in which small business still dominates, let us take a closer look at the garment industry.

Day comes early to the New York garment district. Before the sun pushes up through the haze beyond Fifth Avenue, the streets are alive with trucks jostling for position in front of the fourteen-, sixteen-, and twenty-story Mayan temples, some drivers cursing, others taking their turn with philosophic forbearance. Soon, on the sidewalks, vehicles disgorge their contents, bolts of suit material or print goods, tightly bound bundles of cuttings, racks of finished coats and dresses. Barrows, dollies, hand trucks, and wheeled racks clutter the way. At a street corner, traffic pauses while a mountain of goods propelled by a man-ant bumps down one curb and up another. Or a pair of dress racks, hiding the man pushing them, seem to propel themselves swiftly through the intersection.

The earliest risers are all male—muscular blacks in ancient army uniforms or proud ethnic garb, wiry, open-shirted Puerto Ricans, commanding Europeans. Soon, however, the subways begin erupting thousands of women, some girls barely out of school, others mothers with school-age children of their own, still others women whose child-rearing days are behind them. These are the industry's operators, the women who stitch the seams, attach the trim, and put on the buttons. Once mainly Jewish and Italian, today they are largely black and Puerto Rican. Soon afterward come the aristocracy of the industry, the cutters, the pattern makers, the designers, and the proprietors.

A boss who isn't on the job by 8:30 A.M. or 9 is a rarity, and little wonder. Within roughly a square mile, the area bounded by Macy's and Pennsylvania Station, Times Square, Fifth and Ninth Avenues, toil twelve thousand others very much like himself, two out of five of all the garment industry proprietors in the United States. These are manufacturers, jobbers, and contractors employing a third of a million workers, more than a quarter of all factory workers in New York City. They make men's and boys' suits and coats, shirts and nightwear, underwear and neckwear, trousers and work clothing; women's and children's blouses and dresses and suits, coats and skirts, outerwear and underwear; corsets, gloves, rainwear, leather and sheeplined clothing, belts, Schiffli machine embroideries, knitwear, fabricated rubber products, and artificial flowers.

It is a big market, about $16 billion in 1969, but it is small business. In early 1969 the 20,806 apparel establishments in the United States employed 1,490,676 people, an average of 71.6 an establishment. In the East South Central states the average was 241, in the Middle Atlantic, 46.

Except for knit underwear and work clothing, more than half the concerns in every branch of the industry employ fewer than 50 people. In women's apparel and accessories, more than three-fourths of the concerns employ fewer than 50 people.

Most companies are single-shop operations. In 1967, 277 work clothing manufacturers operated 462 plants, or roughly 1.7 plants a company. For the great bulk of the industry, however, the ratio was lower. In many branches, such as neckwear, robes and dressing gowns, belts, knit outerwear, and women's suits, coats, and skirts, it was virtually one plant to a company.

It is also competitive business, among the most competitive in the nation. Some men get rich making garments, the majority manage to earn a living, and not a few fall by the way. It is estimated that 18 percent of all apparel establishments close their doors each year, because either they have failed, their proprietors have retired, or they have moved to another city.

If it is easy to fail at garment making, it is also easy to get into the business and to succeed. The industry is one of the few remaining areas in manufacturing where a small concern can match its efforts readily with larger competitors, for the technology is simple, little initial capital is required, and most of the machines are little more than mechanized tools. Furthermore, the basic piece of equipment, the sewing machine, hasn't changed in design for much of this century, and operations still remain paced to the speed of the operator, not to the capacity of the machine. Equipment may be purchased on the installment plan, or rented. Men can get started in the business as contractors, obtaining fabric, yarn, buttons, and other materials from the jobbers, who in turn sell what the contractors produce. This avoids the need for tying up large sums in inventory.

Worker training is simple and inexpensive, most of it able to be done on the job, and highly complicated operations are broken down into their simplest elements. A sewing machine operator, for instance, may do no more than stitch a single, short-run seam. After she learns the basic process of controlling the machine—and this takes little time—the rest of her training involves working up to maximum operating speed.

Because the market is big and most companies are small, garment making is a highly specialized business. A man who makes ladies' coats is not likely to make blouses or skirts, just as one who makes men's suits doesn't make shirts or ties. A dress manufacturer won't even make all sizes and price ranges. His specialty may be lower-priced housedresses, sold by the dozen at wholesale, or better-quality half sizes, or copies of high-fashion garments made to sell at retail from $75 to $150.

Garment making wasn't always organized this way. The development and growth of the ready-to-wear clothing industry, taking housewives out of hoover aprons and their husbands out of tailor shops, parallels the rise of the modern department store. The idea that a woman of whatever income or taste might satisfy all of her needs under one roof—the upper floors for the better-heeled, the basement for the budget-minded—led inevitably to buyers who handled a limited line of merchandise. Thus, if a manufacturer wanted to shift from suits to shirts, he would find it necessary to win the confidence of a whole new network of buyers.

Changes in retailing are bringing changes in garment making. Department stores have branched out from single center-city locations to suburban shopping centers, discounters now handle a large part of the volume once accounted for by family clothing stores, and higher incomes and greater fashion consciousness have helped specialty shops proliferate.

Because retailing units are larger, manufacturers have been obliged to increase their ability to assure steady quality, price, and delivery throughout a selling season. The men's suit buyer for a Detroit department store, for instance, wants to be certain that he will have a sufficient range of styles, sizes, and colors at each of four suburban stores as well as at the big downtown unit. At the same time the greater use of name brands, advertising, and franchising has sped the sale of coordinated fashions. Whereas once a sportswear shop might have carried the products of a dozen or more manufacturers, its sales efforts are more likely to be concentrated today on the sweaters, skirts, blouses, and accessories of a single branded and highly advertised line.

These trends, plus Wall Street's fascination with the industry, have led to the creation and growth of large, publicly owned companies, often combining retailing and manufacturing. Although most companies are still very small—almost half of all manufacturers and jobbers have an annual sales volume of less than $1 million—in some sectors of the industry the fifty largest firms now account for one-fifth to four-fifths of all shipments. In 1971 there were one hundred publicly owned companies producing $4 billion worth of women's and children's garments a year. Of these, forty-eight companies concentrated primarily on women's and children's wear, fourteen made other garments but nothing else, and thirty-eight made a host of other products.

Bigger companies command more and cheaper money; they can, for instance, buy fabric for an entire season. They command more sophisticated managers; the computer has begun to creep into some operations. They command advertising and promotion; the names of apparel concerns are no longer unheard on television or unseen in national magazines.

For all this, bigger companies retain many of the characteristics of small business. Production units, typically, are small, and outside contracting, if anything, has become more rather than less important. Styling and selling remain highly personal. Men who have built successful businesses acquired by the new giants don't retire from the field. Instead they remain as the heads of divisions or independent operating units—and vocal shareholders—within the larger amalgamations, former sovereigns who have become dukes and earls within a larger kingdom.

Let us sum up for a moment the traits that have made the garment industry typical—perhaps the most typical—of industries in which small businesses predominate: simple technology, modest capital and skill requirements, ease of entry, and—above all—competition, intense competition. One result of this competition has been the tendency of the industry to suffer from chronic overcapacity. For every entrepreneur ready to call it quits, there is at least one other waiting in the wings, ready to come on stage. At the same time these traits make it possible for the industry to increase its output virtually overnight in response to a sudden surge in demand, or to turn on a dime, abandoning one fashion trend and picking up another.

This, indeed, is the heart of the matter, the life and breath of success. A manufacturer may know how to hire, how to organize production, how to design, and how to sell. But if he lacks the ability to determine what customers, particularly women customers, will want six months or more from now, he may be out of business before the end of a single selling season. Commitments have to be made, and buying too little of a fabric may be just as disastrous as buying too much. Perhaps the most frustrating experience in the industry is to be swamped with reorders for a number that can't be delivered.

How does a manufacturer know what women will buy? If he is big enough or important enough, he will send his designer to Paris. If he is not, he will study the windows at Henri Bendel's and Saks Fifth Avenue. He will follow the women's pages and the department store ads in the newspapers and the trade press. He will watch what women are wearing. He will make a ritual of "schmoozing," or meeting his competitors on the street after lunch to talk and to listen. Some of the effort may involve study and research, but much of it is intuitive. Ask a successful entrepreneur the single factor that contributed most to his judgment and he won't be able to answer. There are so many.

The garment maker operates in a market where the price adjusts so quickly and easily to changes in supply and demand that it seems to be set by an impersonal mechanism. There are so many sellers of a nearly identical product that no single manufacturer contributes a significant portion of the total supply. If any one seller should attempt to raise the price of his output by withholding merchandise from the market, he would quickly discover that he was merely giving up business to his competitors. Therefore, as far as any one garment maker is concerned, the price is set by the market, and there is nothing he can do but accept it. For this reason, such a broad, open, competitive market is sometimes described as a "price-taker's market."

Of course, the garment maker could sell his product at a price lower than the market price, but this would be idiotic, since it would produce a profit smaller than that possible. In a broad, open, competitive market, the market price is the highest price a manufacturer can get for selling any of his product. It is also the price at which he can sell more. He is not obliged to cut his price to increase his volume.

In such a market a successful entrepreneur seldom enjoys a profit bonanza very long. As the news of his success gets around, newcomers are enticed to enter the business as competitors, pushing down the selling price. At the same time efforts are made to woo away key personnel and bid up the price of materials and equipment, raising costs. In the process men, materials, machinery, and management are directed from less profitable activities—those for which consumer demand is less urgent— toward the most pressing requirements of the day. Automatically.

Adam Smith, the great eighteenth-century teacher, moral philosopher, and first of the modern economists, described this quest of profit as an "invisible hand," combining freedom for the individual with order for society. From his chair at the University of Glasgow, he looked out over England and Scotland at the beginning of the Industrial Revolution and saw a land in which the self-interest of the many, not the benevolence of the few, ruled for the good of all.

Adam Smith was more impressed by the advantages of the budding factory system—the division of labor and specialization of tasks that made possible tremendous gains in output per man-hour—than by some of the system's less savory aspects—its tendency toward concentration, its denigration of the workman, its multiplication of the poor. The "invisible hand," it developed, was more an ideal than a fact.

Adam Smith's great work, *The Wealth of Nations,* was published in 1776, the same year that Thomas Jefferson gave pen to the Declaration of Independence. In the two centuries since, the world has changed greatly. If politically it would scarcely be recognizable to Jefferson and his colleagues, it would be because it has changed so much economically from the landscape of Adam Smith. Big, few-concern industries have taken over from industries made up of many small concerns, and giant combinations of workers have offset the diminished bargaining power of the individual. Above both big business and big labor, big government has established itself as the supreme referee, the guardian of the public interest, however variously interpreted. And it has also established itself as the country's biggest customer and its biggest employer.

Anachronistic though they may seem, in the United States the "laws" of the market have never been abandoned. They have been altered, amended, abused, and submerged, given lip service rather than fidelity, and observed in the breach as much as in fact, much as have the Jeffersonian notions of democracy. Businessmen themselves are among the worst offenders. The eagerness of businessmen in 1971 to embrace government control of wages and prices is an example. Nevertheless, the market ideal has persisted. In contrast to the socialist countries, its improvement and perfection, not its elimination, have been the goal.

2. Business Is Big: Autos

The United States, it is often said, is the land of big business. Exactly how big, however, isn't always appreciated.

In 1970, 170 corporations had sales or revenues of $1 billion or more; 31, $3 billion or more; and 13, $5 billion or more. The biggest, General Motors, had sales of $18.8 billion, but this was down sharply because of a strike. In 1969 its sales totaled $24.3 billion, approximately equal to the gross national product of the Netherlands and more than the total output of all but the seventeen largest industrial nations. The next three —American Telephone and Telegraph, Standard Oil (New Jersey), and Ford—each had revenues of $15 to $17 billion, an amount that together equaled the gross income of all farmers in the United States.

Of the more than $1.3 trillion worth of business sales in 1970—retail and wholesale as well as manufacturing—the top five hundred corporations accounted for 36 percent, the top hundred for 23 percent, and the top twenty-five for 14 percent.

Bigness is a synonym largely for manufacturing. All but six of the twenty-five biggest corporations in terms of sales were manufacturers. Of these six exceptions, one was the telephone company and the others were merchandisers. Interestingly, only nine financial corporations had revenues of more than $1 billion. The biggest, the Aetna Life and Casualty Company, ranked twenty-second with $3.7 billion. First National City Corporation, seventy-sixth with $1.7 billion, and Bank-America Corporation, ninety-fourth with $1.5 billion, were the only banks. The others were insurance and finance companies.

In terms of profits, in 1970, fifty-eight corporations reported net profits after taxes of $100 million or more, twenty of $200 million or more, and eleven of $400 million or more. The biggest profit-maker, American

Telephone, earned almost $2.2 billion; the next, Standard Oil (New Jersey), $1.3 billion; and the third, International Business Machines, $1 billion. Because of its strike, General Motors fell from its customary second place in profits to fifth. The ten largest profit-makers accounted for almost one dollar in five of the almost $44 billion of profits after taxes earned by all corporations in 1970, the twenty-five biggest for more than one dollar in four.

Big sales do not necessarily mean big profits. IBM, ranking eighth in sales in 1970, was third in profits, and Eastman Kodak, which ranked thirty-fifth in sales, was eleventh in profits. Except for Sears, fifth in sales and tenth in profits, none of the merchandisers among the top twenty-five corporations in sales was among the top twenty-five in profits.

Big business is a major buyer from and seller to small business—its suppliers and dealers. It is also an important employer, the five hundred largest industrial corporations accounting for 14.6 million of the 19.4 million industrial workers in 1970 or one in five of all nonfarm workers. This share, however, is declining as industry invests heavily in plant and equipment to increase productivity and as employment shifts from manufacturing to health care, education, sales, and other service occupations.

No one is quite sure why big business has grown as it has. Some reasons are obvious: the spread of markets geographically—meaning that such familiar products as bread, beer, and coffee, once made and sold locally, are now marketed nationwide—and the technological economies that result from large-scale operations—for example, a new integrated steel mill, it is said, would cost at least $1 billion.

These, however, are not wholly satisfactory explanations. Companies haven't stopped when they have grown large enough to serve a nationwide market or to realize the savings from large-scale operations, but have grown even bigger. General Motors is not merely the world's largest automobile company, it is five of the world's largest automobile companies. In addition, it is a major appliance maker, the country's biggest builder of railroad locomotives, and its biggest producer of trucks and buses. The Chevrolet Division, by itself, would rank as the nation's third largest automobile producer, ahead of Chrysler and not far behind Ford and General Motors without Chevrolet.

Much the same thing can be said about the other giants. American Telephone is not merely the nation's biggest communications company; by way of its subsidiary, Western Electric, it is also a principal defense electronics manufacturer. Philco bears a similar relation to Ford, their chemical subsidiaries to the major oil companies. Sears, Roebuck, by way of Allstate, ranks as a financial as well as a retail giant.

Why has big business grown so big? Is it because big business can command capital more readily and at lower cost than smaller business?

Is it because it can buy management? Is it because the heads of big businesses command bigger salaries and fly around in more impressive executive jets than the heads of smaller businesses? Is it simply that the heads of big businesses, like the kings of old, gain pride and pleasure in ruling over domains bigger than those of their neighbors? Or has business merely grown, Topsy-like, with no one, least of all management, showing any interest in halting its growth?

Another rationale has been advanced for the growth of big business. According to this theory, big business refuses to accept the verdict of a broad, open, and competitive market. Striving continuously to be the creator, not the creature, of its fate, it leaves as little as possible to chance but seeks to create the conditions that will assure its longevity. It plans, and, since assurance that its plans will not be frustrated increases with size, it seeks size.

The automobile industry should provide an appropriate test of this hypothesis, since, of all big business, the automobile industry is the biggest.

Let's look in at an East Coast assembly plant.

The long assembly line moves steadily on. Near the end, a blue-collared expert, his sleeves carefully rolled up, applies a deft touch with a crowbar to an obstinate hood. Another maneuvers a reluctant door handle. Then the moment arrives. An unspectacular little man, wearing glasses and a cap like a locomotive engineer, sidles behind the wheel of the completed automobile and turns the key. There is a momentary grinding of the starter, a puff of blue smoke, and finally the purring of the engine. A new car has been born.

The scene is one repeated once each minute, sometimes more often, each working day in several dozen assembly lines in automobile plants across the country. And yet, it never ceases to thrill. Only hours before, this had been a lifeless collection of parts, a heap of metal, glass, plastic, and fabric. Now it is being driven off the assembly line under its own power.

Gestation actually starts a day and a half before in a remote corner of the same plant. A tall, muscular black, moving with athletic economy of motion, slides four pieces of stamped sheet metal into a large press. The device automatically aligns the pieces, clamps them tightly together, and then, amid buzzing and sparks, spot-welds them at a hundred points into a single floor-pan. Other sheet-metal parts are hand-clamped together in a form called a "body-buck," and the process of framing, finishing, painting, and trimming is under way.

Actually, the automobile begins not at one place but at several. In another corner of the plant a worker uses a pneumatic hoist to position a frame—upside down at the start—at the beginning of a separate chassis line where springs, wheels, brakes, fuel tank, bumpers, and exhaust system will be added. At another location the operator of a forklift truck moves an engine, mounted in a special cradle, to the beginning of a line where transmission, fuel pump, generator, and fan will be put on. At still another point the front end—fenders, grill, radiator, and headlights—starts to take shape, and, at another, so do the seat cushions.

Eventually the lines will come together, like the tributaries of a mighty river. At precisely the proper moment the engine and the power train will be joined to the chassis. The painted and trimmed body will be picked up by giant, padded hooks, swung down over the chassis and bolted to the frame. The front end, painted to match the rest of the car, will keep its appointment on schedule. The hood and the seats will make their entrance on cue.

This is big business, costly business. The automobile industry directly or indirectly employs one of every six workers in the United States. It supports some 800,000 enterprises. It consumes 60 percent of all the rubber used, 20 percent of the steel. A single plant, employing 5,500 workers and producing 1,100 cars and trucks a day, covers 177 acres, almost as much as the entire New York garment district. The production area, 2.2 million square feet of manufacturing, storage, and office space under a single roof, occupies one-third of the site—enough factory space for hundreds of dress, suit, and coat makers. And this plant, with an annual payroll of more than $50 million in 1970, is only one of a score of such facilities operated by its multi-billion-dollar parent.

This is planned business, business moving with glacierlike inevitability. The car born today had its conception in a time only dimly remembered, when a market researcher, one of a crew of many, knocked on the door of an automobile owner, asking questions:

"Has anything big or little gone wrong with your car in the last thirty days? What was it that went wrong? Have you had it fixed to your satisfaction?"

"Which of these two sketches of future cars do you think is better looking and why?"

"Which would you rather have in your next car—more acceleration while passing or greater fuel economy?"

The answers in hand, a team of product-planning engineers set out to write specifications for a car that will give the customer what he wants and that can be manufactured at a competitive cost, sold at a price customers would be willing to pay, and assure the company's stockholders a satisfactory return on their investment. Their output is a written document setting forth exact targets and limits for the new model: inside and outside dimensions, total weight, carrying capacity, power and equipment requirements, limits on manufacturing costs, and the price limits within which the new car will be sold when completed.

Two years roughly before the new model is unveiled, the designers set to work. Hundreds of pen, ink, and watercolor sketches are prepared, not only of the car as a whole but for all of its different parts. The best ideas are winnowed out and transferred to full-sized clay models. These in turn are finished to a glossy smoothness, covered with a shining plastic that looks like paint, and trimmed. In every respect the mock-up looks almost exactly like the finished car.

Now begins a period of conspiratorial secrecy. When the final design is chosen, many other people are brought into the task of seeing it through to completion. Manufacturing planners determine how the sixteen thousand parts that go into a modern automobile will be made and who will do it—the company itself or some sixty thousand suppliers. Experimental models of every part are hand made, and process engineers determine the machines, tools, and equipment to be used. Months before production gets under way, a pilot plant is set up to make prototypes of the new model, the aim of which is to discover and correct troubles in advance and to train supervisers who will oversee actual production.

The object of all this is to hold mistakes to a minimum, to limit the role of chance. If, at the outset, market research in quantity is employed to help determine what the customer wants, advertising in much more copius outpouring is mobilized later to convince him that what he wants is what the company has to sell.

Even then, however, the outcome is far from certain. Only after the shrouds are pulled back in the dealer showrooms and the customers sit down to write out their orders will the people who have taken part in planning the new model—the financial analysts, purchasing agents, and marketing men, as well as the engineers and designers—get an inkling of how well they have succeeded.

If the process seldom offers opportunity for daring innovation, it also offers little room for serious error. Brilliant successes still occur, and so do dismal failures. But they do not occur often, and when they do they spring from the same source: swings in consumer sentiment that occur after the ponderous process of creating a new model has gotten under way. Thus, Ford's failure to discern a customer trend away from large American cars toward smaller, more economical European models resulted in its disappointment with the Edsel. By the same token, its gamble that a rising generation of younger, better-educated, multiple-car buyers would be ready for it when it arrived resulted in its spectacular success with the sporty Mustang.

Both the Mustang and the Edsel, however, were exceptions. The emphasis more often is on evolution, not revolution; on continuity of styling and engineering, not radical innovation; on making haste slowly. Nothing ventured may mean nothing gained, but big business has reversed the emphasis. Today, more often little ventured means little lost.

This is not to malign big business. It is to describe its most salient characteristic, its attempt to limit uncertainty, its attempt to write its own future. In the automobile business the attempt continues until the last car rolls off the assembly line on the last day of the model year. It involves, among other things, the industry's response to fashion, the growing use of the computer, and the almost incredible organization of men and materials as they come together in the assembly line.

Fashion is no less a dictator in the automobile than in the garment industry. The ancient dictum "You can have any color you choose so long as it is black" has given way to an infinity of engine, transmission, accessory, fabric, and color choices, with the result that a plant producing eleven hundred cars a day on two eight-hour shifts could operate for forty years making a single model without ever producing exactly the same car twice. The number of makes and models offered by each manufacturer has grown correspondingly. The automobile market has been so analyzed and dissected that no longer are there models merely for the old and the young, for those who have made it, and for those who would like to. Today there almost certainly is a car for the affluent middle-ager, burdened at the moment with the demands of children in college but with dreams of freedom and refound youth in the years immediately ahead—for him, possibly, an economy sporty car with doors not too low to permit arthritic entry, four-on-the-floor coupled with an automatic transmission.

For all the permutations and combinations, however, the choice essentially remains "chocolate or vanilla." There is no possibility for an obscure revolutionary, a Dior or a Balenciaga, to rise up from nowhere, capture the imagination of the haute monde, and dictate the industry's styling for a season. There is no possibility for a manufacturer, sensing a trend, to rocket to fabulous riches—or, missing one, to go out of business. The stakes are too high, the commitment too long standing. Moreover, the industry has hedged all its bets. If economy is the motif of the moment, each manufacturer has a model that will meet the demand. If it is opulence, he has another. Some may dine better than others at the table of growth, but none will be left out.

Manufacturing can be viewed as the final stage in a lengthy process of interaction between the customer and the automobile maker. Through market research the maker attempts to predict what the customer will want, and through advertising he attempts to influence it. In the manufacturing process the automobile maker attempts to respond quickly to the customer's decision. This attempt is reflected in the growing use of the computer.

What happens on the assembly line is decided by the choices made in the dealer's showroom, the colors and fabrics a customer selects, the engine he chooses, the package of optional extras. The information, fed into a computer, helps generate orders to many people: company headquarters in Detroit, which allocates production among engine, transmission, stamping, and assembly plants; traffic men, who route a hundred railroad cars, plus additional truckloads, of engines, transmissions, and parts to each assembly plant each day; the stockkeepers, for the company as a whole and for each plant, who keep close tabs on inventory; the purchasing agents, who must buy more.

Before the advent of the computer, it would have been three days before management knew what parts had been pulled from inventory each day and what was needed to replace them. Today, the information has passed through leased telephone lines from a computer in the assembly plant to headquarters in Detroit by 3:30 to 4:00 the following morning. This use of the computer has made it possible for the automobile industry, and business in general, to reduce significantly stocks of goods in transit and in inventory. In the past the tendency of such stocks to accumulate involuntarily when business slowed down was a major source of economic instability.

The computer has done more. It has helped the automobile industry even out work loads. Certain models, such as station wagons, require more labor than others. The market for station wagons varies, however, geographically as well as seasonally. More are sold in the North and East than in the South and West, and in summer than in winter. The computer helps the plant management adjust the daily blend of production.

Visitors to an assembly plant often ask: "How is it they never seem to make a mistake? Don't they ever get a blue fender on a yellow car?" The answer lies in an almost incredible set of orders and controls, so organized, as one supervisor put it, "that the man on the line never has to think." The key to the process is another product of the computer, a teletyped order broadcast to selected locations around the assembly plant. This assigns a number to every car and details every item that goes into it. Thus, late one forenoon, two men looking a bit like creatures from outer space—coveralls taped up the front, squarish caps, goggles, and aspirators—apply three coats of Mediterranean blue enamel, one of more than two dozen colors, to the body of number 356, a racy sports convertible. A football field away, in a smaller enameling booth, another painter will soon spray the same color on a hood and pair of fenders numbered 356. And still later a third—none seeing the finished creation —will apply the identical color to five wheels.

Mass production today follows the same principles that governed Eli Whitney when he set up his rifle plant in New Haven, Connecticut, almost two hundred years ago: the precision manufacture of identical and inter- changeable parts, and the buildup in a carefully timed sequence of a final product from its simplest elements. Mr. Whitney might find it diffi- cult, however, to recognize the present-day descendants of his brainchild. In engine and transmission plants, huge machines utilize precise electronic and hydraulic controls to measure the work in process, automatically ad- just the machines to tolerances as close as one ten-thousandth of an inch, and transfer the work automatically to the next step. This is one version of what is known as automation. In assembly plants, mile-long conveyor systems and huge overhead cranes, operating automatically, contrive to bring subassemblies together at exactly the proper moment. How cleverly such systems are arranged is attested to by the fact that in one plant a body line, feeding into a storage bay, operates just a bit faster than the final assembly it feeds. This permits the body line to shut down while its workers go to lunch without failing to meet its obligation to the final assembly.

All this spells money, vast amounts of money. It is no coincidence that the automobile industry embraces the nation's largest manufacturing business, General Motors. Nor is it coincidence that where seventy or eighty companies once contributed to the industry's output, production today is concentrated among three big manufacturers and one smaller one, the last a giant by the standards of many another industry.

Capital investment in the automobile industry is big, $51,809 per pro- duction worker in 1967. While this is dwarfed by the $204,888 of the petroleum industry, another few-concern industry, it is more than seven times that of the apparel industry, $6,739.

The big investment in plant and equipment, the complicated tech- nology, the long lead times, the discouragement to innovation mean that few, if any, new companies are so foolhardy as to seek entry into a big, few-concern industry. In automobiles the last attempt was made more than twenty years ago by Henry J. Kaiser, whose World War II successes in shipbuilding, steel, and aluminum making gave him not unjustified confidence that he might make it where others had failed. But he did not. Instead, not only Kaiser but Hudson and Studebaker, two long-estab- lished smaller automobile makers, were forced to leave the field.

If a competitive industry like apparel making may be thought of as a game of musical chairs, a constant stream of participants leaving the industry every year to be supplanted by eager young newcomers, a big, few-concern industry may be thought of as an eon-long poker game. The players remain the same or become fewer, but as the remaining participants get to know each other better, they concentrate on each other's idiosyncrasies and labor more and more at devising competitive strategies to make themselves winners. Of late, this has been reduced to mathematical science, the theory of games. If one can anticipate what the others are likely to do, one can plot one's own moves with certainty. The last thing sought, however, is to win so decisively that the other players will withdraw from the game. This might have the unfortunate consequence of bringing that eternal kibbitzer, government, into the game.

Not every big, few-concern industry is the same. Some, like makers of primary aluminum, gypsum products, and tin cans, manufacture products alike as peas in a pod. Others, like the makers of cigarettes, soaps and synthetic detergents, and alcoholic beverages, strive through advertising to create imagined differences when real ones fail to exist. Spending on advertising reflects this fact: the mining industry spends the smallest amount per dollar of sales (0.1 cents in 1967), while the tobacco industry spends the largest amount of any manufacturer (6.0 cents in the same year).

The principal distinguishing characteristic of the big, few-concern industry, its tendency to look constantly over its shoulder at the competition, is reflected particularly in price making. The biggest concern in the industry isn't always the first to raise or lower prices. Some industries seem to practice a minuet, with first one concern, then another, taking the initiative. But none is likely to step out unless it is reasonably sure the others will follow.

This means that, in contrast to an industry like apparel making, price competition tends to be pushed to the rear. Few-concern industries compete; in fact, they compete vigorously. But they do so by trying to create a product different from that of their competitors. Or by emphasizing the services they offer that their competitors do not: for example, unusual credit accommodation, orders tailored more closely to customer requirements, or quicker and more efficient repairs. In their effort to limit uncertainty, the last thing they seek is a price war.

Because prices in few-concern industries are changed infrequently, and then often at the same time, and because one concern may act as a price leader, it is often said that big business arbitrarily administers or fixes prices, the inference being that it uses its market power to produce profits greater than could be obtained in a broad, open, and competitive market. This is one of the usual arguments advanced for price controls.

Is the price that will produce the greatest profit, however, any different in a market dominated by a few concerns from the one that will achieve the same result in a broad, open, and competitive market? In both cases, isn't the price identical—the one that will produce the greatest volume of sales at the lowest unit cost?

There is a difference, of course. Sellers in a few-concern market are denied the twenty-twenty vision provided by a broad, open, competitive market. Since there is no mechanism to determine the exact price at which supply and demand meet, pricing in a few-concern market often involves mistakes. It may be too high to produce the volume needed. It may be too low to cover costs. Nevertheless, sellers in such a market look continuously for the price they hope will produce the greatest profit possible. Their market is thus sometimes spoken of as a "price-searcher's" market.

Sellers in few-concern markets search for the profit-maximizing price —the only price at which transactions take place in a broad, open, and competitive market—unless other considerations take precedence. Because of their high visibility to legislators, regulators, and the public, they may be persuaded to hold their prices below the level that would produce maximum profits. Such a course might win friends in Washington, but it could lose friends in the capital markets. Pursued consistently over a period of time, such a policy of pricing voluntarily below the level that would produce the greatest profit would divert capital and talent away from the industry toward less productive uses. For the economy as a whole, it would mean a drop in potential efficiency and economic growth.

One social critic, a bit over-enthusiastically perhaps, uses the price-fixing argument to contend that big business has succeeded in its ambition of becoming the creator, not the creature, of its fate. Business not only fixes prices to assure itself of a steady stream of profits, he contends, but it uses market research, product design, and advertising to engineer demand. The consumer, he concludes, is no longer the sovereign. He has become the system's slave.

One may admit a point without conceding the argument. Because of its greater freedom in pricing, big business is able to take into account long-term costs small business may be forced to neglect. These include the replacement of aging equipment, the training of management to provide depth and succession, and systematic innovation through research and development. These are costs as important to the future of the enterprise as the direct costs of labor and materials.

The argument would be more persuasive, however, if the landscape were not so cluttered with evidence of big-business miscalculations. The Edsel is only the most highly publicized example. Chrysler made a similar error in misjudging the market only a year or two later, Philco in offering a new television model early in the sixties, Douglas Aircraft when it entered the market for jets, duPont with its synthetic leather, Corfam, and RCA when it tried to build computers. And what leader of the bowling equipment industry would be so bold today as to suggest that consumer demand could be engineered?

The argument would be more persuasive if each year did not bring forth a new crop of businesses—big businesses—in distress, takeover attempts, and shotgun marriages.

There is a difference between big business and small business in this regard. In a few-concern industry miscalculation is less likely to result in the death of the enterprise. But is disaster more acceptable because it is absorbed internally? Are the layoffs and plant closings less painful, the management shake-ups and capital losses less traumatic?

All business has common problems: attracting management and capital, providing incentives and controls, utilizing the most efficient production methods, and organizing for change, which involves developing new products and deciding what markets to enter and when.

Big business has certain additional problems:

1. Communication. In a far-flung enterprise it is hard to assure that management's goals are understood in all places and at all levels. It is even more difficult to obtain the feedback of information needed to gauge success.

2. Control. Given the predilection of free spirits in any bureaucracy to go their own way, it is hard to assure that executives at divisional and lower levels will pursue the company's objectives and not their own.

3. Allocation. Lacking the impersonal mechanism of a broad, open, and competitive market for distributing resources within the company, it is hard to assure that capital and talent are channeled to the most productive of alternative opportunities for profit.

4. Recognition and reward. In a large organization it is not always possible to make full use of talent. Hence it is hard to assure that full value is realized from expenditures on research and development.

Such problems are not unique to big business. They are common also to government, nonprofit enterprises, and socialist states. Much has been written of the effort of Washington to establish performance standards for federal programs, particularly defense programs, within the budget. Even more has been written of the Soviet Union's economic reforms, which seek to create a profitlike structure of incentives and resource allocation.

American big business was the model for both innovations. As early as the 1920s General Motors and duPont were pioneering in the development of the corporation with several independent divisions, each responsible for its own profits. Since then corporations have extended profit responsibility to successively lower levels of management. They have also used profit-maximizing criteria to judge the feasibility of programs that reach beyond the boundaries of a single division or company.

The latest innovation in the response of big business to its problems of internal control and resource allocation would appear to be the multi-market company, or conglomerate, in which minority shareholdings in subsidiaries are not merely tolerated but welcomed. Although the device has come under a cloud because of its identification with cosmetic accounting and other questionable practices, in time its worth may be appreciated. By applying the independent review of the stock market, it provides a new test of the validity of management decisions below headquarters level.

3. Business Is Innovative

Business is constantly changing. Apart from businesses started by farmers and professionals, something like one of eleven concerns are newcomers each year to the business scene. A slightly smaller share depart from it. Nor is change restricted to the bottom. Among the five hundred largest companies, some are moving up in rank while others move down, some are entering the list while others are pushed out. There is a steady coming and going in the business world, a continuous growth and attrition. The whole might be likened to the cells of a body, or more aptly perhaps to the life of an interdependent biological colony.

Within big business, moreover, an appearance of stability may mask vast internal shifts from old products to new, from higher to lower cost production, from one region to another. DuPont's boast that 30 percent of its sales today result from products it hadn't introduced until 20 years ago is one example. Textron's diversion of capital from high-cost New England to low-cost southern textile operations and then out of textiles entirely is another.

Consider for a moment what has happened to some of the famous names of yesteryear. Through mergers and acquisitions their names have disappeared, their capital diverted into entirely new fields of endeavor. Baldwin Locomotive, first merged into Baldwin-Lima-Hamilton, has become a heavy equipment subsidiary of Armour and Company, the meat packers, which is now a subsidiary of Greyhound Corporation. American Locomotive had its name changed to Alco Products and its assets acquired by Studebaker-Worthington. Studebaker itself, one of the last independent automobile manufacturers, is merged with a pump manufacturer and no longer makes cars. Another one-time automobile maker, Graham-Paige, is now the Madison Square Garden

Corporation. A one-time anthracite mining company, Philadelphia and Reading, is now a diversified manufacturing subsidiary of Northwest Industries, itself a spin-off of the Chicago Northwestern Railroad. Glen Alden, another former hard-coal producer, is now part of the Meshulam Riklis retail and dry goods operation. W. R. Grace, which made its name in the Latin American trade, has sold its steamship line, airline and bank, and shifted much of its capital into chemicals and foods. Bangor Punta, once a major Cuban sugar producer, now makes such diverse things as fabrics, process engineering equipment, law enforcement equipment, pleasure boats, camping trailers, and emblematic jewelry. Pullman makes railroad equipment but no longer makes Pullman cars, and Greyhound, the bus company, in addition to owning Armour, is a computer-leasing concern, among a multitude of other things. The recitation is endless.

Innovation is the key to all this movement. The company that fails to innovate stagnates, is overtaken by younger and more aggressive competitors, and falls victim to corporate predators. This is so because only through new products, new ways of making old products, and the discovery and development of new markets can profitability be increased. And only the prospect of continuing and rising profits will assure the capital and talent needed to keep a business growing.

Products tend to move through a predictable cycle. Early in life a new discovery—wonder drugs, digital computers, electrostatic copiers—attracts capital easily. The product, in its simplest design or broadest application, is readily accepted. Hence, the growth of its market is great. Advertising is unnecessary. Everyone wants to be the first in his community or the first in his neighborhood to share in its use. The price, therefore, can be set high enough to recover all long-term costs, plus a genuine profit. Research, in particular, can be directed to the second generation of the product and toward totally new discoveries.

As the product matures, competition from other concerns appears. Even before patent protection is lost, products somewhat but not entirely different and purporting to fulfill the same function arrive on the market. Sales growth becomes difficult to sustain without brand-name advertising, with the result that costs rise as pricing comes under pressure. The usefulness of the product, however, remains unquestioned, the source of capital merely shifting from investors seeking better-than-average growth to those seeking nothing more than steady income.

In old age a product faces increasing competition from entirely new products such as synthetics and other substitutes, which may lack the broad usefulness of the original but outperform it for specific purposes. Special adaptations of the original, in effect new products themselves, continue to do well. As demand shifts to specialties, however, the economies of large-scale production tend to disappear. Marketing of the basic product becomes defensive, its pricing distressed, and capital seeks to leave the industry, in part by way of mergers, in some cases through bankruptcy. The industry turns increasingly to government for protection against competition, particularly import competition.

It has sometimes been suggested that the great waves of innovation are over, that all that lies ahead for business is maturity and old age. Such talk has been heard for one hundred and fifty years or more, each time the burst of economic activity following widespread adoption of a new invention or technique has subsided. The argument, however, is more subtle today. It is no longer said that business is running out of steam, that innovation is grinding to a halt. The facts won't support such a conclusion. Industry accounts for about 70 percent of all the research and development in the United States. In 1970 this was expected to amount to $19.2 billion, 36 percent more than the 1965 level of $14.2 billion.

Instead it is argued that innovation has become so regularized— progress has become such an important part of business, as one large company suggests—that it has become routine. This has sapped the economy of its entrepreneurial lifeblood. And, according to this theory, hardening of the business arteries has set in, just as surely as if there had been no innovation at all. Another version of the stagnation thesis holds that innovation is tolerated by business only as long as it doesn't interfere with a steady and comfortable level of dividends. When the risk increases, the inevitable response of business is to fob off the responsibility for research and development on the government.

This argument is not totally without foundation. Of total industry spending for research and development in 1970, 44 percent, or $8.5 billion, was paid for by the federal government, 56 percent by industry itself. Five years earlier, however, the shares were reversed. In 1965 government was the source of 55 percent of the research and development funds spent in industry, industry itself providing only 45 percent. What is more, federal spending for research and development—for its own, university, and other nonprofit institution use, as well as that of industry—increased only 15 percent, from $13.025 billion to $15 billion, while industry spending for research and development in the same years rose almost 67 percent, from $6.541 billion to $10.895 billion. Government remains the biggest spender for research and development, particularly in the fields of defense and space, but industry is rapidly overtaking it.

The latter-day versions of the stagnation thesis would make greater sense if a company could be sure that by appropriating a fixed percentage of its sales each year for research and development it could produce a steady stream of new and profitable products. Actually, of course, there is very little relationship between research and development spending and its payoff, which may not even lie in the area of technological accomplishment. Often, ground for an important innovation may have been technologically laid years before. But not until a consumer need is perceived, and a way of adapting the technology to meet that need is devised, will widespread diffusion of the innovation occur. Peter Drucker* cites the electric power industry as an example. From Faraday's day on the industry was capable of widespread and rapid growth. But not until Edison invented the incandescent lamp —a cheap, replaceable substitute for existing gas and kerosene lamps— did that growth become certain.

Henry Ford's contribution to the automobile is another example. He is said not to have added a single technological innovation to the development of the automobile, but his introduction of mass production, itself almost a century old, made possible a cheap, easily serviced vehicle—and started the automotive revolution in the United States.

Perhaps more than anything else, those who talk of stagnation minimize or ignore the role of the securities markets in encouraging innovation. The recognition that innovation is the source of all profitability and economic growth has produced a demand pull from the investment community. Investors have come to appreciate that young, research-based companies offer the most spectacular opportunities for investment growth, and have reached farther and farther back in the process of business maturation to indenture likely prospects.

Let's look in on one such enterprise.

Harry Kerwin hung up the phone and breathed a sigh of relief. The underwriter had given him the news he wanted to hear: the first public offering of shares of Process Radiation, Inc., had been an unqualified success. Investors had jumped at the opportunity to pick up 220,000 shares of the fledging enterprise at five dollars a share, and the company had been assured of the funds it needed to begin construction of its new plant.

The result was not unexpected. There was glamour in the company's name and in the company's business, the commercial use of such man-made radioactive isotopes as cobalt 60 to destroy microorganisms, break chemical bonds, create ions, and disrupt the charge balance of atoms on molecules. Some of the company's products suggested the promise of the future. Disposable medical items, such as hypodermic

* The Age of Discontinuity, Guidelines to Our Changing Society, New York, Harper & Row, 1968, p. 24.

needles, no longer had to be handled under aseptic conditions and packaged in clean rooms. Through irradiation, they could be sterilized after being sealed in airtight containers. Wooden flooring and furniture could be made harder and longer wearing. New paints and adhesives could be formulated and their chemical synthesis begun by irradiation. Plastics could be made tougher and more heat resistant, and, what is more, they could be given an uncanny inner memory. A piece of plastic pipe, for instance, could be irradiated, heated, and bent out of shape, and when heated again would regain its original contour and dimension.

If the success of the company's first public offering of securities was predictable, it was by no means certain. Process Radiation, Inc., was still an infant company. Four years before it had still been just a dream in Harry Kerwin's mind. Unlike some other companies "going public," it did have a record of sales and earnings. But these, while growing, were still miniscule. And the offering prospectus required by the Securities and Exchange Commission spoke at great length of uncertainties and risks and hardly at all of bright prospects for the future.

As one of several hundred companies making their initial public debut each year, Process Radiation, Inc., was typical of many. No longer small business, it could not yet be called big or even medium-sized business. Nevertheless, an inexorable logic—new products, sales and earnings climbing at an exponential rate of growth—demanded more capital than the original owners could supply. And so, despite inexperience and misgiving, they had been forced to call on the financial community for help and to invite the investing public to share their rewards and their risks.

For Harry Kerwin this was not his first crisis, or his biggest one. That distinction went to the decision, seemingly eons ago, to quit Amalgamated Nuclear and set up his own shop. For nine years he had been a project manager for the big company, designing equipment to handle radioactive materials, managing government-sponsored pilot projects. A mechanical engineer, Harry had had no previous experience in the nuclear sciences, but in his work for Amalgamated it was "learning on the job all the time," and by the end of his employment he had amassed twenty-two patents that had been assigned to the company.

The break came over commercial application of some of the ideas Amalgamated had pioneered. The big company had competed heavily for government contracts and had an excellent performance record. For a time it appeared to be the Atomic Energy Commission's favored contractor, all else being equal. But the officialdom at Amalgamated, Harry became convinced, was unable to read the handwriting on the wall. Despite the fact that work at MIT and Caltech and pilot projects by several big food and petroleum companies pointed to profitable commercial applications, they seemed to prefer the sheltered life of government contracts.

Harry Kerwin lobbied with management, but without success. There were days, he remembers, when things seemed to be going his way— and others, more frequent, when they did not. Suddenly, one day, he had a "terrible argument" with a vice-president. "I shot my mouth off, but big," he recalls. "I don't know whether I was fired first or whether I quit first."

For two months things were touch and go. Harry rented a small office, borrowed some money, and set out to get some bread-and-butter business. "Don't think I didn't worry," he says. "I took a week before deciding to buy my first filing cabinet. It cost forty-two dollars, and I wasn't at all sure that I should spend the money."

The initial worry and uncertainty ended when an upstate New York university gave Harry a $25,000 contract to build a radiation facility at its nuclear research center. Harry had nothing to offer except his reputation. Nevertheless, the university awarded him the contract on his low bid. "It is very difficult to prove capability," he observes. "The past is your most important asset for the future." A performance bond was required, and Harry borrowed $5,000 "on my pride" to deposit with the bonding company. Harry designed the equipment and subcontracted the manufacture of the hardware. The contract was completed on schedule.

His most monumental decision, Harry says, was to order $50,000 worth of cobalt 60, to be delivered nine months after the order was placed, from the Atomic Energy Commission—without having the money to pay for it. To place the order, Harry had to obtain a license from the AEC permitting him to buy, sell, or handle atomic materials.

"It was the greatest gamble I ever took," he says. "I had to have the material or I couldn't perform the contract. If I qualified for the license, I didn't have to demonstrate ability to pay. I gambled I would get other contracts. I knew I wouldn't go to jail, that all they could do was to keep the stuff. I felt wholly responsible in what I was doing. Still, I lost a lot of hair."

The AEC had supplied Harry with trade credit. In effect, it had provided him with working capital, and to this day he vows his gratitude. The transaction, however, was by no means a giveaway: the delivery date was not guaranteed, quality was assured only within a range of plus or minus 25 percent, and the product was priced to permit the government full recovery of its costs. Today the government is out of the business and prices are much lower. Nevertheless, the AEC's expression of confidence was vital. Without it Harry could not have pushed ahead.

There were other crises and other expressions of confidence. When no one else would lend it a cent, the Small Business Administration advanced Process Radiation, Inc., $15,000. The loan was paid off in full the day the proceeds were received from the company's public offering. When the company's only asset was contracts booked, a large commercial bank—the branch down the block, not the main head-quarters—came through with more. Of the SBA, Harry says: "They were there at the right time and the right place. They really helped." Of the bank: "I gave them an unaudited balance sheet. I couldn't afford an audited one. They gave me a credit that was the making of the company."

In its first three years, revenues rose from $2,329 to $72,214 to $337,749. After losses of $8,906, or 3 cents a share, the first year and $20,126, or 7 cents a share, the second, the company showed a profit of $41,086, or 13 cents a share, the third year—a significant improve-ment but hardly the kind of earnings record to inspire unbridled con-fidence.

Nevertheless, Process Radiation, Inc., was on the move. It had obtained two important contracts from the National Aeronautics and Space Administration, one for equipment to irradiate an entire space-craft at one time in a shielded cell, the other for equipment to protect workers in NASA's Radiation Environment Facility from neutron, beta, and gamma rays. It had made a deal to obtain a radiation facility from a company with one left over from past government work. The rental had seemed dirt cheap, just enough to pay taxes and insurance. But the company had exacted an option to buy 10 percent of Precision Radia-tion's stock at book value, a price that seemed low enough at the time —after all, total net worth was only $60,000—but appeared somewhat different later as the company's sales and earnings began to climb.

Talent had been hired. The marketing manager of the systems depart-ment of a large atomics company was hired as vice-president for market-ing. A chemical engineer, he had taught at Purdue, Louisville, and MIT and had graduated from the Oak Ridge School of Reactor Tech-nology. Other appointments, to be filled later, carried similar qualifica-tions. One was a man hired to head the company's research department, another one named to head a nuclear control systems department. "Everyone is a scientist, everyone a salesman," was the way Harry Kerwin described his choices. Perhaps the most interesting decision was that involving the man named vice-president for technical development. A veteran of more than twenty years' experience in the design and development of complex nuclear engineering systems, he had taught for eight years at MIT and was now employed by a major atomics company. Discreetly, he let it be known that he would consider a change.

"I wanted to hire him," Harry Kerwin says, "but I couldn't afford him. Those were the days when I would have sold out to the first guy who made me an offer. So, reluctantly, I saw him go to another company. He made a big splash there with a major advance in food irradiation. Later I was able to persuade him to join us."

From the beginning Process Radiation, Inc., had plowed back one-third of its earned revenues into research and development, an appropriation that would have shamed many a larger corporation. The expenditure was directed, not merely toward finding new commercial applications for radiation processing, but also at obtaining a more profitable mix between services and products.

As Harry Kerwin explained it, so long as the company remained a service enterprise its opportunity for profit remained small. Processing a hypodermic needle for a pharmaceutical company, for example, might bring the company 5 percent of the manufacturer's price. Making the item itself, although it involved additional packaging and selling costs, assured it 100 percent.

The next move was a giant step. The company, which had previously rented its entire production space, was now ready to build its own plant, a venture calling for the expenditure of $800,000. Harry explored the possibilities. Although the company's relations with the bank remained excellent, the sum was far more than could be obtained merely by expanding its bank line of credit. Moreover, such a course was made impractical by tight money and high interest rates, which factors also ruled against other kinds of straight debt financing. Harry considered issuing debt convertible into common stock. But since there was no public market for the company's securities, the convertible feature did not seem likely to lower interest costs sufficiently to make this kind of financing attractive. He considered the private placement of unissued common stock, but chose not to concentrate a large block of stock in the hands of a few outside shareholders. He also turned down the idea of merger because of the loss of control.

Harry Kerwin was understandably reluctant to become involved in a world of financial, accounting, legal, and Securities and Exchange Commission matters about which, he confessed, "I knew nothing at all." He was reluctant to invite public inspection of everything the company had been doing and was about to do. But he recognized that a public offering of shares, for all his inexperience and misgivings, would be the cheapest and most efficient way to raise the funds. There were, he had to admit, positive compensations. Future financing would be made easier, and the use of stock option plans would help attract and hold the kind of talent Process Radiation, Inc., was attempting to find. He would also be able to diversify his own estate without losing effective control of the company, and he would be able to use the company's stock to acquire other companies.

The last was by no means a minor consideration. If Process Radiation, Inc., was to move from being an equipment and service company to a manufacturer of products, it would have to enter plastics manufacturing, chemicals manufacturing, and metals fabricating. It could do this by starting up wholly new operations, or it could acquire going concerns, utilizing the talent they already possessed. As Harry Kerwin explained it, "We are not buying machines, we are buying people."

The next step was picking an underwriter. Harry's choice was a small firm with a string of successes in bringing to the public the first offerings of science-based companies, including two concerns in the radiation field. His reasoning? "They were already convinced it was a going industry. We knew we wouldn't have to sell them on the idea."

The deal was not unusual. The underwriter was to purchase the entire issue of 220,000 shares at $4.50 a share and resell it to the public at $5.00. In addition, it was to receive warrants for the purchase of an additional 30,000 shares for $300.00. Each warrant would entitle the holder to buy a share at $5.50 in the first year after the offering and at additional premiums of 50 cents a year for four years until the price reached $7.50. The deal was what is known as a "firm commitment agreement." If the offering had been bigger and more speculative, the company might have had to accept a "best efforts agreement." Under such an agreement the underwriter promises merely to do his best to sell the issue.

Since the amount of the offering would exceed $300,000, registration with the Securities and Exchange Commission was required under the Securities Act of 1933, so now came the drafting of the prospectus and other materials necessary for registering the offering, the key men in this project being the company's lawyer, its treasurer, and its independent accountant. The prospectus is a document giving would-be stock purchasers information about the company's history, the products it makes, its competition, employees, sales, markets, and production. In addition it provides financial data concerning the company and the securities to be sold, plus disclosure of the stake officers and directors have in the company, their salaries and stock options, and any contracts or dealings they may have with the company or its affiliates. The SEC requires that the financial data include a balance sheet to the latest year-end, plus a statement of income and retained earnings for the last three years, all of which must be certified by an independent accountant. If the records a company has kept are not satisfactory, the independent accountant will not be able to give an opinion about the company's past earnings and the company will not be able to offer the shares.

As Process Radiation, Inc., prepared to graduate from infancy to youth, it shared a number of characteristics with other young, science-based concerns, perhaps the most notable of which was that it was successful. In contrast to companies in other fields, a majority of which fail in their early years, according to Dun and Bradstreet statistics, concerns spun off from government or university laboratories or from larger science-oriented companies do remarkably well, although those companies relying to a large extent on government contracts were hit hard by the big defense and aerospace cutbacks of 1969–70.

A study by Professor Edward B. Roberts of the Sloan School of Management at MIT in the late 1960s showed that after five years of business life, four out of five of these companies not only were alive but that for the most part they were operating profitably and growing rapidly.

There were other similarities. Almost all the spin-off companies studied had started as government contractors, selling to the defense or space markets. Government business seemed to act as a catalyst, holding together technical forces until a greater proportion of commercial business could be obtained. Defense and space contracts provided financial support before otherwise high prices could be justified by industrial or consumer markets.

The men who founded these spin-off companies, moreover, were found to be remarkably similar. Half were the sons of fathers who themselves were self-employed. Most were well educated but not too well educated, holders of master's degrees but not Ph.D.'s. By and large they were quite young, few much older than their late thirties. Most sprang from development rather than research.

Successful entrepreneurs like Harry Kerwin, the studies showed, sprang from technologies in which the possibility of commercial utilization of ideas was ripe. They gave early and continuing attention to marketing. They recognized the importance of management skills and gave much of their time to finding the right people for the jobs. They set high standards of achievement and leadership, yet they delegated authority effectively.

The road to success that Harry Kerwin and these others found for their firm is by no means certain, however. If innovation rewards some, it discomforts others—such as manufacturers whose products are superseded, workers whose jobs are displaced, and regulators whose conventional ways of doing things are upset—for at all times there are forces favoring change and others opposing it.

Such things, however, are not wholly one-sided. The refusal of construction workers to permit labor-saving automation, for instance, may price conventional housing out of the market. But the willingness of automobile workers to permit cost-reducing techniques to be introduced in the manufacture of mobile homes may achieve the desired result by a different route. Regulation may operate in the same way, inhibiting the growth of rail and seaborne commerce, for instance, but encouraging the expansion of highway, air, and inland water transportation. The resulting tendency in both cases is for whole industries to be junked, their problems being allowed to die with their aging work forces. The process often is slow, the agony prolonged by efforts to make it less painful.

Innovation is a creature also of business ups and downs. During periods of rapid economic growth, securities values tend to rise, creating a strong demand for "growth opportunities." Credit also tends to be more readily available, making it easier for new ventures to gain a foothold and to grow. By way of contrast, however, newer and smaller firms are among the first to be denied credit when the shift is made from easy to tight money.

The trauma is especially great in the shift from a period of inflationary excess to one of business downturn and recession. In boom times hundreds of new issues are brought to market, some with no past record of earnings and only the vaguest hopes of achievement. In 1961–62, and again in 1967–68, a flood tide of issues reached the market, enjoyed price run-ups of as much as 200 percent on their first trading day, and then fell off in price, some below their offering level.

A year later, in both cases, there was virtually no market for these shares. Tight money had made earnings much more difficult to achieve, and the slide in market values had made financing impossible. Unfortunately, the deserving suffered equally with the undeserving. And the standpatters, the established concerns that had chosen to avoid the risks of innovation, got a new lease on life.

4. The Shareowner

The spread of public ownership focuses attention on the role of the shareowner in the modern American corporation. Much has been written about "people's capitalism," the notion that the 31 million people who own shares influence American corporate life in much the same way that voters affect national and local politics. But this is obviously a myth. At the annual meeting there is not even a pretense of one man, one vote. Not only do holders with the most shares have the biggest voice in a company's affairs, but in contrast to politics it is quite proper to buy additional votes.

There is an even more fundamental difference. William C. Freund, the economist for the New York Stock Exchange, estimated that there would be 35 million shareholders by 1975 and 40 million by 1980. Even this large number is dwarfed, however, by the number of those who participate indirectly in share ownership through insurance policies, pension plans, personal trusts, and mutual fund purchases. Their rights as shareholders, to the extent that they are exercised at all, are exercised by others, the owners or trustees of the institutions in which their shareholdings are lodged.

Few shareholders take the trouble to attend or to vote at annual meetings. Except for a few notable dissidents—the so-called corporate democrats and more recently the activists—most shareholders routinely return the proxy requested by management and management votes their shares for them. The managements of large corporations thus tend to become self-perpetuating.

Shareowners are often criticized for permitting management to exercise such control unchallenged. But most shareowners have neither the time nor the inclination to do otherwise. An individual shareowner typically is an owner, manager, or professional who has made money by giving his time to his primary occupation. From the excess funds he puts in the stock market he hopes to obtain a return greater than he might from some alternate use of his funds. If he does, he rewards management primarily through holding his shares or purchasing additional ones. If he does not, he sells. Thus the shareholder population tends to be one of the more transient of the several publics—including suppliers, dealers, workers, customers, lenders, legislators, and regulators—with whom management must deal.

As a result, many managements view the ordinary shareholder with toleration or contempt. For example, for years the chairman, now dead, of a large New York bank scheduled his annual meeting at an hour when many interested shareowners could be expected to attend the meeting of a somewhat larger competitor. Then, each year he attempted to get the meeting over with more quickly than the year before. By his final year, he was able to boast that he had cut the meeting to just under four minutes. Other managements hold their meetings in small towns, far from areas of stockholder concentration. They encourage the stagger system, or election of only a fraction of the directors in any one year. They resist cumulative voting, which would give minority shareholders proportionate representation on corporate boards.

By way of contrast, such giants as American Telephone, General Electric, Texaco, IBM and U.S. Steel move their meetings each year from city to city, arrange transportation and hotel accommodations for shareholders, hire large auditoriums to seat the crowds, and often provide tours of research laboratories and other company facilities. While the free lunch has declined in recent years, the shopping bag of sample company products is distributed more often. Shareholders, after all, may constitute an important captive market.

To the degree that management has opened its doors to the ordinary shareholder, credit must be given to such corporate gadflies as Lewis Gilbert, his brother John, and Mrs. Wilma Soss. By turning the spotlight of publicity on some of the more blatant of management's transgressions, they have helped win more courteous treatment of stockholders as well as some real gains. The permanence of such gains, however, may be questioned. In the merger wave of 1968 and 1969, threatened managements threw up a wall of barriers to greater shareholder influence.

Even to managements that listen, moreover, the voice of the ordinary shareholder is heard only at the annual meeting and at infrequent special meetings called to approve mergers or for other restricted purposes. Making policy and the day-to-day business of running the company is management's prerogative. The shareholders may be informed of what management has done, but except when the bylaws compel it they are never offered a veto. Few others are, either.

This is what the activists seek to change. They want direct representation for consumers, dealers, workers, and others—someone may yet propose the small shareowner—on company boards. Ralph Nader, the consumer advocate, has suggested that perhaps one-fourth of the directors might be popularly elected. In Sweden a minority of the board is now appointed by government.

In the rapidly changing corporate environment, the ordinary shareholder may come to wonder exactly what it is he owns. It is not the company's assets, a lathe or a delivery truck, for instance. Without an employee's badge he probably wouldn't get past the gate at one of the company's plants. It is not the management. He would be laughed at if he tried to assert himself as boss, whether to a foreman or a vice-president.

What he has bought is a bundle of rights, a bundle that may appear bigger than it actually is. Even his right to share in profits is a limited one, enforceable only when dividends are declared. For while the shareholders may seek maximum profits, in their concern for the survival and ongoing life of the corporation the directors may order something less.

One view of the stockholder is that he is merely a special kind of creditor, a lender without a contract. He has given up his claim to the payment of interest at fixed dates and to the return of his capital at maturity of the obligation. But—and this is a question that has troubled legal scholars increasingly—if the shareholder isn't the owner of the corporation, who is?

Management may be able to ignore the ordinary shareowner much of the time. On at least three occasions, however, he comes into his own: when he successfully sues management for malfeasance, when his proxy is sought in a contest for corporate control or minority representation on the board of directors, and when his shares are bid for, through a tender offer, in a take-over attempt.

Management is under no obligation to the shareholder to be efficient or successful. But it is obliged to be honest. It may make mistakes, it may fail to use good judgment, it may lose money—but it may not engage in self-dealing, buttoning up profits for itself at the expense of other shareholders. It may not favor friends or relatives as suppliers or customers when better deals can be obtained from others. Nor may it profit from short-term trading in the company's stock. In the eyes of the law, management stands in a fiduciary relationship to its shareholders. Violation of this principle may bring down upon it a shareholder's suit for recovery of the sums involved.

Such suits are known as "derivative suits." That is, they derive from the rights of the corporation and are brought in the interest of the corporation when its officers or directors decline to do so themselves. They are also known sometimes as "strike suits," or "nuisance suits." This was particularly true in years past when shareholders sued, then settled privately with the company out of court. To prevent stockholder suits themselves from fostering private dealing, the courts now generally require that all settlements be court approved and open and that the proceeds revert to the corporation. Even so, the term "strike suit" persists, because lawyers who bring successful shareholder suits have their fees paid by the corporation. And some, their adversaries contend, are not averse to embarking upon litigation with only a limited chance of success in the hope of eventually earning a fat fee. As a result, small shareholders in many states are now required to post a bond covering court costs if their suits are not successful. No such requirement is made of large shareholders.

The friendless shareholder finds himself suddenly lionized by both management and the opposition when a challenger arises in a proxy contest. In the corporate world such a fight is the closest thing to a political campaign. There are speeches, public statements, position papers. Madison Avenue is enlisted and vast sums are spent on advertising and public relations. For a few months the shareholder finds his vote—for management or against—a matter of tremendous importance to others.

Giant proxy contests—like Robert R. Young's effort to gain control of the New York Central Railroad, which was successful, and Louis E. Wolfson's attempt to win control of Montgomery Ward, which was not —seem a thing of the past. For one thing, they involve huge expenditures. The Central fight cost Young $1,308,000 to mount and the management $876,000 to try to repulse, and in the end most of both sums came out of the pockets of Central shareholders. Then, too, proxy fights involve seemingly endless discussions with the Securities and Exchange Commission over what may be said and what may not be said in the effort to win votes. Finally, they seldom result in a clear-cut victory. A winner in a long and bitterly fought proxy contest often finds that he has to dispute the same issues again at the next and subsequent annual meetings.

A tender offer, by way of contrast, is an attempt to buy control rather than an effort to persuade shareholders to grant it. It offers several advantages to the challenger. For instance, its costs are limited to advertising the offer, to legal fees, and to interest charges on standby financing, costs that ordinarily amount to no more than 3 or 4 percent of the deal. A tender offer is also more respectable because no extravagant campaigning is required or permitted. It produces quick results and avoids uncertainty as well, since it is either successful or unsuccessful. There is no need to return to the shareholders the following year for a repeat performance.

A tender offer, however, is not for the unsophisticated or the timid. It is a complex financial deal involving surprise, speed, and strategy—all elements of war. One way to appreciate what a tender offer involves is to examine a campaign step by step.

The chairman of Old-Line Company received his first telephone call from the head of Predator, Inc., one Saturday afternoon on the golf course. He couldn't talk then, but promised to do so Monday morning.

By the appointed hour it was obvious that the meeting was more than social. Old-Line stock opened up three points on the New York Stock Exchange, and there were rumors that someone was about to make a tender offer.

At the meeting the head of Predator, Inc., informed Old-Line: "We control thirty percent of your stock. Let's talk merger." The chairman of Old-Line thanked him for the information, but refused to talk. Two days later the advertisement of Predator's tender offer appeared in the newspapers.

Here it may be useful to give some of Predator's history. A young company, the founder-owner of which still had a big stake in the ownership, it had grown from $5 million to $40 million in assets in half a dozen years. Much of this growth had been achieved through three previous mergers, none of which, however, had been contested. On the stock market, where it had been recognized as a growth concern, its shares enjoyed a high price/earnings multiple.

Until now, Predator, Inc., had been 100 percent in the defense business. Now, in Old-Line, the company saw an established maker of consumer products to complement its defense business. It saw hidden assets, chiefly a seventy-five thousand store-dealer network. It saw a typical take-over target—a company with poor earnings, dividends, and return on shareowners' investment, an excessive amount of cash, and insignificant management ownership of shares.

In planning its coup, Predator had bought Old-Line shares in the open market over a considerable period of time, being careful to keep its holdings under the 10 percent level that would have required public disclosure. It encouraged institutional investors and friendly individuals to join in the share buying. It proceeded with great secrecy, to keep from driving the share price up.

Until the meeting with Old-Line, Predator had hoped and pretty much expected that it would gain its way without a contest, which is what had happened in each of its previous acquisitions. It hadn't reckoned, however, with the chairman of Old-Line, who was new to the company. Because of family connections, he was thought to be merely a figure-head. Predator didn't realize that he was seeking a chance to prove him-self. Nor did it anticipate the reaction of the directors, mostly retired executives of larger concerns. Because of their age and outside interests, they had been expected to roll over readily and die. They didn't, and Predator found itself fighting an unwanted war.

Before making its offer, Predator had had to ask itself several ques-tions. Would the offer be for cash or securities? How big would the premium be? How many shares would be sought? With their high price/ earnings multiple, Predator shares were attractive, but cash was obviously more so. Moreover, a cash offering, instead of shares or convertible debentures, avoided the immediate problem of dilution of earnings.

On the other hand, Predator had to consider the cost of money and how the cash drain would affect its cash flow and balance sheet. There was also the problem of eventual dilution. If it paid cash for the stock, won control, and then exchanged Old-Line stock for its own, there would still be dilution. But would it be greater or less?

There was also the matter of tax considerations for Old-Line share-holders. They would be selling their stock, which could mean the payment of substantial taxes on capital gains. If a large stockholder did not want to tender because of such a likelihood, Predator might have to take an-other tack.

Perhaps the most important consideration in the ultimate decision was the fact that a securities offering would have involved registration with the Securities and Exchange Commission, both limiting Predator's ability to speak out in behalf of its offer and costing it valuable time. The decision therefore was to make a cash offer.

The next question was how big a premium. The objective obviously is to make an offer so attractive that the shares will come in quickly and the issue will be decided before management has a chance to respond. There is, unfortunately, no magic formula for deciding how high to price an offering, and this, in retrospect, was Predator's first and biggest mistake. It didn't think big enough. Shareholders held off tendering their shares, giving Old-Line management a chance to pull together a defense. It boosted the dividend, juggled the books to make earnings look bet-ter, and split the stock to make Predator's premium appear smaller. It also went into the market with some of its cash to push up the price of its stock and to reduce the number of shares needed to retain control. It launched an antitrust suit, and it brought in competition; Conglomerate A, an unfriendly longtime rival of Predator, upped the bid.

At the prospect of a bidding contest the arbitragers swarmed in like flies. Predator and its associates boosted their holdings by 7 percent to 40 percent, while Conglomerate A was able to attract 15 percent. Together they held 52 percent of Old-Line's stock, but despite some conversations they were unable to get together.

Sensing the impasse, Conglomerate A backed off, selling its shares on the market over a period of weeks—at a big profit. Predator, however, hung on. Although Predator's shareholdings gave it close to majority ownership—the large number of shares in the hands of arbitragers could have swung the result either way—the antitrust suit and other legal involvements kept Predator immobilized. Then, after some time, the market turned. Predator, seeing no way of extricating itself without a big loss while heavy interest costs on its borrowed funds continued, called it quits.

But the story was not quite over. The Old-Line chairman got the chance to prove himself that he had sought. As a reward for his success, he obtained long-term employment contracts for himself and for new key personnel he brought into the company. He also forced superannuated members of the board of directors to resign.

Still to be heard from, however, were the arbitragers, who together were in control of 45 percent of Old-Line's shares. Rather than take a big loss, they sought out still another acquirer, National Company B. And Old-Line management found itself working for new owners after all.

The question remained: what had the purchasers bought? At the first hint of trouble the headhunters—executive recruitment agencies—moved in. Much of middle management and not a few of top management had been wooed away, and Old-Line, a shell of its former self, faced the prospect of building a largely new management team.

Tender offers blossomed in the speculative boom of 1967 and 1968, then withered in the stock market decline and tight money period that followed. Changes in tax laws and accounting practices have made them less advantageous than they once were. More recently, proxy fights have erupted again to undo the ill-considered corporate marriages of the earlier era. For a time, at least, it seems likely that the shareholder may win attention. But just as the era of the giant proxy contest seems past, so the era of successive, rapid-fire tender offers, one following closely on the heels of another, seems gone—at least for a while. For the present, shareholders would appear to prefer a corporation with cash in the bank to one promising pie in the sky.

The changed mood has not exhausted the discussion, however, about the role of the shareholder in the modern American corporation. For example, to cite an issue that has touched off widespread debate both inside the institutions in question and without, should institutional shareholders, the universities and the churches in particular, vote their shares uniformly in favor of management, selling their shares when they disagree with company policies? Or, on the contrary, should those who oppose a company's policies and social goals be encouraged to buy shares and to bore from within, using the forum of the annual meeting to obtain publicity and public response and the mechanism of the courts to obtain legal redress?

Mr. Nader wants stockholder rights and management responsibilities made a concern of the federal government, through a new law requiring federal charters for corporations. This would not only assure public representation on the boards of large corporations, but it would permit the suspension of company executives responsible for corporate infractions of the law—such as permitting offshore oil spills.

The new law would also protect lower-echelon personnel who give evidence against the corporation, throw open a corporation's tax books to public inspection, and establish full disclosure, which now applies to a corporation's securities offerings, as the basic principle underlying all kinds of corporate activity. A corporation would thus be obliged to record its negative contributions to society, such as air and water pollution, as well as its positive contributions, such as its spending on basic research.

The role of the shareholder continues to change—and that of management is changing as well.

5. Profits: Balance Sheets and Income Statements

Big business or small, the object of business is profit. Profit is what is left for the proprietor, partners, or shareholders after the claims of all others—wages, the cost of materials, the replacement cost of aging equipment, plant and office rent, salesmen's expenses, and the myriad costs of just opening the doors every morning—are met. In this sense, profit is reward to the owners for risks taken in the past. In an ongoing business it is also a principal source of funds for new risks that will be taken in the future.

Profit is a measure of efficiency. It tells the management of a business how successful it has been in promoting sales volume and holding down costs to produce the greatest possible margin on sales and return on owners' investment. It enables the present owners to compare results with alternative uses of their capital, helping them to decide if they wish to remain owners, and it helps prospective investors decide whether they want to bid for ownership as well. In this sense, profit is a cost, the cost of risk capital. It is also a measure of the business's viability. If a business cannot cover this as well as other costs—if an investor can do better, for instance, in risk-free bonds—the business isn't likely to last long.

Profit is also a measure of the ability of a business to borrow. A business with high volume and low costs will find credit cheaper and more readily available than one in less robust health. Bankers will be more willing to extend loans, suppliers of materials will be more willing to grant favorable terms, and investment bankers will assign a higher rating to the company's bonds.

It is necessary, then, to have an objective and consistent measure of profits, one that can be applied at regular intervals to an ongoing concern. This is the reason for financial reports and accounting.

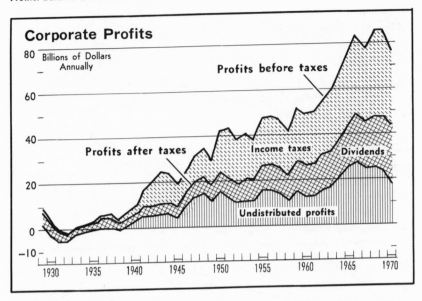

Corporate Profits

80 Billions of Dollars
Annually

Profits before taxes

60

40

Profits after taxes   Income taxes   Dividends

20

Undistributed profits

0

−10

1930   1935   1940   1945   1950   1955   1960   1965   1970

Profits are a reward to owners for past risks, a principal source of funds for future risks, and a major supplier of tax revenues. After rising for three decades, corporate profits leveled off in the mid-1960's.

Many things may affect profit—a change in the management, the opening of a competitor across the street, the threat of a strike. These things may affect the appraisal of a company's prospects—the market value of its shares, in particular—but only things that have already happened or are certain to happen and can be measured in money are recorded in financial statements. Thus, land a business bought several years ago at $50,000 but that is worth perhaps $100,000 now is kept on its books at cost, because there is no certainty that it will be sold at the higher price. But income taxes the company is obliged to pay, although not until next year, are recorded in full.

This points up the fact that, although all the dollars in financial statements look alike and are added together readily, some are worth more than others. This wouldn't be true if prices held steady, if there were no such thing as inflation. But when prices rise year in and year out, as they have in recent years, past transactions involve fewer dollars than present and future ones. This presents special problems in deciding how to value inventories and such long-lived resources as land, buildings, and machinery.

Since financial statements apply to specific periods of time—a month, a quarter, or a year—it becomes necessary to determine when a transaction takes place. Does a sale occur, for instance, when the order is

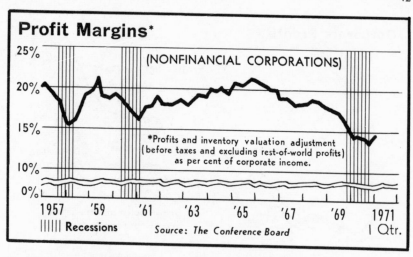

Profit Margins*

(NONFINANCIAL CORPORATIONS)

*Profits and inventory valuation adjustment
(before taxes and excluding rest-of-world profits)
as per cent of corporate income.

|||||| Recessions   Source: The Conference Board   I Qtr.

The part of each dollar of sales going to profit began to drop in 1966.

placed, when the shipment is invoiced, or when the payment is received? Ordinarily it occurs when the contract is made, when the buyer signs the purchase agreement. Other transactions—the payment once every three years of a premium on a fire insurance policy, for instance—can't be assigned to a single accounting period. In the case of the insurance policy, the expense can be spread evenly over thirty-six months. Often, however, it is difficult to determine the time over which a transaction should be spread. What, for instance, is the useful life of a jet aircraft within which its cost should be recovered—eleven years, as one airline contends, or fourteen, as asserted by another?

From the foregoing it should be obvious that accounting is an art and not a science, and that financial statements, especially for short periods of time, give only an approximate picture of a company's profits and the factors contributing to them. The danger of relying excessively on such numbers as earnings per share should be equally obvious.

There would be no problem, of course, if every venture represented only a single accounting period, if the factors contributing to profits and those draining profits were added up and balanced only once and the books closed. This, actually, was the way present-day accounting began, as a way of dividing up the owners' profits from the caravans and voyages that gave rise to Europe's commercial awakening in the fourteenth and fifteenth centuries. The need for a system of accounts that would provide not only a way of measuring ownership changes resulting from the conduct of a business—its profits—but also a continuing picture of those changes over time did not become apparent, however, until several hundred years later. Financial statements as we know them today didn't begin to evolve until the corporation, whose ongoing life was separate from the lives of its owners, began to supplant the sole proprietorship and the partnership as the dominant form of business enterprise.

The two principal financial statements are the balance sheet and the income statement. The balance sheet measures the resources controlled by a business, or assets; the claims against these resources, or liabilities; and the remaining owners' equity, or capital.

This is what a balance sheet looks like:

XYZ Corporation

BALANCE SHEET
December 31, 1970

Assets			Liabilities and Stockholders' Equity	
Current assets			Liabilities	
Cash		$196,000	Notes payable, current	
Accounts receivable		78,000	portion	$ 20,000
Inventories		124,000	Accounts payable	164,000
			Dividends payable	30,000
Total current assets		$398,000	Total current liabilities	$214,000
Plant			Notes payable, due	
Land		$ 48,000	after one year	$160,000
Building	$360,000		Stockholders' equity	
Less: Accumulated			Capital stock	$200,000
depreciation	116,000	244,000	Retained earnings	116,000
			Total liabilities and	
Total assets		$690,000	stockholders' equity	$690,000

The company's resources are divided into two groups, current assets, or cash and items readily converted to cash, and longer-lived assets. Note that the company's building is shown at cost, but that an attempt has been made to reflect its current value by deducting the accumulated expense of replacing it, or depreciation.

The claims against the company's resources, or liabilities, are similarly grouped into current liabilities, those due in one year or less, and longer ones.

The ownership value of the corporation, or stockholders' equity, is also divided into two parts. One part reflects the money invested in the business, the capital contributed by shareholders, and the other reflects the capital accumulated through profitable operations. Although sole proprietors and partners may draw down the funds they have invested, in paying dividends corporations are restricted to the use of retained earnings.

Profit, we have noted, is an increase in the ownership value of a business resulting from operations. Thus, one way of measuring profit would be to compare a succession of balance sheets, being careful to take account of any changes in owners' equity that do not result from operation of the business, such as an increase in invested capital. Another way is to measure revenues and expenses. A revenue is any receipt acquired by a company for goods or services it is in business to produce. It may be cash or an account receivable that will be converted to cash in a short time. An expense is the cost of goods and services used in producing revenues. Wages and salaries, rent, the cost of materials and of replacing aging equipment are some of a business's more important expenses.

The income statement reflects this way of measuring profit, or net income. This is what an income statement looks like:

XYZ Corporation

INCOME STATEMENT
Year Ended December 31, 1970

Sales revenues	$456,000
Dividend revenues	16,000
Total revenues	$472,000
Cost of goods sold	240,000
Operating expenses	137,000
Income taxes	19,000
Total expenses	$396,000
Net income	$ 76,000

The balance sheet and the income statement are really two ways of looking at the same thing, the changes in the ownership value of a business resulting from its operations. One way of thinking of the two financial statements is in terms of a reservoir. The balance sheet represents the level of the reservoir at any given time, the income statement a summary of the flows into and out of the reservoir over a period of time. Another way of thinking about them is in terms of the telecast of a football game. The income statement represents a videotape of the running play-by-play, the balance sheet a "freeze" of the scoreboard at the end of each quarter.

The balance sheet and the income statement are expressions respectively of two interrelated and self-proving equations:

$$\text{Assets} = \text{Liabilities} + \text{Owners' equity}$$
$$\text{Revenues} - \text{Expenses} = \text{Net income}$$

The equations are self-proving because the unknowns in each, as we have observed, are different ways of expressing the same thing. One way of demonstrating this is by subtracting liabilities from assets on the balance sheets at the end of two successive years. The increase in owners' equity should equal the net income derived from the income statement. Another way is to add the net income from the income statement to the owners' equity on the first balance sheet. This should equal the owners' equity on the balance sheet one year later.

The results are necessary—the balance sheet has to balance—because every profit-affecting transaction is entered into the accounting system in two ways, as a change in an asset or a liability and as a revenue or an expense. A sale, for instance, increases a balance sheet asset (cash). It also adds to an income statement item (revenues earned). The receipt of a telephone bill, the payment of which is not required until next month, increases a balance sheet liability (accounts payable). It also increases an income statement item (telephone expense).

The balance sheet and income statement are not refigured after every transaction. For a large business, with thousands of transactions every day, this would be wholly impractical. Instead, each of the principal asset, liability, and owners' equity items on the balance sheet and each of the major revenue and expense items in the income statement are set up as separate accounts.

Each account is set up in the same T-form as the balance sheet. Items on the left side are called "debits," those on the right "credits." There is no pejorative meaning to the word "debit." A credit isn't good and a debit bad. A debit is any transaction that increases the left, or asset, side of the balance sheet or decreases the right, or liability and owners' equity, side. A credit is any transaction that decreases the left, or asset, side or increases the right, or liability and owners' equity, side. There is no special reason why debits go on the left and credits on the right. It is merely a convention, like driving on the right-hand side of the road.

A consequence of this arrangement is that all asset accounts will show a debit balance at the end of an accounting period and that all liability and owners' equity accounts will show a credit balance. Debit and credit treatment of revenues and expenses can be inferred from what has already been said about owners' equity accounts. We have observed that any transaction that increases owners' equity is a credit and any that decreases it is a debit. A revenue must thus be a credit and an expense a debit.

Not all changes in owners' equity result from the operation of a business. They are therefore neither revenues nor expenses and do not affect the income statement. Additions and withdrawals of capital are one example, and gains or losses from the sale of property are another. In addition, certain balance sheet transactions cause a change in total assets and total liabilities without affecting owners' equity. A bank loan is an example. It adds to an asset (cash) on the left side of the balance sheet and to a liability (notes payable) on the right. But it does not result in either a revenue or an expense and so does not affect net income. By way of contrast, interest payments on the loan are an obvious expense.

Other transactions cause a rearrangement of the balance sheet without affecting owners' equity or the left and right totals. The purchase of a delivery truck for cash is an example. One asset (cash) is reduced by the amount of the purchase while another (equipment) is increased by the same amount.

Whether or not a transaction affects profit, it is nevertheless entered twice. This is to satisfy the fundamental balance sheet equation:

$$\text{Assets} = \text{Liabilities} + \text{Owners' equity}$$

Because of this fact the system has been designated "double-entry book-keeping."

Accounting is more than double-entry bookkeeping. If successful mastery of debits and credits were all there were to it, a clerk could become an accountant after several months of training. Instead, an accountant is a professional, like a lawyer, who is accepted only after years of education and experience. Also like the law, accounting involves rules, precedent, and judgment. Double-entry bookkeeping did not result from a highly developed theory. Rather, accounting theory has evolved—indeed, is still evolving—in response to the changing business environment.

It is fascinating that the earliest users of double entry, the merchants of Genoa and Venice, saw no particular necessity in having the two sets of entries balance at regular intervals. A latter-day auditor, retracing the steps of an early Italian bookkeeper, discovered an unresolved error of a dollar or so. In pressing further he discovered the source, failure to post, or enter, the transaction into an account.

Equally fascinating is the early ignorance of why double entry worked. For several centuries practitioners described the accounts as people—Mr. Cash, Mr. Goods, or Mr. Receivables—and transactions among them as a vast series of interlocking movements of imaginary little men. But there was little, if any, appreciation of the utter dependence of these movements on the twin accounting equations:

$$\text{Assets} = \text{Liabilities} + \text{Owner's equity}$$
$$\text{Revenues} - \text{Expenses} = \text{Net Income}$$

Double entry found little use other than historical record keeping until business began to reach beyond the private world of the individual entrepreneur. The huge size of the corporation created the need for better internal control; its separation of ownership from management created the need for better measures of performance; and its increasing impact on the world outside itself—on credit granters, potential investors, tax collectors, and government regulators—created the need for improved surveillance.

With growing frequency, accountants found themselves employed as the right-hand men of management in setting up and monitoring systems for measuring the overall performance of an enterprise and of its several parts. They found themselves hired by banks, commercial credit-rating agencies, unions, tax collectors, and government regulators to pore continuously over management's shoulder. And they found themselves cast in a new role, the role of disinterested appraiser, or certified public accountant, operating in behalf of everyone—but particularly shareholders and would-be investors—needing objective, consistent information of a corporation's financial behavior.

The need for such unbiased judgment was great, for few users of accounting information were inclined to press beyond their own specific requirements. Banks, for instance, were concerned primarily with a company's ability to repay its short-term obligations. They focused, therefore, on the amount of cash and other assets readily convertible to cash among a company's assets and their relationship to the concern's short-term liabilities. Long-term creditors, the holders of bonds and mortgages, were concerned chiefly with the company's ability to pay off its debts in the event of bankruptcy and thus focused on the liquidating value of plant, equipment, and other depreciable assets. The Internal Revenue Service wanted assurance that taxable income wasn't being written off or hidden; bank examiners, that assets were adequate enough and liquid enough to cover any likely claims of depositors; and United States attorneys and investigative agencies, that fraud wasn't being committed. Businessmen, for their part, wanted figures that would minimize taxes, lend least support to union demands, keep credit flowing at lowest cost, placate shareholders, and present the best face to the investing public.

The demands of outsiders and businessmen have come into conflict increasingly. Creditors continue to favor "conservative" accounting, figures that tend to understate the value of assets but fully state the claims against them. This, they believe, gives their claims an extra margin of protection. The operators of closely held concerns often share the same view, feeling that in this way earnings are kept less visible to tax collectors and union negotiators.

Managements of large publicly held corporations, on the other hand, are more and more becoming the victims—often willing victims—of the cult of stock market performance. In recent years a larger and larger proportion of stock market transactions has been accounted for by mutual funds, private pension funds, state and municipal retirement funds, college endowment funds, insurance companies, and savings institutions. At the same time the managers of these funds—plus the investment public in general—have placed increasing emphasis on growth of earnings, particularly earnings per share, in bidding for stocks.

Performance based upon the growth of a company's sales and profits, of course, is the name of the game. However, for a time, at least, quick-money artists discovered that stock market performance need not be limited by insufficient growth in either area, with the result that questionable accounting practices proliferated. Once, it was probably true, the shareholder suffered because "conservative" accounting tended to understate earnings and thus the value of his ownership, making it difficult for him to realize the full value of his shares. But because of overstatement, he was more likely to suffer from inability to buy at a fair price.

Some of the more flagrant variations in accounting practice occurred in such booming industries as franchising, computer leasing and conglomerates. Performance Systems, Inc., once known as Minnie Pearl's Chicken Systems, reported $13.4 million in sales in 1968, $9.34-million from the disposal of franchises. But of the 1,200 outlets sold, only 120 stores were actually operating at the end of the accounting period, which meant that actual franchise sales were probably closer to $900,000 and total sales to $5 million. A subsequent revision of the accounting rules recommended that franchisers recognize as current revenue only the cash actually received from franchise fees, often only 10 to 15 percent of the contract price.

Continental Computer Associates, a computer leasing company, assigned a ten-year useful life to its equipment, using straight-line depreciation. Straight-line depreciation results in an equal charge to depreciation expense in each of the ten years. By way of contrast, IBM charged off similar equipment over four years, using accelerated depreciation. Accelerated depreciation results in heavier depreciation expense in the initial years, declining expense later on. On a $1-million computer, then, Continental would have recorded a first-year depreciation expense of $100,-

000, while IBM would have recorded $400,000. If the computer was leased at $250,000, IBM would have shown a loss, while Continental Computer—leasing identical equipment—would have been able to show a before-tax profit of $150,000. To this day, there is no agreement among accountants about how to determine the useful life of aging assets.

Gulf and Western Industries, the conglomerate, or multimarket, company that operates Paramount Pictures, reported net income of $1.92 a share for the six months ending January 31, 1969, compared with $1.59 a share for the same months of 1968. Only after prodding, however, did the company disclose that 78 cents of the 1969 total came from sales of securities, compared with 13 cents a year earlier. Gulf and Western had done well in the stock market. It had also been active in leasing Paramount films to television. But profits from these sources, as the company itself had noted in an earlier annual report, were far from certain. Without them Gulf and Western's net income for the period would have shown a decline, from $1.46 to $1.14 a share. Two years earlier, an accounting opinion had been published that earnings before and after extraordinary items be given equal prominence.

Lest it be thought that such practices are the province solely of newcomers to the corporate scene, consider the following. In 1968 a number of airlines switched from eleven-year to twelve- to fourteen-year depreciation of their aircraft. Eastern Airlines managed, in this fashion, to cut a loss of $1.91 a share to a loss of $1.06 a share. Pan American, American, and TWA increased their earnings by bookkeeping changes.

The same year the eight largest steel companies all switched from accelerated to some form of straight-line depreciation. At United States Steel the depreciation change increased net income by $55 million. Big Steel also changed its way of accounting for the investment tax credit on purchases of new plant and equipment. Together these accounting changes increased its earnings per share 59 percent, from $2.95 to $4.69. Not long afterward the Allegheny Ludlum Steel Corporation, a major specialty steel producer, went a step further. It applied to the Internal Revenue Service to switch its accounting for materials from last in, first out to first in, first out.

Last in, first out, or LIFO, is a method of valuing inventories based on the notion that goods acquired last are those sold first. This isn't the way things actually work, but there is logic to the idea nevertheless, based on the notion that replacement cost should be matched closely to selling price. In a period of rapidly rising prices, this means that a company isn't deceiving itself by believing that a rise in the price of goods purchased really produces net income. It means that it is allocating sufficient funds for the expense of replacing depleted inventory. LIFO has the additional advantage of minimizing income taxes. By way of contrast, first in, first out, or FIFO, increases a company's tax liability, producing at the same time a larger apparent net income—in other words, real taxes but only apparent profit. The cult of performance being what it is, however, Allegheny Ludlum decided nevertheless to make the switch. Few investors, it apparently decided, would be discerning enough to appreciate the high cost of a better-looking earnings statement.

Businessmen blamed the other fellow for the declining standards. "There is a sort of Gresham's law in operation," one explained. Named for Sir Thomas Gresham, the sixteenth-century English financier, Gresham's law says that when two currencies circulate together, both of the same nominal value but one of greater intrinsic value, the good currency will tend to be hoarded and the bad currency will tend to drive the good currency out of circulation.

In no area, perhaps, was this exemplified so spectacularly as in that of mergers and acquisitions. The classic case involves the acquisition of Wilson and Company, the venerable meat-packing concern, by the then-rising conglomerate Ling-Temco-Vought. LTV purchased 53 percent of Wilson common stock for $81.5 million cash, absorbed the 47 percent remaining by issuing a new convertible preferred stock, and effected a merger of the two companies. Three days later it spun off three new Wilson companies, retaining controlling interest in each but inviting minority stockholder ownership. One new company took over Wilson's meat-packing operations, another its sporting goods business, and the third its pharmaceutical manufacturing. Virtually all the former company's assets and liabilities were handed down to the new entities.

In the process, however, LTV managed to put on its books at $109 million an investment that had cost it $193 million: the $81.5 million cash plus the value of the new preferred measured by its yield, its liquidation value, and its conversion value. The remaining $88 million, in the words of Abraham J. Briloff, professor of accountancy at The Bernard M. Baruch College, The City University of New York, had "for all intents and purposes 'gotten lost' at least insofar as the income statement is concerned and to the extent of $65 million thereof will never ever appear on any statement."*

What LTV had done was to account for the Wilson and Company acquisition as a pooling of interest, not a purchase. In essence, pooling of interest accounting, at least as it was practiced at the time, permitted an acquiring company to record the assets of an acquired company at the value they were carried on the acquired company's books, or book value—LTV added a few wrinkles to do even better—instead of at the actual purchase cost.

* "The 'Funny Money' Game," *Financial Analysts Journal*, May-June, 1969, p. 75.

Book value, a company's net worth as carried on its balance sheet, bears little relationship to the worth of a company as determined by the judgment of buyers and sellers in the marketplace, except for bank stocks and a few industrials.

In LTV's case the difference between book value and the actual purchase cost was recorded as "goodwill," a catchall term that embraces intangibles such as trademarks, patents, brand names, and established market position. Because goodwill didn't have to be amortized, the depreciation expense of the surviving companies was reduced and their net incomes increased—all without anything other than accounting changes.

Such "dirty pooling," as Professor Briloff has dubbed the Wilson and Company and similar acquisitions, seemed doomed ultimately. The Accounting Principles Board of the American Institute of Certified Public Accountants proposed that tangible assets acquired in a pooling of interest be put on the books at market value and be depreciated in exactly the same way as a newly purchased building or piece of equipment. It proposed that remaining goodwill be amortized over forty years, the effect of which would be to pare sharply the boost in net income of the surviving company due solely to accounting changes.

The Accounting Principles Board—to which the Securities and Exchange Commission defers, generally—has been cast in the role of a fire brigade, responding to one alarm occasioned by violation of good accounting practice after another. The board, two-thirds of whose members must approve a recommended change, has scored some notable achievements, perhaps the most significant of which has been its requirement that companies report per share earnings two ways: on a primary basis, in which net income is divided by the number of common shares outstanding, and on a fully diluted basis, in which the number of shares that would result from conversion of preferred stock and debentures and from warrants is taken into account.

The board's efforts did not put out all the fires. Some corporations ignored the rules, others discovered new ways around them. Unfavorable information continued to be hidden in fine-type footnotes to the annual financial statements, and quarterly reports remained sketchy and incomplete. In many cases neither these nor the textual portions of the annual report—including the easily read financial highlights—bore the certification of the concern's independent certified public accountants.

The certification is limited in any case. Unless carefully read and understood, it might suggest more than is actually there. The first paragraph of the certification typically describes the scope of the examination. Even here the auditor's stamp of approval might not apply to the entire enterprise. In bank holding companies, for instance, the certification often indicates that the books of the parent have been examined by the auditors but that those of the subsidiaries have not. The same might be true of multinational companies with several foreign subsidiaries.

The more important paragraph is the second. It offers the opinion, sometimes qualified, that the financial statements are fairly presented and in conformity with generally accepted accounting principles. Note that the independent certified public accountants attest to the fairness of the presentation, not to the accuracy of the figures. The responsibility of accounting firms in assuring the accuracy of financial information they certify has become the subject of several landmark court cases, growing out of apparent failures. It seems quite likely that the courts will decide that a concern's independent auditors bear some measure of responsibility not only for the way the figures are shown but that they mean what they say.

Even so, it is unlikely that there will ever be general acceptance of any one way to determine the useful life of an aircraft or a computer or to value inventory. It seems equally unlikely that there will be total agreement on the way to treat windfall profits and catastrophic losses. The most that an independent certified public accountant can assure is that the figures for a single concern are comparable over a period of years. It can do little to achieve comparability within an industry or with other concerns generally.

This means that, as always, the users of financial information must do more than accept financial statements unquestioningly. The rule "Investigate, then invest" is never more meaningful than when hundreds of concerns—among them some of the oldest and most respected—indulge in cosmetic accounting, a change in accounting methods to improve the appearance of earnings.

Lest the small investor be dismayed at the odds he faces, let him gain consolation, if not confidence, from the fact that some of the wisest and most sophisticated users of financial statements have been fooled as readily as the first-time investor. Westec Corporation continued to pile up debts and its shares continued to trade on the stock market long after sober second-guessing indicated it should have been out of business. The Mill Factors Corporation continued to receive certification from a leading accounting firm and millions of dollars of credit from some of Wall Street's biggest banks despite the fact that for all practical purposes it had been insolvent for several years.

If nothing else, the small investor should realize that the balance sheet does not measure an enterprise's net worth. As a going concern it may understate it considerably; in liquidation it may overstate it. Nor does the income statement give a wholly accurate picture of net income, except over a long period of years.

The small investor should also be wary of the more obvious attempts to improve the appearance of net income, such as failure to amortize such sizable but continuing costs as research and development, efforts to bring infrequent and uncertain windfall gains into income, and the bunching of all kinds of losses in a single year and charging them as extraordinary against stockholders' equity, not income. He should eschew as investments the shares of companies that fail to disclose necessary comparisons and other pertinent information or hide it in the fine print. He should favor those companies that strive for clarity, completeness, and comparability.

Happily, an increasing number of concerns are providing substantial information not only on their overall operations but on those of their major divisions. Bangor Punta, MGM, and National Distillers were among the pioneers in taking such steps. But while some companies are coming to appreciate the importance of better financial reporting, a large number continue to employ less defensible practices. More than many other consumers, the user of financial statements must keep before him constantly the admonition: Let the buyer beware.

6. Government, Business, and National Income

Business may be big, but government is bigger. It is also faster growing. At the turn of the century one out of every twenty-four workers was on a government payroll, but presently the ratio is closer to one in six. Federal government spending has grown eight times as fast as the national output, and government debt—federal, state, and local—has risen from six to thirty cents of every dollar of indebtedness of the American people.

At the beginning of the century federal outlays amounted to about one-half billion dollars a year, enough to run the government a little less than one day at the 1970 expenditure rate. Indeed, total administrative budget expenditures from the beginning of the republic in 1789 to 1900 amounted to $15.5 billion, less than one month's outlays at the 1970 unified budget rate of $195 billion.

A better measure of government size and influence lies in the relationship between its spending and the total national output of goods and services. While estimates of this so-called gross national product (GNP) are somewhat uncertain for the early years of the republic, except for the Civil War and World War I federal spending probably averaged no more than 5 percent of GNP from the beginning of the country to 1929.

The percentage of federal spending to GNP, 2.5 percent in 1929, rose rapidly through the years of the depression and the New Deal. But despite the boasts of the New Dealers and the anguished cries of their opponents, federal spending never got much above 10 percent. World War II, however, changed things. By 1945 federal spending had jumped to 45 percent of GNP. Since the war federal spending has risen above 20 percent of GNP only twice, during the Korean War and again during

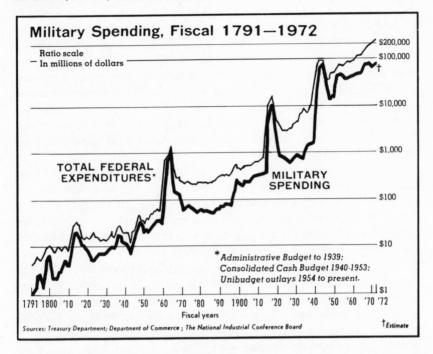

Military Spending, Fiscal 1791—1972

Ratio scale
— In millions of dollars

$200,000
$100,000
†

$10,000

$1,000

TOTAL FEDERAL
EXPENDITURES*

MILITARY
SPENDING

$100

$10

*Administrative Budget to 1939;
Consolidated Cash Budget 1940-1953;
Unibudget outlays 1954 to present.

$1

1791 1800 '10 '20 '30 '40 '50 '60 '70 '80 '90 1900 '10 '20 '30 '40 '50 '60 '70 '72

Fiscal years

Sources: Treasury Department; Department of Commerce ; The National Industrial Conference Board   † Estimate

Wars and preparations for wars have played an important role in Federal spending programs. Since World War II, the proportion of total outlays going to the military has remained higher than in previous peacetime periods.

the Vietnam conflict, and in each case only slightly. But except for a brief period in the late 1940s, it has never fallen below 17 percent.

The relationship of federal spending to the total output of goods and services tells only part of the story. From a low point of 3.6 percent of GNP in 1944, state and local spending has increased almost without interruption until it stands close to 10 percent of total output. This means that the spending of all government units—50 states and 80,000 localities as well as the federal government—has grown from 10 percent of GNP in 1929 to more than 30 percent today.

Wars and the preparation for wars have played an important role in federal spending. In only four periods in the nation's history—from the founding of the republic until the War of 1812, between the Civil and the Spanish-American wars, between World Wars I and II, and between World War II and Korea—have military outlays fallen below 40 percent of total federal outlays. During wars they have leaped as high as 90 percent. Since World War II defense-related activities—among them atomic energy, military assistance to foreign governments, the space program, and foreign economic aid—have gained steadily in importance.

New functions and new concepts of the role of government have also affected federal spending. In years past, when America was largely an agricultural country, older persons were cared for by their children. Today, with most people living in cities and families often widely separated, Social Security has taken over much of this function. At one time education was entirely the concern of local governments and private individuals. Today, in part to establish national standards and in part to assure that needy children aren't denied an education, the federal government advances considerable aid to schools.

More and more, the emerging problems of the final quarter of the century are problems arising from the growth of population and the country's increasing urbanization. These include such widely differing things as the training of undereducated manpower for useful jobs, the elimination of air and water pollution, and the ending of air traffic congestion over metropolitan areas. Many of the problems are one of a kind, calling for an integrated approach by many different specialists. Eliminating air and water pollution, for example, may bring together chemical engineers, industrialists, city planners and medical men, representatives of both the public and private sectors. Often the problems are national, or at least interstate, in their scope—hence the increasing reliance on the federal government as organizer and arbiter.

Government services have certain characteristics. They include those in which the benefits are spread widely among a large group of users and those in which private property rights are not well established. Interstate highways, public health programs, flood control, and the national defense are examples. Some kinds of services, however, are commonly used but privately owned. A baseball game is an example. Thousands of spectators share in the common enjoyment of the game, but each pays an individual admission price. The difference between public and private goods, then, is not common as opposed to personal benefit. Many privately owned goods—the flowering shrubs around a home, for instance—result in public benefit and enjoyment.

Armen A. Alchian and William R. Allen* of the University of California, Los Angeles, say that the difference between public and private goods arises additionally from the inability to exclude people who would share in the benefit from a necessary common service but are unwilling to pay. A classic example of this is a lighthouse. If a lighthouse keeper could control the light rays so that any nonpaying shipowner would be unable to see the light, he could price his services in relation to what users were willing to pay. Since he cannot, government has taken over the task.

* *University Economics,* Belmont, Calif., Wadsworth, 1964, p. 751.

Even then, however, public operation is not essential. Take the case of television. In the minds of most people, it offers a common benefit. And yet, so long as anyone with a receiving set can view a program sent from a central transmitter, broadcasters are unable to charge individual viewers for the programs they see. In a number of other countries this has meant government operation, while in the United States it has led to the underwriting of operating costs by advertisers, although the advent of cable television is changing the nature of the game. As broadcasters increasingly offer programs only to viewers who pay to connect their sets to a cable, the need for tax support or advertising declines, and a charge for a specific program or service, in effect an admissions charge, is substituted.

Even when government recognizes a service as essential, it does not necessarily have to provide it itself. As in higher education, it may subsidize private operation through grants to students and universities. Or it may provide tax subsidies.

In the United States government hasn't limited itself to the goods and services it best can provide. It has intervened increasingly in the private sector. Government intervention in the economy began initially as an attempt to establish the rules of the game. It started with laws defining property and governing its transfer. Without such laws there would be no exclusive possession and transfer of scarce goods, the essential condition of a market economy, and there would be no contracts. And misrepresentation and fraud would go unpunished.

Government intervened further by becoming an active referee. To enforce its own notions of competition in areas where property rights were easily defined, it passed the antitrust laws. Where property rights were less easily defined—the allocation of air routes and radio frequencies, for example—it used its powers to limit the number of suppliers. Seldom, however, did it restrict itself to establishing property rights where none had existed before. Having embarked on regulation, it more often went on—frequently with perverse results—to try to simulate market performance. It legislated prices, output, standards of service, and profits.

Where private industry has been slow to join the game—high-research, high-technology areas on the one hand, health care and economic opportunity on the other—government has found it necessary to assume the role of entrepreneur. Unlike the socialist countries, however, it has eschewed the ownership of business enterprise—why, it is hard to say. The decision may reflect superior intelligence, an appreciation of the inefficiencies of bureaucracy. It may reflect the ancient American distrust of big government. Or it may reflect nothing more than luck.

Government has chosen to avoid the pitfalls of bureaucracy by dealing as much as possible with private contractors as suppliers. While this may have sidestepped one kind of problem, it has led to another. In its dealings with contractors the government now faces the unenviable task of attempting to keep an arm's-length relationship, although it may be the contractor's sole or principal customer.

The result of this amalgam of private services and government services is a mixed economy. It is not laissez-faire—that is, an economy in which individuals and businesses make decisions limited only by the dictates of competition—nor is it socialistic—that is, an economy in which decisions are made solely by the state.

Although there is no detailed planning, as in a socialist country, it would be a mistake to imply that the American economy is unplanned. Planning in the American economy began as necessity, to meet the challenges to survival posed by two world wars. The wars, as had earlier conflicts, presented huge problems in allocating scarce resources and in meeting the costs of the conflicts. Almost accidentally, they demonstrated the considerable impact of government spending on overall growth and stability.

If government spending could so stimulate economic growth in wartime, would not similar spending have a comparable impact in peacetime? If government purchases of goods and services and the efforts to finance those purchases led to wartime boom and postwar bust, couldn't the same forces be applied countercyclically in peacetime to help offset business ups and downs? These questions were asked during the great depression of the 1930s and again after World War II.

The result, embodied in the Employment Act of 1946, was the conscious decision of government to use its considerable spending and taxing powers to counter the forces of inflation and recession and to use its money-creating powers for the same purpose. This required planning.

Planning as it has come to be practiced in the United States does not mean that all activities are ordered from on high, that Washington gives a command and that all units in the economy, private as well as public, march off in the same direction at the same moment. Rather, it means that an implicit attempt is made to agree on common goals, that policy makers as well as followers must often search for the ultimate direction, and that units attempt to align themselves to the common aim. The parade may look much the same as that in a socialist country, but the lineup of marchers and their route is far less predictable.

The desire of government, then, to promote both growth and stability involved more than the use of its own resources. It meant inducing the private sector to keep more closely in step with the common plan, a necessary prerequisite of which was some way of linking the public and private sectors, some way of determining whether the economy was moving up or down and how fast.

The answer was national income accounting. The national income accounts are a series of accounts, not unlike those relating to the income statement of a business concern, which attempt to sum up regularly the receipts and expenditures of all the major groups in the economy—consumers, businesses, governments, and foreigners—in effect, to apply the language of the businessman, accounting, to the economy as a whole and to its major parts.

The similarities between national income accounting and business accounting are considerable—money value providing the common denominator for all transactions, with several exceptions only actual transactions being recorded, the use of a system of double entry, and the accounts being set up to balance—but there are some notable differences. For the present, there is no system of accounts to measure assets and liabilities, the national wealth and the claims against that wealth.* The result is an income statement only. There is no balance sheet.

Profit, where it occurs, is treated as a return to capital. It is not the final balancing item of the statement. Although transactions are recorded initially in dollars of present value, an attempt is made to restate them in dollars of constant value. This is done by calculating the rate of price increase—or as during the 1930s the decrease—and "deflating" the current dollar figure for total output to offset this rise.

The essence of the national income accounts is the realization that every receipt by one person involves a cost to someone else. Wages, rent, interest, and dividends are income to workers, landlords, creditors, and shareholders. They are costs to employers, tenants, debtors, and corporations. The sum of expenditures on all goods and services produced equals the sum of all incomes earned.

Two sets of accounts, then, have been created, one to measure money spent in creating the national product, the other to measure incomes earned. Since total product equals total income, the two sets of accounts must balance.

The expenditure, or product, accounts record spending by consumers on goods not previously used, spending by businesses on new goods not intended for resale, all purchases of goods and services by federal, state, and municipal governments, and net spending by foreigners for American goods and services. The receipt, or income, accounts add together wages, rents, interest, and profits.

The result is the national product. It is described as the gross national product (GNP) before an allowance for depreciation, or the expense of replacing aging plant and equipment, is subtracted. It is described as net national product (NNP) afterward. Net national product is a better in-

---

* There are wealth estimates and also estimates of debt.

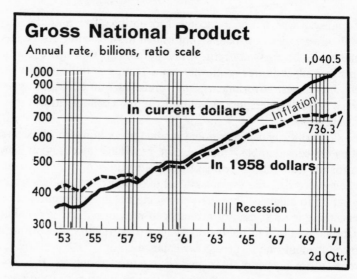

Gross National Product
Annual rate, billions, ratio scale

1,040.5

In current dollars

Inflation

736.3

In 1958 dollars

||||| Recession

'53 '55 '57 '59 '61 '63 '65 '67 '69 '71
2d Qtr.

The gross national product is calculated in current dollars and, after adjustment for price changes, in dollars of constant value. Real growth was high in the early 1960s but slowed as inflation took an increasing toll.

dicator of current output than gross national product. But depreciation figures are hard to obtain quickly, and over the years NNP has borne such a steady relationship to GNP—about ten-elevenths—that GNP is equally usable.

To assure that the accounts measure current production, but nothing more, final sales are recorded. Thus, the purchase of an automobile by a consumer or a truck by a business goes into the accounts, but the purchase of steel used to produce the vehicle does not. Similarly, the sale of already existing assets—a used car, an old house, shares of stock—are excluded from the accounts, as are welfare, social security, veterans' payments, and other transfers of income not related to current production.

Government expenditures are treated differently from private. No attempt is made to determine how much government expenditure represents investment and how much depreciation should be charged against it, and no attempt is made to determine how much government product is final. All government expenditures on goods and services are included at their cost to the government, which means everything the government pays to its employees plus all it buys from private industry, from typewriters to space vehicles. Pensions for war veterans and other transfer payments, however, are excluded.

Much useful production gets accomplished without anyone's getting paid, housewives' services and those of do-it-yourself home repairmen, for example. Most such activity never gets into the accounts. In certain cases, however, an attempt is made to estimate the value of goods that are not marketed, such as the food produced by a farmer for his own family use or the rent a homeowner would have to pay if he were not his own landlord.

This results in some amusing, if not always logical, consequences. If a man marries his housekeeper, the GNP goes down by the amount of her pay. But if she subsequently takes another job outside the home and someone else is hired to come in and clean, the GNP goes up by the amount of both wages.

By way of contrast, some payments are made for output of questionable value. The production of a company that dumped pollutants into a stream would go into the accounts in exactly the same way as that of a more civic-minded competitor although the effort of a community downstream to remove the contaminants would also be recorded in GNP. And wages paid to a worker who spends most of his time at the water cooler aren't distinguished from those paid to one who declines to utilize his coffee break.

This does not mean that the national income accounts are stupid or useless. It means that they should be approached with the same caution one should use in examining the income statement of a business, and with the same awareness of the accounting conventions underlying each. It means that as much attention should be paid to the components of GNP as to the total, and that attention should be paid to the direction they are moving and to how fast they are changing. With other economic indicators—including industrial production, new orders for durable goods, capital spending, and the money supply—such movements can give valuable clues to the state of the economy and its likely future direction.

In fact, no general business downturn—with the possible exception of the 1873–79 contraction—has been recorded in which GNP, after adjustment for price changes, moved up. Because of this fact, the National Bureau of Economic Research, the private research organization whose pioneering efforts helped to create the national income accounts, now requires a drop in real GNP for two quarters in a row as a necessary precondition for calling a downturn a recession.

Most of the items are self-explanatory, but a few extra words may be needed. In addition to business purchases of machinery and equipment, net private domestic investment includes all—not merely business—construction and inventory changes. The rationale for including apartment houses is that rented dwellings, like business properties, are income producing. Since owner-occupied homes provide a service indistinguishable from that provided by apartment houses, they are included, too. As for inventories, since the national income statement is a summary of goods and services produced, not of those sold, goods made but not sold must be added to the sales figures. Similarly, goods removed from store and warehouse shelves for sale but not produced in the year must be subtracted from sales figures.

This is what the national income statement looks like:

Gross National Product

(in billions of dollars)
1970

Personal consumption expenditure		$616.7	Compensation of employees	$599.8
			Rental income of persons	22.7
Durable goods	$ 89.4			
Nondurable goods	264.7		Net interest	33.5
Services	262.6			
			Proprietors' income	67.6
Government purchases of goods and services		220.5	Corporate profits and inventory valuation adjustment	76.5
Net private domestic investment		51.4	National income	$800.1
			Indirect business taxes	92.1
Gross investment	135.7			
Less: Depreciation	84.3		Transfer payments	3.6
Net export of goods and services		3.6	Miscellaneous and statistical discrepancy	−1.8
Exports	62.2		Subsidies less current surplus of government enterprises	−1.8
Less: Imports	58.6			
Net national product		$892.2	Net national product	$892.2
Depreciation		84.3	Depreciation	84.3
Gross national product		$976.5	Gross national product	$976.5

Employees' compensation includes all wages, salaries, bonuses, royalties, commissions, and tips. It also includes the Social Security contributions of both workers and their employers, fringe benefits, and payroll taxes.

Interest includes payments on private debt obligations but excludes payments on the public debt, the rationale being that private debt is capital creating and that interest payments on such debt represent a proper charge against current production. By way of contrast, government debt is considered to represent largely the past costs of operating the government.

Corporate profits resulting solely from a rise in inventory prices are subtracted from the corporate profit total.

Some taxes, like personal and corporate income taxes, are levied directly on the principal income items—wages, rent, interest, and profits. Being taxes on income, they are considered part of income, disbursed first to workers, landlords, creditors, and business owners and then collected by the government. Other taxes—like the federal excises on liquor and tobacco, state gasoline and general sales taxes, and local property taxes—are levied directly. They are not considered to reflect any contribution of resources to current production. But since they are already included in the expenditure total on the left-hand side of the national income statement, they have to be added in on the right-hand side as well.

Here is the gross national product, restated to reflect these concepts:

Gross National Product and Personal Income

1970
(in billions of dollars)

Gross national product		$976.5
Less: Depreciation		−84.3
Net national product		$892.2
Less:		
Indirect business taxes	$92.1	
Business transfer payments	3.6	
Statistical discrepancy	−2.1	
Plus:		
Subsidies less current surplus of government enterprises	1.8	
		−91.8
		$800.4
National Income		
Less:		
Corporate profits and inventory valuation adjustment	76.8	
Social insurance contributions	57.1	
Plus:		
Transfer payments to persons	73.9	
Interest paid by government and consumers	31.8	
Dividends	25.2	
Business transfer payments	3.6	
		+0.6
		$801.0
Personal Income		
Less: Personal tax and nontax payments		−116.2
Disposable personal income		684.8
Less: Personal outlays		−634.6
Personal saving		$ 50.2
Saving rate		7.3%

Subtracted from net national product, direct business taxes produce national income, the income earned by workers, landlords, creditors, and business owners for their contribution of productive resources.

Personal income, the total income received by households in a year, is obtained by subtracting from national income income earned but not received—Social Security contributions, undistributed corporate profits, and other items—and by adding income received but not earned—principally personal transfer payments. Disposable personal income is obtained by subtracting personal tax and nontax payments from personal income.

Personal saving is obtained by deducting personal consumption expenditures and certain other items from disposable personal income. The saving rate is personal saving as a percentage of disposable personal income.

The national income accounts tell how rapidly a country's income is rising. By themselves, however, they tell little about its people, how rich or poor they are and how their lot is changing.

By dividing real gross national product—GNP deflated for price increases—by population, a good measure of how the citizens of one country compare with those of another in the division of current income may be obtained. By calculating the rate of change in this per capita real GNP we can determine how rapidly they are improving their circumstances.

The national income accounts say almost nothing, however, about how well off a people are at any time. Thus, they tell little about the sacrifices needed, for instance, to achieve a more rapid rise in GNP and little about the ability of the less-developed to catch up with their industrialized neighbors or of the ability of the Soviet Union to overtake the United States.

The need here is for a national balance sheet, a way of adding up a nation's resources and the claims against those resources, subtracting the liabilities from the assets, and arriving at the nation's wealth. The problem in accomplishing such a balance sheet centers largely in the fact that much of a nation's wealth lies in its people, in its supply of working men and women and in their level of training. The scholars have been working on a national balance sheet but have not yet perfected it to the point where practical and reasonably complete reports can be published regularly.

The national income accounts, as we have seen, record only final sales. Intercompany transactions are excluded. Suppose, however, a shipping strike were to block off imports of copper. What effect would this have on the production of automobiles, electrical equipment, and plumbing supplies? One way of telling is input-output analysis.

Input-output analysis divides the economy into a number of industrial sectors, usually several hundred. The sectors are then entered in a table, once vertically and once horizontally, like the names of cities on a road-map mileage table. Amounts purchased by each industry are listed vertically under the industry from which they are bought. Amounts sold by each industry are listed horizontally alongside the industry to which they are delivered. The total purchases, or input, of each industry are summed up at the bottom of each column. The total sales, or output, are summed up in a separate right-hand column. The sum of all inputs and outputs comes together in a single figure in the lower right-hand corner. This is the total output of all goods and services in the economy, or GNP.

Here is the basic form of organization of the input-output tables:

Input—Output Table

	Producers								Final Markets			
Sellers \ **Buyers**	Agri-culture	Mining	Construc-tion	Manufac-turing	Trade	Transpor-tation	Services	Other	Persons	Investors	Foreign-ers	Govern-ment
Agriculture												
Mining												
Construction												
Manufacturing												
Trade												
Transportation												
Services												
Other												
Employees												
Owners of Business and Capital									Gross National Product			
Government												

A discerning reader will observe that the items under final markets at the right comprise the left-hand side of the national income statement in balance-sheet form while those at the bottom comprise the right-hand side. Because of the complexity of the data and because inter-industry relationships change slowly, the Department of Commerce, which com-

[In millions of dollars at producers' prices]

For the distribution of output of an industry, read the row for that industry.

For the composition of inputs to an industry, read the column for that industry.

Industry	Motor vehicles and equipment (59)	Radio, television and communication equipment (56)	Electric lighting and wiring equipment (55)	Machine shop products (50)	Metalworking machinery and equipment (47)	Other fabricated metal products (42)	Stampings, screw machine products and bolts (41)	Primary nonferrous metal manufacturing (38)	Primary iron and steel manufacturing (37)	Glass and glass products (35)	Rubber and miscellaneous plastics products (32)	Paints and allied products (30)	Miscellaneous fabricated textile products (19)
Livestock & Livestock Products													
Other Agricultural Products													
Forestry & Fishery Products													
Agricultural, Forestry & Fishery Services													
Iron & Ferroalloy Ores Mining								15	1,168				
Nonferrous Metal Ores Mining			5					891			9		
Coal Mining	15	1	1		1	1		13	470	(*) 3	10	5	4
Crude Petroleum & Natural Gas						2	1		70	37			(*)
Stone and Clay Mining and Quarrying	2	(*)		(*)		2		18	12	1	(*)		1,245
Chemical & Fertilizer Mineral Mining				(*)		(*)		(*)					315
New Construction													61
Maintenance & Repair Construction	71	11	3	7	11	13	6	44	173	13	27	6	272
Ordnance & Accessories	16	108			1	5	20	6	5		(*)	100	8
Food & Kindred Products											181		
Tobacco Manufactures							(*)		(*)	(*)	394	1	2
Broad & Narrow Fabrics, Yarn & Thread Mills	15	1	8	2	(*)	1	5	12	20	4	22	1	23
Miscellaneous Textile Goods & Floor Coverings	129	(*) 10	3	3	6	44	36	13	35	58	6		28
Apparel	17		3	2	1	9		7	3		28		(*)
Miscellaneous Fabricated Textile Products	397	3	1		6	1	3	22	7	11	4	1	1
Lumber & Wood Products, Except Containers	27	6	1	(*)	1	57	6	2	16	14	3	19	28
Wooden Containers		193		3	1	5	18	(*)	2	2	(*)		1
Household Furniture	7		54	2	2	13	55	21	7	134	53	499	(*)
Other Furniture & Fixtures	(*)	18	17		11	7	1	12	411	130	161	228	2
Paper & Allied Products, Except Containers	1	30	30	5	1	61	36	1	(*)	1	2	21	28
Paperboard Containers & Boxes	10	29	16	1	14	88	24	148	(*)	5	383		1
Printing & Publishing	13	15	31		(*)	4	3	128	157	8	1,790	105	(*)
Chemicals & Selected Chemical Products	2	46	79		1	123	27	1	15	62	5	10	28
Plastics & Synthetic Materials	42	1	(*)	(*)	3	(*)	18	82	5	(*)	10	(*)	1
Drugs, Cleaning & Toilet Preparations	11	2	(*)	5	20	5	65	16	45	190	21	1	(*)
Paints & Allied Products	2	25	110	9	43	66	(*)	2	4,897	78	445	11	2
Petroleum Refining & Related Industries	194	101	32	(*)	84	32	(*)	(*)	528	7	5	6	102
Rubber & Miscellaneous Plastics Products	69	(*)	201	(*)	443	124	1	1		16	13	23	5
Leather Tanning & Industrial Leather Products	893	38	241	27	131	(*)	19	35			24	148	1
Footwear & Other Leather Products	(*)	(*)		196	1	10	1,047	136			74		11
Glass & Glass Products	1	73		92		13	287	4,883			50		6
Stone & Clay Products	366	224		(*)		72	18				24		23
Primary Iron & Steel Manufacturing	79					1,543					2		148
Primary Nonferrous Metal Manufacturing	3,453					742							
Metal Containers	547				1	1							

Item													
Other Fabricated Metal Products	1	(*) 1	62	62	2	184	44	202	71	338	209	88	174	1,120
Engines & Turbines	3		66	66	1	424	67	16	16	4	139		175
Farm Machinery & Equipment						2	11	20	4	14			21
Construction, Mining & Oil Field Machinery	(*)	(*)	(*)	(*)		32				7			25
Materials Handling Machinery & Equipment	(*)	(*)	2	2	1	20	(*)	(*)	(*)	6	1	23	1	17
Metalworking Machinery & Equipment			6	6		13	4	1						542
Special Industry Machinery & Equipment					3	80	73	51	1	92	381	6	99	3
General Industrial Machinery & Equipment	1		14	14		47	7	7	29	3	33	1	4	203
Machine Shop Products	1		1	1		126	42			17	188		45	416
Office, Computing & Accounting Machines	(*)		6	6		172	109			224	13		38	16
Service Industry Machines	1							1	1		45	1	38	16
Electric Industrial Equipment & Apparatus			(*)	(*)	10	15	3	1	1	(*)	3	3	19	207
Household Appliances	(*)		6	6		139	27	5	3	23	130	97	229	51
Electric Lighting & Wiring Equipment	(*)		7	7	(*)	5	6	5	5		9	9	9	22
Radio, Television & Communication Equipment					1	5	31	1	15		53	101	16	180
Electronic Components & Accessories	2		11	11			22		2	1	(*)	8	140	111
Miscellaneous Electrical Machinery, Equipment & Supplies			2	2	(*)					16	3	35	776	73
Motor Vehicles & Equipment	(*)		5	5	(*)	5	50	2	122	12	2	94	1,966	422
Aircraft & Parts			34	34	(*)	77	70	1	2	9	66	19	3	13,166
Other Transportation Equipment										14	12		160	13
Scientific & Controlling Instruments	(*)		(*)	(*)	2	1	6	(*)	(*)	7	11	(*)	(*)	8
Optical, Ophthalmic & Photographic Equipment	4		9	9	2	22		17	17	25	15	7	62	247
Miscellaneous Manufacturing			8	8	2	2	1	1	1		1		23	7
Transportation & Warehousing	17	50	65	65	6	31	9	10	1	35	11	2	9	2
Communications; Except Radio & TV Broadcasting	21	13	170	170	65	1,146	330	71	38	105	38	42	73	637
Radio & TV Broadcasting	11		33	33	10	103	45	25	25	35	25	11	78	67
Electric, Gas, Water & Sanitary Services	12	11	106	106	113	624	325	44	82	39	20	19	49	166
Wholesale & Retail Trade	141	121	299	299	106	737	425	112	251	143	127	56	384	922
Finance & Insurance	17	16	49	49	21	214	72	35	59	34	9	19	44	119
Real Estate & Rental	26	21	76	76	24	55	56	52	85	42	24	29	122	76
Hotels; Personal & Repair Services exc. Auto	3	9	11	11	2	12	3	3	5	5	1	2	5	15
Business Services	28	67	231	231	66	328	144	79	163	87	65	41	320	482
Automobile Repair & Services	2	2	8	8	3	19	7	3	8	5	3	2	17	388
Amusements														
Medical, Educational Services & Nonprofit Organizations	1	2	5	5	1	9	4	3	5	4	2	2	14	8
Federal Government Enterprises	5	4	10	10	4	16	7	5	9	7	3	3	22	30
State & Local Government Enterprises	(*)	(*)	2	2		8	3	1	1				1	4
Directly Allocated Imports		13	241	241	59	715	1,103	44	161	18	42		236	103
Transferred Imports	(*)	1	88	88		8				61				
Business Travel, Entertainment & Gifts	15	45	81	81	20	83	47	31	78	51	33	25	123	112
Office Supplies	2	3	9	9	3	15	6	4	8	6	2	6	18	15
Scrap, Used & Secondhand Goods			4	4	14	661	610	4	12	10		7		43
Government Industry														
Rest of the World Industry														
Household Industry														
Inventory Valuation Adjustment														
Intermediate Inputs, Total	2,422	1,571	5,478	5,478	1,325	14,166	10,292	2,718	5,220	2,632	1,121	1,803	6,499	28,139
Value Added	752	891	4,413	4,413	1,607	10,453	3,980	2,237	3,743	2,512	1,137	1,279	5,942	11,892
Total	3,174	2,462	9,891	9,891	2,932	24,618	14,272	4,955	8,963	5,144	2,257	3,081	12,440	40,031

* Less than $500,000

piles the figures, makes no attempt to do so each year. The most recent information, for 1963, is available in detail in a 370-industry breakdown and in an 86-industry summary. Material from the latter is condensed in the chart on the two preceding pages. The purchases of selected industries are listed in full; however, sales of these industries only are shown. The data is in millions of dollars at producers' prices.

From the table, it should be apparent that a change in the output of one industry affects almost every other industry. A rise in the demand for automobiles, for instance, will produce an increase in the demand for steel, fabrics and tires. The steel increase will produce a rise in demand for sulphuric acid, limestone and coal. The fabric increase will produce a rise in demand for cotton yarn, synthetic fibers and chemicals. The tire increase will produce a rise in demand for rubber, nylon and chemicals. Input-output analysis permits us to follow the ripples throughout the economy.

Don't be surprised at the fact that the automobile industry buys more from itself than any other industry. This reflects primarily the huge purchases automobile assemblers make from the suppliers of parts and other equipment. In addition, some part of every industry's product is consumed by itself. The automobile industry uses cars to convey its own personnel and trucks to haul materials to and about in its plants and to carry assembled vehicles to its dealers.

With supplementary data, input-output analysis helps companies to determine likely needs for additional workers and new plant and equipment, to calculate the direct and indirect impact of cost and price changes in any industry, to evaluate market prospects for established and new products and to spot prospective material shortages. It can help in long-range economic forecasting, detailing, for instance, the effect of import competition on industries and regions or the impact of a new industry on a region's water and energy resources.

Still other kinds of economic accounts are the flow-of-funds accounts which measure the sources and uses of money and capital flows and the balance of payments accounts which measure one country's standing financially in relation to other nations of the world. More about each later.

7. The Federal Budget

The federal budget is more than a recording of government receipts and outlays and the resulting surplus or deficit. It is a summing up of past commitments of the nation's resources and an outline of future commitments as well.

The nation's resources, not merely the government's, are involved, for Washington's taxing and spending policies and the steps taken to finance them affect far more than the federal government. The budget reflects decisions, not always explicit, about the size of government and the production of public versus private goods and services. It reflects decisions about the level—federal, state, or local—at which public goods and services will be produced.

The budget reflects decisions about how the benefits of this production will be distributed, both among those now living and between the present and future generations, the latter choice involving how much of the nation's income will be consumed and how much saved and invested. In this sense the budget involves a commitment to faster or slower economic growth.

The budget exerts this influence beyond the halls of government because Washington takes in and redistributes far more in taxes than it spends on its own needs. In 1970 the federal government purchased goods and services amounting to 9.3 percent of the real gross national product, at the same time collecting about 21 percent of the national output in taxes and Social Security contributions. The rest it turned back to state and local governments as grants and to individuals and families as transfer and interest payments. Federal contributions financed 19 percent of state and local purchases of goods and services, and about 10 percent of consumer expenditures.

The fiscal reach of the federal government extends beyond the distribution of excess tax collections among state and local governments, consumers, and the capital markets, for it influences considerably how this largesse will be spent. The turning back of many of the billions of dollars to states and localities in grants is conditioned upon their use for specific purposes. Taxes take income from some consumers and transfer payments redistribute it to others. Taxes on specific items, such as automobiles and cigarettes, discriminate against some kinds of consumption, while subsidies favor others. Government guaranties, insurance and interest rate subsidies give an advantage to some kinds of investment over others.

The fact that the federal government exerts this important influence on other sectors of the economy gives the budget much of the character of a national, not just a government-sector, plan. But the federal government is not the only force whose decisions affect the economy. Millions of individuals regularly decide how they will divide their time between work, training for work, and leisure; their incomes between current consumption and saving; and their expenditures among the many items competing for them to purchase.

These decisions by individuals trigger other decisions by businessmen: what products to make and how to price them, how much labor to hire, what materials to buy, how much plant and equipment to purchase. These private decisions are far more numerous, far more complex, and far more significant in total than those of government. They decree that whatever plan government may have for the future allocation of resources will be as much a product of what private decision makers do as a blueprint of what government planners think should be done.

The planners, then, must keep an eye at all times on the consumer and businessman and attempt to forecast their behavior. If the forecasts are accurate and the government takes steps to complement private economic activity, what actually happens will match closely what the planners had hoped would happen and the plans will be fulfilled. If the forecasts are not accurate and the government takes actions conflicting with those of the private sector, there will be disappointment.

Forecasts are more likely to be wide of the mark if the economy is swinging wildly than if it is pursuing a course of steady growth. It is in the interest of the planners, then, to attempt to smooth out business ups and downs, a motivation that is in addition to the mandate of Congress, expressed in the Employment Act of 1946, to promote "maximum employment, production, and purchasing power"—to avoid, in effect, the waste that results from overemployment as well as underemployment of the nation's human and material resources.

The Employment Act was something of a milestone in American history. Until the 1930s, economic downturns with their accompanying unemployment and human misery were thought to be inevitable, the consequence of largely autonomous influences operating in the private economy. During the Great Depression the notion of creating a budget deficit to raise private incomes and thus reverse business downturns gained recognition, but it was not until after World War II, when the ideas of the British economist John Maynard Keynes became widely accepted on this side of the Atlantic, that such use of the government's taxing and spending powers won formal approval from Congress.

The Employment Act was also something of a grab bag. As a result of the political pulling and hauling that preceded its passage, the act set price stability, growth, and the "promotion of free competitive enterprise" as objectives, in addition to full employment.

How these objectives were to be accomplished wasn't specified. The President was given a Council of Economic Advisers to assist him in the task and was directed to make an annual economic report in which, presumably, he and his advisers would outline their plans and procedures. There was little doubt, however, that Congress intended to use the budget to counter business ups and downs.

What is the nature of business ups and downs? At all times some areas of business are advancing and others are declining. There may be a slowdown in aluminum, for instance, when most other industries are moving ahead strongly. Overcapacity resulting from an excessively optimistic appraisal of sales prospects could be the reason. The fact that more industries are advancing than declining, however, characterizes the period as one of expansion. It is accompanied by rising production, employment, incomes, and other measures of aggregate economic activity. When more industries are declining than advancing, the period is described as one of contraction. It is accompanied by declining measures of aggregate economic activity. The succession of periods of expansion and contraction is spoken of as "the business cycle."

The government has come to intervene in the business cycle in two ways, through the so-called built-in stabilizers and through discretionary changes in spending and taxes. The built-in stabilizers are called that because they go to work automatically, without the need for congressional action, cushioning the decline in personal incomes during contractions and restraining the growth during expansions. Most important of the built-in stabilizers is the personal income tax, which takes progressively more of incomes as they rise and progressively less as they fall. Others include the corporate income tax, which includes some measure of progression, unemployment compensation, and welfare payments. The built-in stabilizers are more effective on the downside, absorbing an estimated one dollar in three of the decline in personal incomes resulting from a business downturn.

During the 1957–58 recession, one of the more severe of the post-war downturns, for instance, the physical output of the nation's factories and mines fell 14 percent, the physical output of commodities and services fell 5.4 percent, and the dollar volume of total output fell 4.3 percent. But personal incomes, because of the built-in stabilizers as well as other factors, declined less than 1 percent. In an earlier recession, that of 1954–55, because of a broad-based tax cut they declined not at all.

Because the built-in stabilizers by themselves are not powerful enough to counter the forces of inflationary boom or recession, Congress must take discretionary action if the ups and downs of the business cycle are to be smoothed out. In a recession it must cut taxes or increase spending, moving in the direction of a budget deficit. In an inflationary boom it must cut spending or increase taxes, moving in the direction of a surplus.

A dollar of tax changes equals a dollar of spending increases in the movement of the budget toward surplus or deficit, but they are by no means the same thing. A spending increase means bigger government, an increase in federal decision making. To the extent that it is not simply redistributed to consumers, it means a rise in the output of public versus private goods and services: more defense, more health care, more education. By way of contrast, a tax cut increases private decision making. It tips the scales in favor of choices made directly by consumers: more new homes, more automobiles, more college educations for their children.

How a surplus or deficit is financed is as important as how it comes about. To the extent that there is no inflationary increase in the money supply, a deficit pulls investment funds from the capital market to buy government bonds that otherwise might have been used to finance home construction and build new factories, power plants, railroad cars, aircraft, and other business plant and equipment. A surplus releases funds for private investment.

A budget deficit, however, is sometimes financed by an increase in the money supply greater than the growth of the productive capacity of the economy. This means inflation, a rapid rise in the prices of almost everything. Under these circumstances a deficit has the effect of an across-the-board tax increase, affecting those least able to pay as much as those most able to pay. Particularly because of the effect of the progressive income tax on rising money incomes, government grows at the expense of the private sector, and with the increase in business investment that often accompanies inflation, consumption is throttled. While the economy is still booming, then, the seeds are sown for eventual recession.

Not long ago it was impossible to know what was meant in hearing that the budget was in surplus or deficit by several billion dollars because there were three competing budget concepts, each seemingly used to permit the government to present the most favorable face to the public. To end competition among the three concepts and to make the budget a more meaningful document, the unified budget was conceived and adopted. The unified budget concept acknowledges that the budget has differing uses: determining the effect of government spending and taxes on income and employment, managing the Treasury's cash, determining debt management policies, and evaluating specific programs. But it embodies the principle that needed information should be obtained from a single document.

It begins, then, with what used to be known as "the consolidated cash budget," the total of all funds received and disbursed by the federal government. It separates appropriations requiring action by Congress —the exclusive domain of the old administrative budget—from those not requiring congressional action. Next it totals up all receipts and expenditures to produce an expenditure account surplus or deficit, and to this it adds net federal lending. This gives the budget surplus or deficit, the only surplus or deficit under the unified budget approach.

The document includes, in addition, a summary of how a deficit is to be financed—by reducing cash balances or adding to the debt—or how a surplus is to be used—by adding to cash balances or reducing the debt—and ends with a summary of outstanding federal debt and loans.

The budget measures government spending, directly and by way of the loan account, at three points in time. When Congress makes an appropriation or otherwise authorizes federal agencies to spend, it records the action as "budget authority," referring to it in the expenditure account as "new obligational authority" and in the loan account as "new loan authority." When an agency signs a purchase contract or otherwise makes a spending commitment, the budget records the transaction as an "obligation incurred." Finally, when the Treasury issues a check in payment for goods delivered or services performed, the budget records the transaction as an "outlay."

The unified budget accepts as a goal the notion that insofar as possible all government receipts and expenditures should be on an accrual basis. Thus, expenditures would be recorded when the government incurs obligations, not later when it makes actual outlays. Similarly, receipts would be shown when individuals and businesses incur tax liabilities. Initially, however, there have been administrative difficulties in putting the accrual principle into practice.

Here is what the unified budget looks like:

BUDGET SUMMARY (in millions of dollars)

Description	1970 actual	1971 estimate	1972 estimate
Budget authority (largely appropriations):			
Available through current action by Congress:			
Previously enacted	141,592	156,418	--------
Proposed in this budget	--------	9,553	170,162
Available without current action by Congress	85,373	88,524	97,796
Deductions for offsetting receipts [1]	−13,992	−18,233	−18,994
Total budget authority	212,973	236,263	248,965
Receipts, expenditures, and net lending:			
Expenditure account:			
Receipts	193,743	194,193	217,593
Expenditures (excludes net lending)	194,456	211,143	228,286
Expenditure account deficit	714	16,951	10,693
Loan account:			
Loan disbursements	8,313	8,807	9,440
Loan repayments	6,182	7,196	8,494
Net lending	2,131	1,611	946
Total budget:			
Receipts	193,743	194,193	217,593
Outlays (expenditures and net lending)	196,588	212,755	229,232
Budget deficit	2,845	18,562	11,639
Budget financing:			
Net borrowing from the public	3,814	17,600	10,600
Other means of financing	−969	962	1,039
Total budget financing	2,845	18,562	11,639

Description	1969 actual	1970 actual	1971 estimate	1972 estimate
Outstanding debt, end of year:				
Gross Federal debt	367,144	382,603	407,033	429,400
Held by the public	279,483	284,880	302,480	313,080

MEMORANDUM

Description	1969 actual	1970 actual	1971 estimate	1972 estimate
Outstanding loans, end of year:				
Direct loans:				
Loan account	29,484	31,615	33,226	34,172
Expenditure account	17,042	19,463	20,564	22,299
Guaranteed and insured loans [2]	[3] 104,014	106,382	119,449	140,300
Government-sponsored agency loans [4]	27,024	37,584	45,370	53,233

[1] These consist of interfund and intragovernmental transactions and proprietary receipts from the public.
[2] Excluding loans held by Government and Government-sponsored enterprises.
[3] Includes $1.6 billion of certificates of interest as reclassified agency debt (Commodity Credit Corporation, Agriculture) July 1, 1969.
[4] Excluding Federal Reserve banks.

The unified budget is an improvement, a major one, in measuring the impact of federal spending and tax policies on the economy. But it isn't the whole story, because a deficit of $5 billion, say, may mean one thing under one set of circumstances and something quite different under another. In a severe recession it might not be enough, while in an inflationary boom it might be too much.

What has to be realized is that a budget surplus or deficit is as much a result of the general level of the economy as a creator of that level. Tax receipts rise much faster than national output in a rising economy and fall much faster in a declining economy. This is simply another way of looking at the built-in stabilizers—from the Treasury's point of view, not the private sector's.

Whether a particular spending and tax mix is appropriate for stability depends on where business stands and whether it is expanding or contracting. A helpful way of considering such a mix is to calculate what kind of surplus or deficit it would produce if the economy were employing its manpower and industrial capacity fully. Such a full-employment budget is stimulating to the economy when it moves from surplus to deficit and restraining when it turns upward again.

The proper size of the full-employment surplus will not always be the same. When private demand is strong, a large full-employment surplus will be appropriate to hold down inflation while maintaining full employment. When private demand is weak, a small surplus or even a deficit may be called for. Moreover, a surplus that may have been adequate in one boom may be inadequate in the next simply because of the growth of the economy. The full-employment surplus as a percentage of full-employment gross national product, it has been suggested, might be a more meaningful measure.

Acknowledging the usefulness of the full-employment budget analysis in measuring the impact of the federal budget on the economy, it is necessary to emphasize that it, too, isn't the whole story. To measure the short-term effects of federal spending, much needs to be known about its nature. How much, for instance, involves direct purchases of goods and services and how much transfer payments? Direct purchases not only have an immediate impact on the economy but they have a multiplier effect as the income they generate is spent and respent. By way of contrast, transfer payments await a spending decision by someone else before their effects are felt—the retired person who receives a Social Security payment, for instance, or the state government that gets matching funds for highway construction.

Timing is also important, but as the accrual principle is put into practice in the budget process, recording spending as obligations are incurred, it will become less so. Meanwhile, it is essential to know how

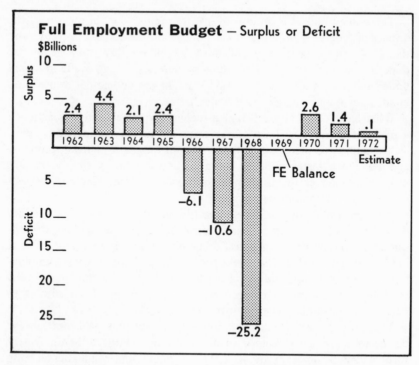

Full Employment Budget – Surplus or Deficit

$Billions

How stimulative a particular tax and spending policy may be can be determined by calculating the surplus or deficit it would produce at full employment. Such a budget is stimulating when it moves from surplus to deficit, and it is restraining when it moves oppositely from deficit to surplus.

much spending involves payment for goods and services produced promptly, such as the pay of government employees and off-the-shelf purchases of existing items, and how much payments on large government contracts. When the government places a big contract the effects are felt first in the private sector as the contractor begins to order materials, hire workers, and let subcontracts. As the work moves ahead the influence is seen as an increase in business inventories, both goods in process and finished orders. Not until the government inspects and makes full or partial payment for the submarine, aircraft, or space vehicle, according to the reckoning that has prevailed until now, is the outlay recorded as government spending.

This discussion of the impact of government spending on the economy has centered so far on the federal government. As noted earlier, however, state and local government spending has grown until its purchases of goods and services are now larger than those of the federal government.

This is important to economic stability because state and local spending tends to move in line with, not contrary to, business ups and downs. As state and local spending grows, then, an increasing burden is placed on the federal government to counter inflationary booms and recessions. By 1975, according to estimates by the Council of Economic Advisers, state and local purchases of goods and services should be two-thirds again as large as those of the federal government.

As it is, the federal government accounts for almost one dollar in five the state and local governments spend. In part, this reflects Washington's generosity. Federal grants to the states and localities doubled in the six years from 1964 to 1970 and now account for more than one-fifth of all federal spending for nonmilitary purposes. Education, highway safety, law enforcement, medical assistance, rural rehabilitation, and welfare are only a few of the broad categories in which such assistance falls.

Generosity, however, isn't all. The federal government benefits from a tax structure much more efficient in extracting revenues from its citizens than those of the states and localities. The income tax, on which the federal government chiefly depends, generates tax receipts faster than the growth of the economy. The sales tax, on which the states rely, and the property tax, on which the localities depend, do no better than match the growth of the economy.

The situation is bad enough in times of stable prices, but inflation adds an extra dimension to the problem. Even when real incomes do no more than stand still, the progressive nature of the income tax—the fact that people with higher incomes are taxed more than people with lower incomes—diverts an increasing share of rising money incomes to the federal government. At the same time the prices of things states and localities buy—new schools and hospitals, teachers', policemen's, and garbage collectors' wages—rise much faster than tax receipts. The federal government grows fat while the states and localities become paupers. With inflation at an annual rate of 5 percent, it has been estimated, state and local government costs outdistance receipts by at least $2.5 billion.

The revenue-generating propensity of the federal tax system has proved an embarrassment to Washington. The federal tax structure does a good job in meeting the requirements of war, but when human problems, not national defense, become the nation's number-one concern, it continues to pull funds into the federal coffers when the need is at the state and local level.

Revenue sharing is one answer. If adopted, the proposal would turn back to the states, with no strings attached, a percentage of taxable personal income. In the first year the states would get $500 million, and five years later they would get $5 billion. The plan would provide more generous payments to states that tax their citizens heavily than to those that do not. Heavily taxed localities would benefit similarly from a "pass-through" provision. The plan, however, as the critics were prompt to note, makes no attempt to weigh the quality of services obtained. Graft or inefficiency, simply because it cost more, would be more highly rewarded than good government.

Revenue sharing isn't the only answer to increased state and local needs. Simply by cutting taxes, Washington would give the states and cities an opportunity to meet rising demands for their services by increasing their own taxes. It is unlikely, however, that taxpayers would permit local taxes to go up as much as federal taxes were cut.

Another answer might be to permit taxpayers to credit a part of their state and local taxes against their federal tax bills. Mayors and governors would still have to take their programs to the people and the legislatures for approval, but resistance to increases in state and local taxes might not be as great as now.

Government use of tax and spending policy to counter business ups and downs suffers from certain inherent difficulties. It depends, as we have noted, on forecasts of private economic behavior, and this is an inexact science. Much government spending—on highways, dams, and other public works, for instance—takes a long time to plan and even longer to set in motion. A public works program undertaken to combat a recession may exert its greatest influence when it is least needed—at the height of the subsequent boom. Finally, because they require congressional approval, spending and tax changes take months, sometimes years, to accomplish.

A notorious example of this is the income tax surcharge proposed to combat the inflation resulting from the Vietnam War. The buildup of American armies in Vietnam began in 1965. In January 1967 President Johnson first recommended a surtax to Congress. But it was not until a year and a half later, after the country had incurred its biggest budget deficit until then and inflation had become rampant, that the surtax was passed.

This raises a broader question. There is little doubt that Congress can be induced to cut taxes and increase spending to combat a recession. But will it take action important enough and prompt enough to hold down inflation? An equally interesting question is whether changes in tax and spending policy have any influence at all if they move opposite to the Federal Reserve's expansion or contraction of the money supply. Whether fiscal policy is the separate and independent force it was once thought to be has become the subject of an important debate among economists.

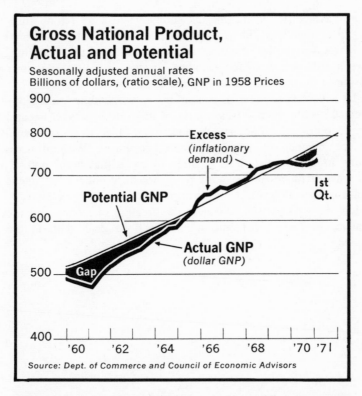

**Gross National Product,
Actual and Potential**

Seasonally adjusted annual rates
Billions of dollars, (ratio scale), GNP in 1958 Prices

Source: Dept. of Commerce and Council of Economic Advisors

When the economy operates below its potential, government
policies can be directed toward closing the gap. Too much
stimulation, however, will produce excess demand, resulting in
inflation, as in the late 1960s.

The monetarists, those who believe changes in the money supply are
the most important influence in the economy, find no direct link between
government tax policies and the real world of output, jobs, and incomes
and only a minor link between government spending policies and the
real world. But even those who believe that fiscal policy may exert
considerable influence will concede that historically the evidence is mixed.
The 1948 tax cut was followed by a recession. Most of the Korean
War inflation occurred while the budget surplus was rising, and the inflation abated when the surplus turned to deficit. The 1954 recession,
which occurred with a rising high-employment surplus, was milder than
the 1957–58 recession, which coincided with a falling high-employment
surplus.

Perhaps the greatest disappointment to the fiscalists was the refusal
of the economy to slow down in 1968 despite the abrupt turnaround in
the high-employment budget from a record deficit of about $15 billion

before passage of the income tax surcharge to a $3 billion surplus by the end of that year. The fiscalists, can, however, cite some successes: the slowdown in the economy and in inflation after President Eisenhower's 1959–60 drive for a budget surplus, as well as the strong expansion of the economy following the 1964 tax cut.

The monetarists' answer is that tax and spending policy produced expected results when it was translated first into a parallel expansion or contraction of the money supply and that it failed to do so when it was not accompanied by such a parallel movement. Without necessarily joining in this verdict, it is possible to agree that fiscal policy works best when it moves in harmony with monetary policy and stands least chance of success when it moves opposite to monetary policy.

How the government influences the creation of money and uses this influence to foster economic stability will be dealt with in the next chapter.

8. Money

The role of money in helping to smooth out business ups and downs is a recent one, no more than a moment in the long history of man.

Over the centuries money has come to mean much more than something material. Men have married for money, murdered for money, sold their children for money. They have connived, embezzled, extorted, demeaned themselves, trafficked in love, betrayed their God, their country, and their best friends. They have enslaved others and themselves. They have reduced ancient civilizations. Wars have been started for money, and no war of any size has ended without the expenditure of vast sums of it. The American, French, and Russian revolutions and the rise of Hitler each came to pass at least in part because of problems of money.

If all of the baser aspects of man are mirrored in money, many of his nobler aspects are reflected there as well: his aspirations for himself and his children; his charity, generosity, and concern for his fellows; his identification with the less fortunate peoples of the world. Money, however, represents power, as is recognized by anyone who has borrowed a hundred dollars from a brother-in-law, doled out allowances to children, or supplicated the boss for a raise. If people through the ages have examined gift horses with suspicion, it is because they have experienced difficulty distinguishing generosity from the quest for power, the noble motive from the base—and because, in their stubborn humanity, they resist ceding their independence to anyone.

Money, then, is much more than a thing. It may be a weapon or a deterrent or, on the other hand, an incentive or a goad. At the least, it is an instrument or tool without which the modern world would not function.

In primitive civilizations goods moved by barter. The maker of an earthenware pot, for instance, had to find someone wanting an earthenware pot who at the same time offered something he himself needed or wanted, food perhaps. Trade was strictly person to person, and was limited by the ability of sellers to find appropriate and willing buyers.

Consider the problems that would result if the barter system still prevailed. One might find the price of meat expressed in bushels of wheat, the price of butter in pounds of wool, and the price of household detergent in gallons of gasoline. At one store the price of topcoats might be expressed in automobile crankshafts; at another, in minutes of computer time; and at a third, in European vacations.

Money eliminates the need for such item-by-item comparisons. It serves as a common denominator. The dollar-and-cents listing of only 100 items in a weekly food store advertisement keeps a housewife from having to make 4,950 item-by-item comparisons in deciding how to distribute her grocery purchases. The listing of 1,600 share prices in the New York Stock Exchange's daily listing keeps an investor from having to make 1,779,200 issue-by-issue comparisons.

Money has another practical advantage. It obviates the need for anyone to tie up a substantial part of his wealth in trading goods and of his time and energy in seeking buyers and sellers. Consider the pack of samples you might have to carry on your back if you could not carry money in your pocket or in your checking account. In addition to serving as a common standard of value, then, money is a convenient and economical common medium of exchange.

Money makes it possible to compare values not only among widely differing goods and services but over time as well. This encourages savings and investment, the withholding of incomes from current consumption to create the resource base for consumption by future generations, and permits the extension of credit. If there were no way of assuring that what was borrowed would be repaid at values at least close to those at which the debt was incurred, there would be little incentive to save, and little hope of obtaining credit.

Money, as we noted earlier, makes it possible to apply a yardstick to the measurement of business profits. The conventions of business accounting have been altered and amended to create the national income accounts and other economic accounts. In all, money serves as the common unit of measurement.

The uses of money help to determine its characteristics. It must be highly valuable, widely accepted, and easily transported. The ancients discovered that people would be willing to accept scarce, durable commodities—gold, silver, and copper, for instance—in exchange for their goods and to hold them for the purchase of other needs and wants. Surviving terms such as "pound," "livre," and "mark" were measurements that applied originally to this commodity money. The difficulty of assuring adequate measurement led to coinage, the application of the king's, or sovereign's, stamp to the metal, guaranteeing its weight and quality. The fact that one British coin is still called a sovereign attests to this function.

The government guarantee of value persists, but little else. In the United States gold and silver are no longer used to make coin. And banknotes—engraved paper certificates originally exchangeable for gold and silver—are no longer redeemable in the precious metals.

Money, then, has become steadily more abstract and sophisticated. By the end of the present century it may be largely pips in the memory cores of a network of electronic computers, which would be linked by telephone, microwave, and satellite communications to banks, homes, and businesses. Today, however, the great bulk of money—three dollars of every four—consists of checking account deposits in the nation's thirteen thousand commercial banks. These are also called "demand deposits," because a depositor may ask for and obtain his funds merely upon request. By way of contrast, time deposits are accepted for fixed periods of time, usually thirty, sixty, or ninety days or more, and cannot be obtained sooner without loss of interest. In the United States time deposits bear interest, demand deposits do not.

Although money changers were important in biblical times, modern banking had its origin in the Italian cities of the early Renaissance. The initial function of the banker was to offer a safe place for the storage of gold, silver, and other valuables. He would accept bullion or coin, issuing a receipt to the depositor. In time, because the receipts were more uniform than the worn, sweated, and clipped coins for which they were exchanged, they came to be preferred for the settlement of debts and other payments. Then some banker made an important discovery: not all people with valuables on deposit wanted them back at the same time. He could issue more receipts, or banknotes, than he had gold or silver in his vaults. He could, in effect, create money.

Commercial banks do much the same thing today. A commercial bank, with a few exceptions, is any bank that accepts checking account, or demand, deposits. When any lender other than a commercial bank— a savings bank, a savings and loan association, or possibly a finance company—makes a loan, it has to reach into cash for the funds. On the books, loans go up and cash goes down, but deposits, total assets, and total liabilities stay the same. In simplified form, this is what a savings bank balance sheet looks like before and after a $10,000 loan is made:

Homeowners Savings Bank

Cash	$ 1,000,000	Deposits	$61,000,000
Loans and investments	65,000,000	Capital	5,000,000
Total assets	$66,000,000	Total liabilities and net worth	$66,000,000

Homeowners Savings Bank

Cash	$ 990,000	Deposits	$61,000,000
Loans and investments	65,010,000	Capital	5,000,000
Total assets	$66,000,000	Total liabilities and net worth	$66,000,000

When a commercial bank makes a loan, however, an officer of the bank simply credits the borrower's checking account with the amount of the loan. He creates a deposit, or new money, just as spendable as any the borrower might have put into the account himself. On the commercial bank's books, loans, deposits, total assets, and total liabilities all go up by the amount of the loan, but cash—with an important exception to be noted later—remains the same. In simplified form, this is what a commercial bank balance sheet looks like before and after a $10,000 loan is made:

Hometown Bank

Cash	$ 800,000	Deposits	$4,000,000
Loans and investments	3,600,000	Capital	400,000
Total assets	$4,400,000	Total liabilities and net worth	$4,400,000

Hometown Bank

Cash	$ 800,000	Deposits	$4,010,000
Loans and investments	3,610,000	Capital	400,000
Total assets	$4,410,000	Total liabilities and net worth	$4,410,000

With this magnificent ability to create money, literally at the stroke of a pen, why don't commercial bankers go beserk, lending and creating more and more? One answer is that they have a considerable amount of their own funds, their invested capital, at stake, and presentation of claims beyond the bank's ability to meet them would render the bank insolvent and jeopardize this investment. In addition to keeping some of their funds in cash, then, bankers keep a significant additional amount in highly liquid assets, short-term government and other securities that may readily be converted to cash.

There is an even more important restraint on the ability of bankers to create new money, the fact that member banks—as a group, not necessarily individual banks—of the Federal Reserve System must increase their cash balances with the central banking system by one dollar for each six or seven dollars of new deposits they generate. Thus, an increase in lending and deposit creation at one bank may be more than offset by the retirement of loans and the extinguishing of deposits at others.

A member bank's reserve account at the Federal Reserve is a checking account not unlike a customer's checking account at the bank itself. All banks must average their deposits to determine reserve requirements and their reserve balances to determine reserve adequacy once each week. Currency and coin member banks keep in their vaults to meet their regular operating requirements are included in the calculation of reserve adequacy. A member bank wanting to increase its loans and deposits may find that it has reserves in excess of its requirements. If it does not, it may borrow reserves from other member banks in the so-called Federal Funds market, or from the Federal Reserve at the discount window.

No member bank, however, is the sole master of its fate. The reserve account at the Federal Reserve may be viewed as something akin to a joint husband-and-wife checking account, in which the wife is free to make deposits or withdrawals without telling her husband what she is doing. He finds out only when he sees the balance at the end of the accounting period. The wife, in this case, is the Federal Reserve. Its actions can add to the total of member bank reserve accounts or subtract from that total. A policy of adding steadily to member bank reserves is spoken of as "easy money," while a policy of restricting the growth of member bank reserves is spoken of as "tight money."

It may be helpful to examine in somewhat greater detail what happens when the Federal Reserve permits the reserves of member banks to increase. Let us assume that Hometown Bank is a member of the Federal Reserve, that for simplicity it is required to maintain 10 percent of its deposits as reserves, and that its reserve account shows a balance of $410,000. Here is its reserve position:

Deposits	$4,000,000
Required reserve ratio	10%
Total reserves	410,000
Less: Required reserves	400,000
Excess reserves	$10,000

Hometown Bank has excess cash of $10,000, which it is free to lend or invest. Let us assume that it lends the $10,000 to a local retailer. The bank takes the merchant's note for $10,000 and gives him credit in his checking account for a like amount. The bank makes the following entries in its books:

Hometown Bank

Assets		Liabilities	
Loans and investments	+ $10,000	Deposits	+ $10,000

The retailer had a purpose, of course, in seeking the loan: he wanted to buy merchandise from a wholesaler. When he does, he pays for the purchase by writing a check for $10,000 on his account at the Hometown Bank. The wholesaler deposits the check in his bank, the City Bank, which enters it for collection through the Federal Reserve. At the district Federal Reserve Bank, the reserve account of Hometown Bank is charged $10,000, and Hometown Bank in turn charges the checking account of the retailer:

Hometown Bank

Assets		Liabilities	
Cash	− $10,000	Deposits	− $10,000

Hometown Bank has lost its excess reserves and cannot make additional loans without being short of reserves.

Before the transaction, this was the City Bank balance sheet:

City Bank

Cash	$26,000,000	Deposits	$100,000,000
(Including total reserves: $10,000,000			
Loans and investments	84,000,000	Capital	10,000,000
		Total liabilities and	
Total assets	$110,000,000	net worth	$110,000,000

This was its reserve position:

Deposits	$100,000,000
Required reserve ratio	10%
Total reserves	10,000,000
Less: Required reserves	10,000,000
Excess reserves	0

City Bank was loaned up. It could not lend or invest another cent without incurring a reserve deficiency. The wholesaler's deposit, however, changed things. It increased deposits by $10,000, and when the check cleared through the Federal Reserve Bank, City Bank received a $10,000 addition to its reserve account:

City Bank

Assets		Liabilities	
Total reserves	+ $10,000	Deposits	+ $10,000

Of the $10,000 increase in deposits, City Bank had to use 10 percent, or $1,000, to increase its reserves. This gave it $9,000 with which to make new loans or investments. If this entire amount were redeposited in a third bank, that bank would have to increase its reserves by $900, giving it $8,100 for new loans and investments. If the banking system were permitted to make full use of the added reserves, the $10,000 increase would mean a $100,000 expansion of money and credit. A 20 percent reserve requirement ratio would mean a $50,000 expansion.

Several points might be made. For maximum monetary expansion, all banks acquiring excess reserves as a result of the initial transaction would have to lend the full amount of such excess reserves. The expansion of money and credit is a response of the banking system as a whole. No one bank could lend ten times the amount of its excess reserves without running seriously short of reserves. As the volume of commercial bank lending increases, some reserves are absorbed by an increase of currency in circulation.

Although there is a link between the quantity of reserves and the money stock, it is not a rigid one. If a borrower chooses to take the proceeds of a loan in cash rather than as a deposit to his checking account, excess reserves are absorbed, reducing the lending capacity of the banking system and the growth of the money supply. If the banks elect to remain less than fully loaned, excess reserves remain idle—a not unusual situation when business turns downward and fears grow that borrowers may default. If banks are unable to find qualified borrowers, another possible result of a downturn, the result is the same. In both cases the growth of the money supply is restricted.

The ability of an institution like the Federal Reserve to ease or restrict the flow of money into the economic lifestream is known as "central banking," an art comparatively new in the history of the world. In his landmark volume, *Lombard Street,* Walter Bagehot told how directors of the Bank of England exercised this power, largely unconscious of the fact that they were doing so. That was barely a hundred years ago. In the United States and most other countries central banking is a product of the twentieth century.

A central bank is usually a monopoly, the sole institution privileged to issue banknotes, the single lender of last resort to the banking system. It is usually also government owned or controlled. The Federal Reserve System is a strange hybrid. It is not one but a network of twelve regional central banks. When the system came into being more than fifty years ago, there was some thought that each Federal Reserve Bank would operate independently, making its own policy and setting its own lending rate, but this notion was quickly dispelled.

The Federal Reserve System is also both private and public in character. Member banks, which are private, are obliged to subscribe for the shares of their district Federal Reserve Banks. In turn, they are privileged to elect six of the nine directors of each bank. Control of the system, however, is vested in the seven-man Board of Governors, of whom the President, with the consent of the Senate, appoints one every other year to a fourteen-year term. Monetary policy, moreover, is made by the Federal Open Market Committee, a body in which the Board of Governors is a voting majority. Other voting members are the president of the Federal Reserve Bank of New York and, by rotation once each year, four of the remaining eleven Federal Reserve Bank presidents.

Not all commercial banks are required to be members of the Federal Reserve System. Banks chartered by the federal government, so-called national banks, are, but state-chartered banks are not. As a result, of the more than thirteen thousand banks in the United States fewer than six thousand are members. The ability of nonmembers to avoid Federal Reserve control is a matter of continuing concern to the central banking system, mitigated by the fact that almost all large banks are members and also by the fact that four out of every five dollars of total deposits are under system control.

The Federal Reserve has three principal instruments at its command for influencing the level of member bank reserves. The Board of Governors may raise or lower the percentage of daily average deposits required as reserves. (Congress has established a reserve range of 10 to 22 percent of checking account deposits for banks in large cities, designated as reserve city banks, and of 7 to 14 percent for banks in smaller places, designated as country banks. It has established a reserve range of 3 to 10 percent on time and savings deposits at all member banks.)

The board may raise or lower the interest rate charged member banks to borrow reserves at the discount window of the district banks. (Discount rate changes are initiated by directors of the district banks, but they are "reviewed and determined" by the Board of Governors.)

The Federal Open Market Committee may issue a directive to the manager of the system open market account, an officer of the Federal Reserve Bank of New York, that over a period of time will require him to add to or reduce the system's holdings of government securities. In September 1971, the system began trading additionally in Federal agency obligations.

Reserve requirement changes are infrequent, and are considered a blunderbuss in the central banking system's arsenal of monetary weapons. Discount rate changes also do not occur often, and have thus lost much of their influence in encouraging or discouraging member banks to borrow. (The interest rate at which member banks borrow reserves from other member banks, the so-called Federal Funds rate, moves up and down continuously and thus is considered far more indicative than the discount rate of money market conditions.) Changes in the discount rate have become important chiefly as a signal of the Federal Reserve's intentions. A drop in the rate after a series of rises, for instance, would indicate an easing of monetary policy, while a rise after a series of drops would indicate a tightening.

The principal weapon at the command of the central banking system is the purchase and sale of government securities in the open market. How does the Federal Reserve's purchase of government securities result in an increase in member bank reserves? To understand, let us examine a transaction.

The system open market account manager places an order with one of the more than a dozen government securities dealers to buy $1 million in Treasury bills, short-term instruments that trade daily in tens of millions of dollars. The dealer obtains the bills from a large international oil company that regularly keeps cash other than that needed for immediate use in these, or similar, interest-earning obligations.

The Federal Reserve pays for the government securities by drawing a check against one of the district Federal Reserve Banks, in this case the Federal Reserve Bank of New York. This is the way the transaction is recorded:

Federal Reserve Bank of New York

Assets	Liabilities
U.S. Government securities	Deposits
Bought outright + $1,000,000	Member bank reserves + $1,000,000

The government securities dealer deposits the check in a large New York City bank:

Bank of Wall Street

Assets	Liabilities
Cash + $1,000,000	Deposits + $1,000,000

Again for simplicity, let us assume that the bank has a required reserve ratio of 20 percent. Of the $1 million addition to its deposits, then, it can make $800,000 in additional loans. If the full $800,000 were redeposited in a second bank, it could make $640,000 in additional loans. A third bank could support another $512,000. If full use were made of the additional reserves, the $1 million purchase of government securities would support $5 million in additional loans.

On the other hand, a $1 million sale of government securities by the Federal Reserve would extinguish $5 million worth of bank loans or investments.

We have assumed in this example that the Federal Reserve made its purchase from an individual or business other than a bank. What if it buys government securities from a bank? On the books of the Federal Reserve Bank the transaction is exactly the same:

Federal Reserve Bank of New York

Assets	Liabilities
U.S. Government securities	Deposits
Bought outright + $1,000,000	Member bank reserves + $1,000,000

On the books of the bank, however, there is no change in liabilities. The transaction represents a shift from one class of assets to another:

Wall Street Bank

Assets		Liabilities
Cash	+ $1,000,000	
Loans and investments U.S. Government securities	− $1,000,000	

Since there is no increase in deposits, there is no increase in required reserves. Hence, the bank is free to lend the entire amount of cash it receives.

The Federal Reserve performs a number of functions. Among other things, it distributes currency and coin for the Treasury, clears checks for commercial banks, serves as the principal depository for federal government funds, holds gold for foreign governments and central banks and invests their short-term dollar holdings, regulates stock market credit, and has a say in bank and bank holding company regulation. Its primary function, however, is making monetary policy.

9. How Monetary Policy Is Made

In economic affairs the Federal Open Market Committee is one of the most powerful bodies in Washington, yet it is also one of the least known. What goes on at its meetings must be pieced together from the accounts of members, former members, and their staffs. Because information concerning the committee's thinking and decisions concerning the future course of monetary policy might prove unusually profitable to securities speculators, great efforts are made to keep the sessions secret. What happens doesn't become known until the publication, once every three months, of summaries of the meetings held in the previous quarter, and details don't become public until publication of the minutes, about five years later. Let's drop in on one of the meetings, generally held every third Tuesday in the Federal Reserve's white marble headquarters building on Constitution Avenue.

The meeting takes place in a room studded with charts, blackboards, and other visual displays. Seated at the table are the twelve voting members of the committee plus the seven nonvoting district bank presidents. At 9:30 A.M. precisely, the chairman—who is chairman also of the Board of Governors—calls the meeting to order. First to be heard from is the open market account special manager, who reports on foreign exchange market conditions and operations, then the open market account manager, who reports on domestic transactions. After this, three senior staff members report and present their recommendations on the economic situation, financial markets, and international payments.

After members of the committee criticize the staff reports and the staff members defend them, the members present their own analyses and recommendations. (At one time, this discussion began with the president of the Federal Reserve Bank of New York, who is vice-chairman of the committee, and then moved from member to member, in order, but recently it has become less formal.) At the end the chairman attempts to summarize all that has gone before and to fashion directives to the open market account manager and special manager. A vote is then taken. Most often the directives are approved unanimously, but occasionally members will vote against approval, giving their reasons for doing so.

The directive to the open market account manager is couched in general terms, such as "maintaining firm conditions in money and short-term credit markets." How he achieves the objective—whether he buys or sells government securities, which ones, and how many—he must decide for himself. (Because of the breadth of the market, most operations are in short-term obligations.) Influencing his decisions are a number of market factors affecting the level of member bank reserves. A widespread snowstorm, for instance, may delay the airlines, slowing the presentation of checks for collection in hundreds of cities across the country and adding to the float. "Float" is Federal Reserve credit that is extended to member banks when checks are not collected by the Federal Reserve before member bank reserve accounts are credited in accordance with an established time schedule. This is a factor adding to member bank reserves. Or, because of an impending holiday weekend individuals and businesses may withdraw larger amounts of currency from their banks, adding to currency in circulation. This is a factor subtracting from member bank reserves. An increase in Treasury deposits with the Federal Reserve at quarterly income tax payment dates subtracts from member bank reserves, while withdrawals to pay the government's bills, frequent in the final half of each calendar year, add to reserves. An outflow of monetary gold, in settlement of an international payments deficit, subtracts from reserves.

The system open market account manager tries to forecast the behavior of these market factors, to offset them, and then to buy or sell enough government securities to carry out the Federal Open Market Committee's directive. Every day, in a telephone conference call with members of the Board of Governors, senior staff members, and other high Federal Reserve officials, he reviews such things as new offerings entering the markets, dealer financing needs, and the demand for Federal funds and tells what steps he intends to take to carry out the committee's instruction. His operations, then, are subject to daily updating, evaluation, and correction, if necessary.

With such careful attention to the formulation and execution of open market operations—a prodigious amount of effort goes into the preparation of positions for presentation at committee meetings—how can the Federal Reserve be criticized? The answer is that it not only can be criticized but has been, on a number of grounds.

Some of the criticism centers around the organization of the central banking system. The district banks have been called anachronistic, although it is usually acknowledged that they have been an important source of innovation within the system. The Federal Open Market Committee has been called unwieldy. No nineteen-man debating society, it is argued, can move swiftly enough or decisively enough to do what is often required. The Commission on Money and Credit, a group of distinguished scholars and businessmen who made a comprehensive review of money and credit markets, concluded that three men were all that were needed to formulate monetary policy.

The Board of Governors, it has been said, should be relieved of its responsibilities for the structural regulation of the banking system, such as, for instance, the approval of bank mergers and holding companies. Members should be selected because of broad, general qualities, not to represent agriculture, housing, or other specific industries.

The big criticism, however, has centered around monetary policy. Far from stabilizing the economy, its most dogged critics contend, the Federal Reserve itself has been a major source of instability, having exaggerated, not flattened, business ups and downs. This criticism results from a cleavage between economists who contend that the supply of money has little influence on the real world of output, incomes, and jobs and those who hold that the money stock is the most important influence. The two bodies of thought have become known as the fiscalist and monetarist schools, after their advocacy of tax and spending policy as the principal weapon for economic stabilization, on the one hand, and control of the money supply, on the other. They are also known as the Keynesian and Friedmanite schools after their mentors, John Maynard Keynes, the British economist, businessman, and public official whose thinking influenced greatly the depression and postwar years, and Milton Friedman, the University of Chicago professor whose extensive historical research helped establish the empirical support for what has come to be known as the modern quantity theory of money.

Half a dozen years ago the Keynesians held sway both in government and the economic world. Discussing the 1964 tax cut a year afterward, Arthur Okun, a member and later chairman of the Council of Economic Advisers, conceded that the monetary effects had not been considered. He rationalized the omission as follows: ". . . in practice, dealing with the period of the last year and a half, I cannot believe that the omission of monetary variables can make a serious difference."*

* "Measuring the Impact of the 1964 Tax Reduction," a paper presented September 10, 1965, to the American Statistical Association. Reprinted in *Perspectives on Economic Growth*, Walter W. Heller, ed, New York, Random House, 1968, p. 42.

Two events shattered the Keynesian satisfaction. In most years, like the tax-cut year of 1964, fiscal and monetary policy had moved in the same direction. It was impossible to say, therefore, whether one or the other had been dominant. In 1966, however, an interesting test developed. A sharp increase in the budget deficit was accompanied by a significant slowdown in expansion of the money supply, pitting the influence of fiscal policy against that of monetary policy. If monetary policy was insignificant in the real world of output, incomes, and jobs, the economy should have continued to boom. Instead it went into a tailspin, the downturn culminating in the minirecession of 1967. Indeed, a more serious recession was avoided only by a prompt and massive reversal of monetary policy.

Again, in mid-1968 passage of the income tax surcharge and the cuts in government expenditures insisted upon by Congress as a condition for passage produced a substantial increase in the full-employment budget surplus. Fearful of "overkill"—the thought that fiscal restraint would prove excessive—the Federal Reserve, which had been keeping a tight rein on member bank reserves, permitted the money supply to expand rapidly again. Instead of overkill, the result was renewed inflationary expansion. Once more monetary policy was the winner.

Until these demonstrations the monetarists had been regarded—when they had received any attention at all—as an amusing and not quite respectable group of eccentrics, an obscure cult with headquarters in Chicago. Milton Friedman's great work, with Anna J. Schwartz, *A Monetary History of the United States, 1867–1960,* was acknowledged to be a work of prodigious scholarship, but Professor Friedman's monetary views received little critical comment, either favorable or unfavorable, and his thoughts on other matters were usually ignored. Among these were such innovations as the negative income tax to provide minimum incomes for earners of low wages or no wages; the auction of radio and television frequencies like seats on a stock exchange; the issuance of educational vouchers to parents, permitting them to choose among public and private schools of varying cost and quality for their children; and the imposition of rebatable air- and water-use taxes on potential polluters of the environment.

The events of 1966 and 1968 changed things. The views of the monetarists began to receive attention. Professor Friedman found himself a frequent platform figure and his counsel sought at high levels of government. The fiscalists, forced to work money into their equations, were forced also to defense of the Keynesian dogma. From "Does money matter?" the debate shifted 180 degrees to "Does fiscal policy matter?"

It was not as if unsettling events had produced uncomfortable questions for the purveyors of the established truth. Waiting in the wings was a highly developed alternative doctrine, supported by a great mass of empirical data, ready to be substituted for what had been accepted.

Although there are fiscalists and monetarists of a thousand stripes, the two schools differ principally in their views of the proper role of government and the market in the economy; of the sources of output, incomes, and employment; and of the steps needed to assure stability. They differ, in other words, in ideology, in theory, and in policy prescription.

Most monetarists, although not all, see the economy as essentially stable, with little need of help from government to keep it moving ahead. They emphasize the desirability of individual choice in the marketplace over majority rule in the political arena. Most fiscalists see the economy as essentially unstable, needing government effort both to smooth out business ups and downs and to power economic growth; they emphasize the desirability of increasing the output of public over private goods and services. Another way of categorizing the two schools is in terms of their fears. Most fiscalists seem more concerned about the possibility of recession and unemployment, while most monetarists fear unrestrained expansion and inflation.

In terms of economic theory as well as ideology, the monetarists see the world quite a bit differently from the fiscalists. The latter focus on the discrepancies between actual and full employment of the nation's manpower and material resources, paying no attention to the effect of inflationary price increases on the demand for real goods. Since they believe the money supply to be as much a result of economic activity as a source of it, they give it no special role in their calculations of overall activity. When they do give attention to money, it is in terms of the effect interest rates may have in encouraging private investment. Investment is the key to their theory because of the so-called Keynesian multiplier, which is the relationship between investment and the national income adduced by the British economist.

Investment, in the Keynesian view, represents dollars that—spent on factories, machinery, office buildings, and homes—touch off a chain of expenditures by the wage earners who produce these things, by the other wage earners who produce the things they in turn buy, and so on down the line. A dollar of investment, in this view, means perhaps three dollars of GNP. Keynes assumed that consumption was a highly stable function of income and that this relationship derived from a "fundamental psychological law." If this was true, it followed that any autonomous increase in investment would produce a greater increase in income.

The monetarists challenge these ideas head-on. Changes in private investment, they say, have proved a much less accurate barometer of business ups and downs than changes in the money supply. People—

both individuals and businesses—have a good idea of the cash balances they need to operate comfortably and are extremely reluctant to change them. In the United States they hold a little over four weeks' income in currency. In India, despite the fact that money plays a far smaller role in the economy, they hold roughly seven weeks' income, and in Yugoslavia they hold six. Whether a country be high income or low income, market oriented or socialist, its people's preferences for holding cash are remarkably similar to those of people elsewhere. What is more, the monetarists contend, the differences narrow further when the greater role that checking accounts play in the industrialized countries is taken into account.

Because people are so stubborn in their notions about the amount of wealth they want to keep in the form of money, the monetarists say, it is important to distinguish between nominal money, or money of varying purchasing power, and real money, or money the value of which is adjusted for changes in the price level. The key to the monetarist doctrine is that people want to hold a predictable real-money balance not a nominal-money balance. The amount of money the public demands at any time depends on prices and price expectations, interest rates, income, and wealth. If the Federal Reserve supplies more money than the public demands, the excess supply increases spending. At first this increases real income and employment, but if the excess supply persists increased spending will push up prices until the stock of real money is reduced to the point where demand equals the supply. Conversely, if the Federal Reserve supplies less money than the public demands, spending will be diminished and employment, incomes, and prices will fall to the point where, once again, the demand for real money equals supply.

The monetarists focus, then, on discrepancies between the real money balances the public actually hold and those they would like to hold, between the nominal stock of money the Federal Reserve can control and the real stock of money it cannot. They fasten their attention on the money supply, member bank reserves, and other monetary aggregates rather than upon interest rates. For the monetarists, the key to smoothing out business ups and downs is steady growth of the money supply.

The fiscalists have retreated. They have begun to give money a more prominent, although still not a causal, role, but they have not given ground without a stubborn fight. They express doubts that a central bank can control even the nominal money supply. Don't member banks exert some influence over money creation when they undertake to borrow reserves, they ask, and credit users even more when they decide to seek loans? They ask why the monetarists sometimes use the narrow definition of the money supply—private checking deposits plus currency outside banks—and sometimes a broader definition that includes time deposits at commercial banks. And if commercial bank time deposits are included in the definition, why not similar deposits at savings banks and savings and loan associations? The fiscalists also question the usefulness of money as an indicator because of the long and variable lags between changes in the money supply and changes in GNP. And these by no means exhaust their catalogue of complaints.

In the pulling and hauling between the fiscalists and the monetarists, the Federal Reserve finds itself in the role of an unlikely member of the chorus thrust suddenly into the role of leading tenor. While it waited in the wings, tolerated but largely ignored, there was no question about how it exercised its talents, but now, on center stage, it finds itself the object of tireless criticism.

The monetarists give the Federal Reserve high marks for good intentions, but they argue that its actions have tended to add to, not diminish, business ups and downs. One reason, they say, is that the central banking system has attempted to stabilize interest rates rather than assure a steady growth of the money supply. Thus, in the summer of 1965, when escalation of the war in Vietnam was adding rapidly to credit demands, the Federal Reserve began supplying reserves to keep interest rates from rising. The result, perversely, was a still greater demand for credit and still higher interest rates.

Historically, the critics contend, the Federal Reserve has reversed policy abruptly whenever inflation or deflation began to get out of hand —tightening money sharply, as in 1959, 1966, and 1969, or expanding it rapidly, as in 1967, the final half of 1968 and in 1971—which has added to the roller-coaster effect. A more effective course of action, they say, would have been to move sooner but less abruptly in the same direction.

Another criticism is that the Federal Reserve sometimes puts other objectives—help to the Treasury in marketing its debt and support of certain institutions, such as the savings banks and savings and loan associations, and certain sectors of the market, such as housing—ahead of stabilization. Assuring the health of the financial structure and assisting the Treasury are both older objectives; indeed, the Federal Reserve came into being as a direct result of the panic of 1907 and met its initial test in helping the Treasury finance World War I. At times of war, therefore, the Treasury's needs still take precedence, and at times of deep deterioration in public confidence, such as the bank holiday of 1933 and following the Penn Central debacle in 1970, the questions of liquidity and health of financial institutions come to the fore. A successful program of stabilization, however, should obviate greatly the need for such concern.

At times other than war or panic, the critics insist, Federal Reserve attention to the needs of the Treasury, financial institutions, or specific sectors of the market may conflict with its primary obligation to stabilize business ups and downs. As an example they cite even-keeling, the Federal Reserve's policy of avoiding changes in monetary policy during periods of Treasury financing. The Federal Reserve specifically disavows support of any Treasury marketing, success or failure of which depends on the terms set by the Treasury and their acceptance by investors. But it does agree to refrain from moves immediately before, during, and immediately after a Treasury financing that might cause losses to government securities dealers underwriting the issue and possible failure of the financing.

At first glance, even-keeling seems to make sense. Why should one arm of the government, the central bank, deliberately create difficulty for another arm, the Treasury? In years of substantial budget deficits, however, the Federal Reserve may find itself supporting Treasury financings so often that it is unable to pursue its own objectives. In 1968, a year of strong inflationary pressures, for instance, the Federal Reserve found itself obliged to maintain a policy of even keel for a total of 134 days during six Treasury financings. In only four months, March, June, September, and December, was it free to move on its own.

The critics raise another objection to even-keeling. The record shows, they say, that the Federal Reserve has intervened more actively in the Treasury's behalf when interest rates have been rising than when they have been falling. Far from remaining neutral, they say, the central banking system has sought to help the Treasury in its understandable desire to hold down the cost of servicing the public debt. This, however, has imparted an inflationary bias to even-keeling.

The issue of Federal Reserve support of nonbank thrift institutions and housing is more complicated. It hinges on whether the central banking system should operate primarily through broad, general measures that affect the overall cost and availability of credit or through measures designed to aid specific institutions and sectors of the market. The interest-rate ceilings on commercial bank savings and time deposits— the so-called Regulation Q ceilings—are the most prominent example of the latter. The ceilings grew out of the 1933 banking difficulties and the competition among banks and thrift institutions for deposits. Regulation Q was designed to bring such competition under control. The ceilings were lowered twice, then for twenty-one years—from 1936 to 1957—they remained unchanged, largely ignored and forgotten. These were the depression, war, and early postwar years, the years of low interest rates and little competition for savings.

By the mid-fifties market rates of interest—no longer pegged at artificially low wartime levels—rose above the ceilings and the ceilings were raised, the object being to permit commercial banks to compete more effectively with savings banks and savings and loan associations. Permitted to pay higher rates than commercial banks, these nonbank thrift institutions and the housing market they served had been getting the lion's share of time and savings deposits. In time, agreement was reached among the Federal Reserve and the federal and state agencies regulating the thrift institutions to maintain a rate differential in favor of the thrift institutions.

The Regulation Q ceilings were raised seven times in the 1960s, in part in response to rising market rates of interest and in part in response to a new development, the creation and sale of large, negotiable certificates of deposit by commercial banks. These are money market instruments, sold usually in denominations of $1 million or more, which compete with Treasury bills, commercial paper, and other short-term obligations for the temporarily idle cash of corporations, state and local governments, and others.

The interest-rate ceilings, then, came to have still another function, the rationing of funds between commercial banks and open-market instruments. During the 1960s the idea gained ground that by keeping a lid on interest rates the Federal Reserve could limit the growth of credit. All that happened actually was that borrowers were driven from the banks to open-market instruments such as commercial paper, the unsecured promissory notes of finance and industrial companies sold to raise short-term funds. In 1969, a year in which market rates climbed well above the ceilings, the volume of large, negotiable certificates of deposit (CDs) outstanding dropped $12 billion, but that of commercial paper outstanding rose $11 billion.

At the same time, the drop in time deposits caused by Regulation Q drove the banks to seek alternate sources of funds. Through subsidiaries and holding companies they entered the commercial paper market themselves, and through European branches the large banks siphoned vast quantities of Eurodollars—dollars on deposit at banks and branches overseas—from Europe. These efforts triggered attempts by the Federal Reserve to plug the loopholes, which were followed by still further efforts by the banks to find ways of evasion.

In mid-1970 the ceiling was abruptly lifted on large negotiable CDs after the Penn Central Railroad petitioned for help under the Federal bankruptcy laws, defaulting on its obligations and putting the entire commercial paper market under a cloud. For a time there was a question whether other large issuers of commercial paper, notably the Chrysler Corporation, would be able to obtain funds. To allay such fears the Federal Reserve reemphasized its role as lender of last resort, pledging whatever resources might be needed to avert a liquidity crisis.

In retrospect, it was hard to discover what useful thing the ceilings had accomplished. The Federal Reserve had succeeded in driving borrowers from regulated to unregulated sources of funds, increasing the risks to borrowers and inhibiting its own efforts at control, and had diverted bankers and its own personnel from productive effort to consideration of a maze of legal complexities. It had caused worldwide disruption of the money and capital markets, rekindling distrust of Americans overseas, and had brought the American economy to the brink of a liquidity crisis. But the ceilings had accomplished little, if anything, in restricting the overall flow of credit.

Even in their primary objective, the protection of the thrift institutions and the sources of housing credit, the ceilings were of doubtful help. As market rates of interest rose above the ceilings, depositors withdrew savings from banks and savings institutions and borrowed against the cash value of life insurance policies, reinvesting the proceeds directly in higher-yielding bonds and other obligations, which process was given the jawbreaking name of "disintermediation." Among others, the market for Treasury bills in denominations of $1,000 and $5,000 blossomed as savers sought higher returns than the banks and savings institutions were permitted to pay. To discourage the participation of small investors in the bill market, the treasury raised the minimum denomination of Treasury bills to $10,000 in March 1970.

The criticisms of the Federal Reserve cannot be lightly dismissed. Perhaps the most devastating is the judgment of Professor Friedman that the central banking system is unnecessary, that the country would be better served if discretionary control of money and credit were abandoned and the money supply permitted to grow by a fixed percentage each year, one suggestion being about 4 percent each year, roughly in line with the long-term growth of the economy.

This approach acknowledges the chief deficiency of the money supply as a policy-making tool, the long and variable lags between changes in the money supply and changes in business activity, and acknowledges as well that economic forecasting is an imprecise art. Policy makers, the monetarists say, should abandon fine-tuning, the effort to stabilize the economy through short-term adjustments, but should permit interest rates, for example, to vary widely.

In rebuttal the Federal Reserve and its defenders say that money won't manage itself, that even if steady growth of the money supply is accepted as a desirable objective someone must supply reserves to or withdraw them from the banking system.

The central banking system has, however, begun to adapt to the new thinking. The system open market account manager has been directed to give greater weight to the monetary aggregates in his day-to-day operations and less weight to interest rates. Since January 1970 the Federal Reserve has committed itself to maintain an annual rate of growth of the

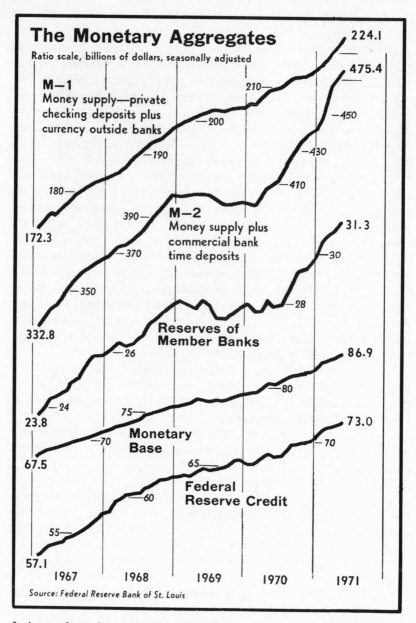

The Monetary Aggregates

Ratio scale, billions of dollars, seasonally adjusted

M—1
Money supply—private
checking deposits plus
currency outside banks

M—2
Money supply plus
commercial bank
time deposits

**Reserves of
Member Banks**

**Monetary
Base**

**Federal
Reserve Credit**

224.1
210—
—200
—190
180—
172.3

475.4
—450
—430
—410

390—
—370
—350
332.8

31.3
—30
—28

—26
23.8
—24

86.9
—80
75—
67.5
—70

73.0
—70
65—
—60
55—
57.1

1967   1968   1969   1970   1971

Source: Federal Reserve Bank of St. Louis

In its conduct of monetary policy, the Federal Reserve has given greater
attention to the growth of the money supply and other closely linked items.

money supply of at least 5 percent. Even so, the directives issued by the
Federal Open Market Committee continued to place maintenance of
orderly market conditions and influencing long-term interest rates ahead
of growth of the aggregates. This could explain the system's inability to

keep growth of the money supply at its target rate early in 1971, when it jumped ahead sharply. In the first seven months of 1971, the money supply narrowly defined advanced at an annual rate of 11 percent.

Until recently the Treasury bill rate, the Federal Funds rate, and the net reserve position of member banks were the best indicators of monetary policy. The net reserve position is calculated by subtracting member bank borrowings from the Federal Reserve from reserves in excess of requirements. It is described as "net free reserves" when excess reserves are greater than borrowings, and as "net borrowed reserves" when borrowings are greater than excess reserves. A big net free reserve position for the banking system indicated easy money, a big net borrowed position tight money.

Now the rate of change of the monetary base is becoming an important indicator. The monetary base, that part of the money supply over which the Federal Reserve has greatest control, includes member bank reserves and currency held by the public and nonmember banks, adjusted for reserve requirement changes and shifts in deposits. Ordinarily the monetary base and the money supply grow at similar rates.

Can the fiscalists and monetarists be reconciled? Will a common prescription for stabilization of business ups and downs, as useful in curbing inflation as in curing recession, evolve? With its emphasis on underemployment of resources, the fiscalist remedy seems best suited now to a depressed economy, while, with its concern for the effect of changing prices on cash holdings and interest rates, the monetarist remedy seems best suited to an economy straining under inflationary pressures. A reconciliation will depend importantly on the ability of the theorists to separate the monetary effects of a budget deficit, for instance, from the purely fiscal effects, and will depend on their ability to state the monetary effects in quantitative terms. Already, however, the two schools are coming closer together, and a new synthesis seems entirely likely.

10. Antitrust

Antitrust plays an important role in the mixed American economy. The body of common law, statutes, and court interpretations outlawing price-fixing, group boycotts, geographical division of markets, and other monopolistic practices reflects the primary American commitment to private enterprise in the mix of governmental and private decision making and to competition as the chief regulating force in the economy. This commitment contrasts with that of socialist countries, where state ownership of all or a major part of industry is the objective, and with that of countries where the state's power has been used to enforce private market-sharing arrangements, or cartels.

Antitrust reflects an American aversion to monopoly that reaches back to the Boston Tea Party and beyond, at the same time embracing the notion that life perhaps was better in a simpler America, that the village blacksmith should not have been deprived of a livelihood by the automobile, the corner grocer by the supermarket.

One group of economists sees no conflict between the two ideas, believing as they do that the concentration of American industry in three great waves—one after the Civil War, another in the 1920s, and the third only recently—threatens the basic economic freedoms. As industries come to be dominated by an ever fewer number of concerns, producers find it possible to restrict output and charge higher prices than they could under fully competitive conditions. The sovereignty of consumers, who might buy more of a product if prices were lower, is thwarted, and the freedom of entrepreneurs to establish businesses and of workers to find employment within an industry is restricted. The adoption of more efficient means of production loses its necessity.

An opposing group of economists finds the affection of Congress and the courts for the small businessman often at loggerheads with the encouragement of competition. The growth in size and reduction in number of concerns, they say, stems not so much from a hope for monopoly profits—these occur less often than supposed—but from an attempt to realize the economies of large-scale operations. In the 1880s and 1890s the savings were largely in production, in the amalgamation of such capital-intensive industries as railroads, steel, and petroleum and in the extension of markets nationwide. In the 1920s the economies were achieved primarily in distribution, in the interconnection of vast public utility networks, and in the spread of chain store retailing. More recently the savings have resulted from the application of management science and computer techniques to diverse enterprises, particularly those arising from the growth of a service economy.

Competition, this opposing group argues further, should not be measured solely by the number of concerns in an industry or by their size. Admittedly, the more concerns in an industry the less likely is anti-competitive behavior. Collusion becomes more expensive, more susceptible to detection, and more likely to break down. But other factors may exercise an even greater influence on competition. If new concerns can enter the industry quickly and cheaply, monopoly profits are likely to be small and short lived, and, if the industry's buyers are big, competitive pricing is apt to prevail. Perhaps most important, if other products can be substituted readily for those an industry produces—or if purchases can be postponed indefinitely—anticompetitive behavior is not likely to be effective.

After all, the maker of an automobile is not competing primarily *with* other automobile makers, but *for* the consumer's dollar. If his product is not new enough, stylish enough, or efficient enough, the consumer will be tempted to spend his dollar elsewhere—on a summer home, perhaps, or a vacation in the Orient. Or he may simply put his money in the bank. By the same token, if steel producers permit their product to be priced out of the market, they invite competition from foreign steel producers—assuming that tariffs or quotas don't keep out imports—and from aluminum, concrete, plastics, or some other material waiting in the wings.

With the economists so far apart, is it any wonder that Congress and the courts appear to be confused? Under the Sherman Act, for instance, price-fixing became a crime. Under the Robinson-Patman Act, however, wholesalers were forbidden to pass along to retailers and retailers to consumers the full economies arising from mass buying, and under the Miller-Tydings Act and the McGuire Act retailers were forbidden to pass along any. If a single retailer of branded and trademarked merchandise signed a so-called retail price maintenance contract, all other retailers in a state were bound by it—assuming such contracts were made permissible by state law. If General Electric, say, obtained an agreement from a retailer to refrain from selling its $21.95 toaster below list price, then all other retailers in a state were enjoined from cutting the price. Fortunately, in many states the courts have ruled the enabling laws void.

The Robinson-Patman Act was aimed at the chain stores, the Miller-Tydings and McGuire acts at the discount houses. In each case it was argued that these large merchandisers were using monopoly power to obtain large and unjustified price decreases from suppliers. The result actually was to suppress retail competition and to sustain inefficient store owners.

Congress has not been alone in expressing sympathy for competitors, if not for competition. In the Aluminum Company of America case, Judge Learned Hand conceded that Alcoa had not engaged in monopolistic practices. What it had done was to anticipate increases in demand, doubling and redoubling its capacity, and as a result of its foresight and efficiency it had managed to keep 90 percent of the market for aluminum ingot not made from scrap. This, however, was contrary to the purpose of the Sherman Act, as interpreted by Judge Hand. As he saw it, that purpose was the preservation of a system of small producers "for its indirect social or moral effect," in spite of some possible cost in efficiency.

More recently the Supreme Court has struck down mergers that would have added only slightly to industrial concentration. In the Brown Shoe case it denied Brown, primarily a manufacturer, the right to merge with the G. R. Kinney Company, primarily a retailer. In an industry of more than eight hundred manufacturers, the two concerns accounted for less than 5 percent of the industry's output and operated only 2.3 percent of all retail shoe stores. In the Von's Grocery case the Court denied Von's, the third largest supermarket chain in the Los Angeles area, the right to merge with Shopping Bag Stores, the sixth largest. In an area where one hundred fifty chains competed, the two companies accounted for 7.5 percent of the market. The Court gave no weight to the fact that the two chains were in different parts of the area and thus did not compete directly, and it swept aside the argument that food retailing by department stores and discount houses had introduced new vigor into competition. The increase in the number of food chains and the decline in the number of independent retailers, it said, was reason enough to block the merger.

The Supreme Court's fondness for the independent local company and its dislike of large national concerns reached a height of some sort in the Utah Pie Company case. Utah Pie had sued Continental Baking and two other national concerns for treble damages under the Robinson-Patman Act. Their sin? Vigorous competition, which had reduced prices to consumers and was chipping away at the 66.5-percent share of the Salt Lake City market enjoyed previously by Utah Pie. The Court thought unimportant the fact that Utah Pie itself had initiated much of the price cutting, that it had made profits continuously, and that it had greatly expanded its absolute sales volume. The deciding factor, apparently, was that in a growing market Utah Pie's share, although still substantial, had decreased.

The situation is not hard to explain. Small businessmen are people, easier to identify with than the abstract principle of competition, and may also be constituents and voters. If perchance they are also monopolists—the village blacksmith and the corner grocer often were—their sins may appear less grievous than the calculating efficiency of a distant manufacturer or chain store operator. And to a community or region, consolidation oftens means the loss of a company headquarters, along with much of the banking, stock transfer, legal, and other business a headquarters generates. It may also mean the elimination of uneconomic plants and jobs.

There is another strain in antitrust law that cannot be ignored—the fear that economic monopoly will subvert political liberty, the belief that many centers of power are better than a few. If the cost of this insurance against autocracy is some sacrifice of economic efficiency, according to those who make the argument, then so be it. In any rational analysis, the benefit outweighs the cost.

Like the Constitution itself, the antitrust laws are susceptible of varying interpretations. It is difficult to accept the judgment of some critics that their chief effect has been to restrain, not further, competition. It is equally hard, however, to assert with assurance that they have been a major force impelling the economy to greater productivity and growth. About the most that can be said is that the United States has seldom embarked on an avowedly anticompetitive policy, the National Recovery Act being one such instance. By applying Marquis of Queensbury rules, some of the brutality has been removed from competition, but it is doubtful that by themselves the antitrust laws have done more than give a little extra time—or a few extra rounds—to inefficient competitors.

The Sherman Act (1890), the cornerstone of antitrust law, was designed to combat the great industrial combinations, or trusts, that had sprung up over the previous decade—the Whisky Trust, the Sugar Trust, the Lead Trust, the Cotton Oil Trust and, above all, the Standard Oil Trust. In the words of Senator John Sherman of Ohio, the sponsor of the act, a trust could "control the market, raise or lower prices, as will best promote its selfish interests, reduce prices in a particular locality and break down competition and raise prices where competition does not exist."

The trusts, he said, disregarded the interests of consumers, dictated terms to railroads, and beat down wages without fear of strikes, all because they had eliminated competition. In a single generation, he added, they had created inequality of condition, of wealth, and of opportunity. They exercised great influence at state capitals, he said, and like Briareus, the hundred-handed giant of mythology, they reached out "to every part of our country."

The Sherman Act has two principal sections. Section 1 declares: "Every contract, combination in the form of trust or otherwise, or conspiracy, in restraint of trade or commerce among the several states, or with foreign countries is hereby declared to be illegal. . . ." Section 2 says: "Every person who shall monopolize, or attempt to monopolize, or combine or conspire with any person or persons to monopolize any part of the trade or commerce among the several states or with foreign nations, shall be deemed guilty of a misdemeanor. . . ."

There is no recitation of price-fixing, group boycotts, geographical division of markets, tie-in arrangements, or other prohibited practices, and no definition of an illegal combination or monopoly. This was for the courts to determine. The act merely adopts a phrase and a word, "restraint of trade" and, "monopolize," which over the years had acquired meaning in the common law. What the Sherman Act did, in the words of one commentator, was to nationalize the common law, which was to prove the act's strength—and its great weakness. Because it was entirely flexible, adaptable to changing times and conditions, in wise judicial hands it could become a Magna Carta of competitive freedom. The deliberately vague language of the statute, on the other hand, offered lesser minds an opportunity to negate its purpose—or worse, to so burden its interpretation with hairsplitting that it would be employed only infrequently.

The courts quickly determined that, despite the wording of the Sherman Act, not every restraint of trade was outlawed. A contract for the sale of a restaurant, for instance, which prohibited the seller from establishing another restaurant in the same community for several years, was held to be entirely proper, the object being the reasonable one of protecting the value of the purchase. If, on the other hand, the contract had required the seller to stay out of the restaurant business for all time and in all places, the restraint would have been unreasonable. Unreasonable restraints, the courts held, were prohibited.

The courts determined that certain restraints of trade were so pernicious in their effect on competition and so lacking of any redeeming virtue that their unreasonable nature didn't have to be proved but were illegal per se. Such types of conduct included price-fixing arrangements, group boycotts, agreements to divide markets, and tie-in sales.

The Sherman Act permits the government to initiate both civil and criminal actions, the latter punishable by jail sentences as well as by fines. It also permits injured parties to bring civil suits for three times the amount they have been damaged.

The effectiveness of the Sherman Act in the area of per se violations and the severity of its penalties was demonstrated to the business community in 1960 when twenty electrical equipment manufacturers and forty-five of their executives were indicted on charges of price-fixing, bid-rigging, and market-sharing in the sale of products ranging from turbine generators to circuit breakers. The next year, after General Electric, Westinghouse, Allis Chalmers, and other manufacturers entered guilty pleas, the companies were fined and a number of executives were sentenced to jail. But this was only the beginning. Treble-damage suits running into millions of dollars were brought against the companies by public utilities, state and local governments, and other injured equipment buyers.

The Sherman Act has also been used—not often but spectacularly —to break up existing combinations. Perhaps the most important cases involved the Standard Oil Company (New Jersey) and the American Tobacco Company. In 1911 the Supreme Court ordered the dissolution of each, setting forth in the process the "rule of reason." This said, in effect, that big was not necessarily synonymous with bad, that only trusts that had achieved size through predatory practices—as, the court determined, had Standard Oil and American Tobacco—were to be dissolved. "Good" trusts, as it found United States Steel to be nine years later, would be permitted to continue.

The Alcoa decision (1945), in effect, reversed the rule of reason. Alcoa's crime was size, not predatory behavior. Judge Hand ordered Alcoa to cut its ties to the Canadian aluminum producer, Aluminium Ltd., and to open the industry to new competition by licensing other domestic producers under its patents. The government subsequently sold its own war-built plants to the new competitors, Reynolds and Kaiser. Subsequently, other producers have entered the field.

The United Shoe Machinery decision (1953) echoed Alcoa. Through economies of scale, ability, and research, among other things, the company had come to dominate its market. The Court ruled that the company should not be broken up but that conditions should be placed upon it "to restore a competitive market." The company, according to agreement, returned to the Court a dozen years later, slimmer but, in the eyes of government antitrust lawyers, not slim enough. After an unfavorable Supreme Court ruling, the company in 1969 consented to sell off assets, reducing its size to one-third of the industry total.

In 1969, in one of the most significant antimonopoly actions ever taken under the Sherman Act, the Department of Justice—joined by several private companies—charged the International Business Machines Corporation with monopolizing the market for digital computers. And more recently, the Federal Trade Commission which shares the responsibility for prosecution with the Justice Department has begun studies of the breakfast cereal, drug, automobile, steel, electrical machinery, chemical, and petroleum industries to determine the effects of concentration on competition. (Aware that the spin-off of Chevrolet as a separate automobile manufacturer has been a long-run aim of some would-be trust busters, General Motors has embarked on a program to make Chevrolet facilities indistinguishable from those of its other divisions.)

The Sherman Act outlawed existing contracts, combinations, or conspiracies in restraint of trade. The Clayton Act (1914) was designed to nip incipient combinations in the bud. As amended by the Celler-Kefauver Act (1950), section 7 prohibits the acquisition by a company of the stock or assets of another company "in any line of commerce in any section of the country where the effect of such acquisition may be substantially to lessen competition or to tend to create a monopoly."

From one point of view the Clayton Act has checked a dangerous trend toward concentration. Since 1950 more than eight hundred mergers—most of them involving acquisitions by the five hundred largest manufacturing companies—have been challenged. In a single year, three out of five billion-dollar companies have had one or more of their acquisitions challenged. Horizontal mergers, those between direct competitors, which in the immediate postwar years accounted for 41 percent of all mergers, have been virtually eliminated. Through the prevention of such giant acquisitions as the proposed take-over of the Youngstown Sheet and Tube Company by Bethlehem Steel, concentration in such important industries as steel has actually been reduced.

From another point of view there is no dearth of antimerger activity, but little of it makes economic sense. In their effort to expedite litigation, the courts make little or no effort to subject challenged mergers to the Clayton Act's test of illegality, the probability of a substantial lessening of competition or a tendency toward monopoly. Instead they focus on numbers of sellers and size of market shares to the exclusion of more meaningful real-life measures of competitive efficiency. They stretch the use of analogy as well, applying to banking, for instance, measures of anticompetitive behavior applicable to gasoline sales, motion pictures, and fashion patterns. They permit gerrymandering of markets to create the least favorable pattern of market shares and throw around terms like "market power" and "potential competition" without giving them specific meaning. They reach back to old decisions and ancient rules of law but ignore readily obtainable present-day facts. In sum, antimerger actions have become a lawyer's paradise but an economist's nightmare.

Without taking sides, it is possible to agree that defense of an antimerger suit has become a formidable undertaking, saddling a company with legal fees often running into six figures and draining executive talent for years. By itself, the likelihood of a challenge may be enough to dissuade a company from undertaking what it otherwise might consider to be an efficiency-promoting merger.

Until recent years most mergers were of three kinds—vertical, horizontal, or market extension. A vertical merger involves a union between buyers and sellers. When a large concern moves in the direction of acquiring its sources of raw material, the move is said to involve backward vertical integration, and, when it moves in the direction of acquiring consumer outlets, to involve forward vertical integration. A horizontal merger involves sellers of the same product in the same market, or direct competitors, while a market extension merger involves sellers of the same product in different geographical markets—milk wholesalers, say, in New York and Florida.

Of late, many mergers have involved the union of concerns in entirely different industries. Such a merger is known as a "conglomerate merger," and should be distinguished from a merger resulting from an effort to utilize a common source of raw materials, a common technology, a common research and development effort, or common marketing facilities. Such a merger is known as a "concentric merger."

Conglomerates have won a bad name because of their identification with high-flying financial promoters. In the boom period of the late 1960s, promoters capitalized on glamour, cosmetic accounting, and a gullible investment public to create vast enterprises with the appearance of certain expansion and ever-rising share prices. A frequent technique was to have a "growth company"—one whose stock was selling at a high multiple of its annual earnings—acquire another with a low price/earnings multiple. Through the use of pooling of interest accounting and other techniques, earnings per share of the merged company were increased and the price of the stock bid up. This created the "funny money"—stock of inflated market value—for further acquisitions. It also created the basis for the issuance of convertible debentures and other debt, which made possible further expansion of earnings per share.

But, with the stock market decline that followed the boom of the late 1960s, the game for many came to an end. The decline in share prices, much more severe for the conglomerates than for the market as a whole, made new acquisitions impossible. Shorn of the benefit of new mergers and pooling of interest accounting, the growth of earnings per share fell off. At the same time, the burden of a top-heavy debt structure in a time of steeply rising interest rates often created a severe cash squeeze. Many large conglomerates did well merely to remain alive.

Before this happened the promoters had often unloaded their shares on less sophisticated investors. Add to this other charges against the conglomerates—that their take-over of major banks threatened the access of other borrowers to credit, that their acquisition of television networks introduced a new barrier to freedom of information, that they were being used by the Mafia to extend its control over legitimate business—and the reluctance of some companies to be identified as conglomerates becomes wholly understandable. Most of these chose instead to be known as multimarket or multi-industry concerns.

Many of the high-pitched voices raised against the conglomerates have been those of entrenched old-line managements, often with poor or mediocre records of performance, who have sought to ward off attack. Less emotional voices, however, have also been raised in accusation, and these say that conglomerates will use predatory pricing, cutting prices in one industry until competitors are driven from the field and subsidizing the temporary losses with profits from other lines of endeavor. Apart from the fact that such behavior violates the antitrust laws, it flies in the face of accepted principles of management incentives and rewards. In a multi-industry company a manager is paid on the basis of profits earned by his subsidiary or division. To ask him to accept lower prices and profits now in the hope of higher ones later is tantamount to asking him to take a pay cut without any assurance of having it restored. This is especially true when a rise in prices later is likely to bring new competitors into the field.

A similar criticism is that conglomerates will force the companies they acquire to buy and sell from each other to the disadvantage of independent competitors. The answer, again, is that in terms of management incentives and rewards such a policy makes no sense, except when the terms are no worse than could be obtained elsewhere.

Conglomerates, critics also say, can use their substantial resources to finance such things as expensive product development and large-scale advertising. Such advantages not only operate against the ability of smaller concerns to compete but prevent the entry into the field of anyone except another large company.

This kind of argument figured importantly in the decision of the Supreme Court denying Procter and Gamble the right to acquire the Clorox Company. The Court found that Procter and Gamble, the nation's largest soap and detergent maker, was not in direct competition with Clorox, the nation's largest manufacturer of household liquid bleach. But Procter and Gamble, with annual sales of $1.156 billion, was many times the size of Clorox, with sales of $40 million a year, and what is more, Procter and Gamble's expenditures as the nation's largest advertiser alone were twice Clorox's total sales. The Court decided that, because the field was already highly concentrated, the acquisition would have reduced the likelihood of competition and made a bad situation worse.

The Procter and Gamble case has been cited as an argument against conglomerates. Actually, of course, it is an argument against all large concerns. Interestingly in this regard, in 1970 avowed conglomerates accounted for only six concerns of 73 industrial companies with sales of $1.5 billion or more. These concerns and their ranking were: International Telephone and Telegraph, eighth;* Ling-Temco-Vought, fifteenth; Tenneco, thirty-fourth; Litton Industries, thirty-sixth; Gulf and Western Industries, sixty-fifth; and Textron, sixty-sixth. If public policy requires a breakup of the biggest conglomerates, should not ten times the same number of other concerns as big or bigger also be dismantled?

The argument takes on special significance when it is realized that conglomerates are the only concerns big enough to command the management talent, utilize the financial resources, undertake the research and development, and engage in active promotional activities needed to compete with concerns in already highly concentrated industries. The conglomerate, in the words of one commentator, sits on the edge of all markets, ready to enter, and thus keeps the establishment on its toes. Another economist, a German, sees conglomerate mergers as a self-correcting force in American capitalism, denying the prophecy of Karl Marx that monopoly is inevitable.

Professor Neil Jacoby of the University of California notes that the Census Bureau classifies American industry into 470 industries comprising 21 manufacturing groups. If there were only one concern in each industry, there would be 470 monopolies. If there were companies in each industry producing related products only, there would be 22 concerns in each of the 21 major manufacturing groups. If, on the other hand, conglomerates were universal, every one of the 470 concerns would be competing in each of the industries.

The example is extreme, since economies of scale would limit competition of this kind. Nevertheless, Professor Jacoby concludes: "Conglomeration helps to keep down industrial concentration in manufacturing and mining in the face of macro-economic concentration. For any assumed level of macro-economic concentration, a population of

---

* In settlement of an anti-trust suit brought by the Justice Department because of its acquisition of The Hartford Fire Insurance Co., ITT agreed in August 1971 to divest itself of several of the largest corporations it had acquired in recent years and to refrain from other large domestic acquisitions.

conglomerate firms will produce lower average concentration than would a population of single-industry or concentric firms."*

The thought is worth pondering because, many observers believe, there is an inherent contradiction in antimerger policy. To the degree that efforts to deter mergers are successful, they help to hold down existing levels of concentration, but on the other hand they tend to "lock into the candy store" large concerns already on the scene.

Public policy makers may thus be forced into one of two choices: to dismantle the giants, particularly those that have achieved size through mergers unchallenged in the past, or to encourage new large-scale competition. Washington administrations of both political stripes have for many reasons been reluctant to begin a new campaign of trust-busting. The encouragement of conglomerate competition, although contrary to recent thinking of Congress and the courts, could offer an interesting alternative.

* "The Conglomerate Corporation," *The Financial Analysts Journal*, May-June 1970, p. 45.

11. Regulation

Competition is established as the public goal for most business in the United States, however men may differ about the ways competition should be defined and civilized. The impersonal mechanism of adjustment represented by the competitive ideal, however, does not rule everywhere. In transportation, communications, energy production, and certain other areas carved out by government, public regulation has been substituted for the market process.

In a regulated industry, private ownership remains. But many of the functions of management are limited by or ceded to government. The regulators control prices and standards of service and restrict both the right of newcomers to enter an industry and of established companies to withdraw service. They determine safety requirements and the qualification of personnel, and they may also pass judgment on financing plans and on what they believe to be a fair and adequate return on investment.

Regulation, which sprang from the clamor of farmers and workingmen to control the high and discriminatory pricing practices of the nineteenth century monopolies, the railroads in particular, has become a major—some say the principal—anticompetitive force in the economy today.

Who are the regulators? They are members appointed to some fifty or so federal boards and commissions, occasionally a lone official. Many are responsible directly to a cabinet officer, and thus are members of the executive branch. The most important, however, are the so-called independent agencies, those to which Congress has delegated some of its most important responsibilities under the Constitution—the power to create money, for instance, and the power to regulate interstate commerce. Some of the best known of the independent agencies are the

Federal Reserve Board, the Interstate Commerce Commission, the Civil Aeronautics Board, the Federal Communications Commission, the Federal Power Commission, the Atomic Energy Commission, the Federal Trade Commission, the National Labor Relations Board, the Federal Deposit Insurance Corporation, and the Securities and Exchange Commission.

The independent agencies are unique. When they promulgate rules within the powers delegated to them by Congress, they are exercising a legislative function. When they seek out and accuse violators, they are performing an executive function. When they sit in judgment on violators and prescribe penalties for the infraction of rules, they are exercising a function of the judiciary. The theory that gave rise to the form—an original American contribution to constitutional evolution—was that the independent agency would provide expertise and continuity to business regulation neither Congress nor the courts could provide. The Congress could not be responsible for day-to-day administration, and the courts could act only on cases brought before them. What was needed was a body of experts, independent of politics and the industry they served, equipped through education, experience, and temperament to behave both as legislators and jurists.

This was the theory. In practice both expertise and judicial behavior have often been lacking. Men and women have been appointed to the independent agencies as rewards for political favors, and have regarded their posts as stepping-stones to higher political office or better-paying jobs in industry. Because reappointment is not automatic, they have been forced to give undue heed to influential members of Congress— the chairmen of appropriations committees and of committees to which their agencies are directly responsible—to presidential aides, and to the leaders of the industries they regulate. A regulator may survive the criticism of politicians, but he will seldom weather the condemnation of an entire industry. And in their conduct of business the independent agencies have been accused of permitting undue delays, of failing to delegate trivial responsibilities, and of permitting a huge backlog of work to pile up.

To the degree that the independent agencies have fallen short of their high promise, both Congress and the President must bear some of the blame. They have refused to appropriate sufficient funds or assign adequate personnel when needed—the appropriation for the Securities and Exchange Commission, for instance, was cut sharply in the early 1950s, just before the big rise in stock market activity—and they have wilted under industry pressure. In 1963, for instance, the Federal Communications Commission was forced to withdraw a proposed rule limiting the length and frequency of television commercials. The standards would have been no more severe than those already accepted by subscribers to the radio and television codes of the National Association of Broadcasters, but the industry complaint was so insistent that Congress not only forced the FCC to end its rule-making proceeding but passed a law forbidding it to take up the matter again. Chiefly, both the President and Congress must appreciate that regulators can't be appointed and treated as lackeys and be expected to behave as courageous independents.

Even if the regulators were ideally qualified, handsomely supported, and free of all pressures, however, they would still have problems. This is because of the flaws in regulatory theory, the conflicts in agency purpose and jurisdiction, and the cloudy crystal ball with which the independent agencies most often seem to view the future.

Regulatory theory proceeds from the premises of public utility and monopoly. The concept of public utility was spelled out by the Supreme Court in a landmark decision, *Munn* v. *Illinois* (1877):

When . . . one devotes his property to a use in which the public has an interest, he in effect grants to the public an interest in that use, and must submit to be controlled by the public for the common good, to the extent of that interest.

A public utility is under the extraordinary duty to render reasonably adequate service to all who apply. . . .

Again, a public utility is required to serve up to the limit of its capacity. . . . It may not let customers' wants go unsatisfied. Nor may it attach unreasonable conditions to contracts for service which in effect negate its duty "to serve all comers."

Monopoly, as has been discussed, is the antithesis of competition. It is the ability of a seller to restrict his output to achieve prices and profits greater than would be possible in a competitive market.

Public utilities are sometimes described as natural monopolies. It would be difficult to envision a dozen telephone companies—or even two—running their poles down the same street. Nevertheless, public utility monopolies are seldom natural. Some result from charters and franchises. A company is chartered to supply a city with water, then granted exclusive permission to lay its mains in the streets and connect them to businesses and dwellings. Others result from patents. The contest between Alexander Graham Bell, Elisha Gray, and hundreds of other inventors to determine who legally invented the telephone—and thus gained the right to offer telephone service—is one of the more colorful chapters in American business history. Still other public utility monopolies result from the award of such things as air routes and television frequencies.

In each case a property right has been established where one did not exist before, and in each case it was accomplished by government action. It should come as no great surprise, then, that in any industry the earliest cries for government regulation come from businessmen. Give the public better service, they plead. Improve passenger safety. End ruinous competition.

At this point the public finds itself torn. It wants none of the frequency grabbing, drowning out of competitors, and occasional jamming that characterized the early days of radio. It wants none of the corner-cutting on safety that marred the early history of both railroads and aviation. On the other hand, it is fearful that, once granted monopoly power, a public utility will abuse the privilege.

The lure of the new service—be it a ride across the prairie behind a spark-belching locomotive or live transmission of an Olympic contest on television by way of satellite—usually is enough to decide the issue. The franchise, route, or license is created and awarded, and often the taxpayer also provides generous subsidies to help the infant industry get on its feet. Soon, however, the love affair ends. The utility is charging too much, consumers complain. It is discriminating unduly between various classes of users. Government regulation is needed to keep prices reasonable and fair.

This was what happened in the first regulated industry, the railroads. The Act to Regulate Commerce (1887) decreed that rates should be reasonable, that one person should not be charged more than another for the same service, that shippers shouldn't pay more for a short than a long haul, and that traffic shouldn't be pooled and allocated according to an agreed formula among competing railroads.

The act also established the Interstate Commerce Commission, the first independent regulatory agency. Over the next three decades the commission's powers to keep rates reasonable and fair were strengthened and extended. The ICC was also given power over the railroads' service and safety standards, but not until passage of the Transportation Act of 1920—after government operation of the railroads during World War I—was it empowered to fix minimum as well as maximum rates or to establish what it considered to be a fair rate of return on the railroads' investments. Finally, the ICC was given power over the right of entry into the industry—it had to approve all extensions of service—and over the railroads' issuance of securities.

The Transportation Act of 1920 went even further. It sanctioned the consolidation or common control of competing roads, looking to the day when the nation's railroads would be brought together in a dozen or so large systems. A later law, the Reed-Bulwinkle Act (1948), specifically exempted railroad rate-making conferences—and those of other carriers regulated by the ICC—from the antimonopoly provisions of the Sherman Act. Railroad regulation, then, had swung 180 degrees from its original direction. From assuring passengers and shippers of fair and reasonable prices it had turned to defining and attempting to assure the carriers an adequate return on their investments.

The decision to treat the railroads as a monopoly couldn't have come at a less opportune time. The automobile, aided by vast public road expenditures, was about to begin cutting into the railroads' passenger business. Interstate trucks and barges, the latter helped by additional public expenditures on inland waterways, were to begin making deep inroads into the railroads' freight business only a bit later.

As these trends became evident, what was Congress's answer? Was it to permit the railroads once again to compete? Not at all. It was to enact the Motor Carrier Act (1935) bringing interstate trucking and the Transportation Act of 1940 bringing domestic water carriers under ICC control. Henceforth the commission would fix rates for trucks and barges much as it already did for the railroads—with two important exceptions. Haulers of agricultural products were exempted under provisions of the Motor Carrier Act, and haulers of bulk commodities were exempted from application of the inland waterway rules. The railroads, then, were denied the privilege of competing for the kind of business they are best equipped to provide, long distance haulage of bulky, low-value commodities. As a result freight was diverted to less efficient, higher-cost transportation, railroad capacity was underutilized, and the cost of transportation, which figures into the price of each of the thousands of items a consumer buys, was higher than it would have been otherwise.

At about the same time, 1938, Congress passed the Civil Aeronautics Act, establishing regulation of the airways similar to, but separate from, that of ground transportation by the ICC. The Civil Aeronautics Board, created by the act, was under no obligation to consider the effects of its promotion of the airlines, aided by substantial direct as well as indirect subsidies, on other forms of transportation. The act proved to be the death knell for intercity railroad passenger service.

The story isn't over yet. The railroads continue to lose ground in their struggle with competing carriers. The ICC, still viewing them as a monopoly, has permitted them to abandon service and right of way and to merge with competing lines. The railroads, however, haven't been able to retrench fast enough to avoid losses and, in some cases, bankruptcy. The collapse of the $6.8 billion Penn Central, the nation's largest railroad, marked the culmination of the process.

The ICC has permitted the railroads to do almost anything except to compete. Things had gone so far at the time of the Penn Central debacle that one prominent railroad executive was able to recognize the possibility of merit in nationalization. State ownership, he conceded, might untie the railroads' hands in their competition with other carriers. The National Railroad Passenger Service (Amtrak) stops just short of nationalization. Although the corporation is private and intended to be profit-making, eight of its fifteen directors are appointed by the President and it has access to government-guaranteed loans.

The CAB, by way of contrast, is under statutory injunction to foster competition. It also, however, doles out subsidies to unprofitable local service airlines if it considers the action in the public interest. The two functions conflict. Unless it is prepared to dip into a bottomless well of subsidies, then, it must restrict entry into the industry. In practical terms it has resolved the conflict by limiting competition between many major cities to three airlines and between many secondary cities to two. Other cities enjoying scheduled air service are served by a single line only.

In regulating transportation, whether the objective has been control of a monopoly that no longer exists or the fostering of competition in the face of restricted entry, the result has been the same: too much capacity. For the carriers this has meant a continuing profit squeeze, for passengers and shippers, rates higher than necessary.

In the regulation of energy production, a result exactly the opposite has obtained. Efforts of the Federal Power Commission to establish fair and reasonable prices for natural gas at the wellhead have led to widespread curtailment of exploration and fears that existing supplies will be inadequate to meet growing consumer demand.

In regulating radio and television, the Communications Act of 1934 said that broadcasting was not a public utility. That is, rate and other forms of competitive regulation did not apply. Neither the domination of individual stations by the networks or of programming by advertisers was foreseen when broadcasting originated. Nevertheless, the Federal Communication Commission's control over entry into the industry according to "the public interest, convenience, and necessity"—a standard first enunciated in the Act to Regulate Commerce—has produced vast riches for some, little or none for others.

If regulators suffer a common failing, it is their considerable lack of success in foretelling the future. Their performance may be no worse than that of a race track bettor, a Wall Street speculator, or the operator of a private business, but the consequences may be infinitely more serious. When an individual or business makes a mistake in forecasting, the results are predictable and prompt, a loss of wealth or earnings. When a regulator makes a mistake altering the shape or viability of an industry, the results may not become apparent for a decade.

Examples of this are endless: the FCC's judgment in the formative years of television that thirteen very-high-frequency channels would suffice; the CAB's verdict in the early 1950s that a third airline could be squeezed profitably into the New York–Miami route; the Atomic Energy Commission's opinion that nuclear fuel would quickly become competitive with coal and oil for the generation of electricity; and the Federal Power Commission's judgment that interconnection of power grids produced little risk of blackouts.

The vast and unpredictable consequences of change tend to ally the regulators with the regulated as defenders of the status quo. The chief fear of a public utility with considerable monopoly power is that it will fall victim to obsolescence, which was the reason for the American Telephone and Telegraph Company's determined effort to dominate the communications satellite program. The giant utility—one of the nation's few unquestioned national monopolies—succeeded both in getting the satellite program lodged in private hands and in barring the aerospace companies, which had contributed greatly to the early development of communications satellites, from sharing in their operation. It managed also to gain the lion's share of the ownership of the unique corporation established under congressional auspices to operate the satellite program.

AT & T was unable to prevail, however, in its view that the nation should embark quickly on a low-level satellite program. The low-level program would have utilized satellites that rotated in orbit instead of occupying a fixed spot in the sky. It would have required many more vehicles and, therefore, much greater launching expense, and much more costly ground equipment. From the viewpoint of a regulated public utility, however, the greater expense was a boon, not a deterrent, since it lessened the likelihood of diminution of the rate base, the valuation placed upon a utility's plant and equipment upon which in turn it is permitted to calculate a fair and reasonable rate of return.

AT & T's initial success in winning domination of the communications satellite program may prove a limited victory, for Comsat—the concern in which its ownership dominates—found its exclusive territory limited to overseas communications. The domestic market, the real prize, seemed likely to be shared with one or more competitors. Even more of a threat, from the utility's viewpoint, was the possibility that the number of ground stations might number in the hundreds, instead of the few proposed by AT & T, lessening the need for connecting telephone lines. There was even a remote possibility that every home might have its own satellite antenna, eliminating the need for wires entirely.

Comparable to the fight to control satellite communications is the effort of the motion picture industry and the television networks to prevent the establishment of pay TV, an effort that seems likely to be negated by the spread of community antenna television systems, or cable TV, and their widespread offering of special programs. An even more serious threat to the networks is the home video recorder. By permitting a viewer to watch one program and tape another for watching later, the recorder undermines the effort to build the big prime-time audiences upon which present-day network economics rests.

All technological change is a challenge to a monopoly utility, but the possibility of do-it-yourself operation presents a special threat. Just as the private car and truck ended the railroad monopoly, so the growing use of individual and company planes may create a danger for the airlines. (Phonevision, perhaps is an even greater threat to business air travel.) The home satellite device, the home fuel cell, and the home computer, although farther down on the horizon, engender the same kind of fears for other utilities.

The substitution of private for public services raises questions of economics and of ethics. The cost of operating a private car or plane may be greater than patronizing a railroad or airline, and the safety certainly is lower. The greater convenience of do-it-yourself, however, is usually more than enough to offset these disadvantages.

Do-it-yourself services are not equally available to all. The less affluent are the last to obtain private cars, private planes, and home communications centers. As demand shifts away from public services, should they be forced to bear the necessarily higher cost of those that remain? This is a problem that does not trouble socialist countries like the Soviet Union. Private cars are few, private planes nonexistent. If there is less freedom of consumer choice, there is greater opportunity to keep public services operating efficiently. Compare, for instance, the superior Moscow and Leningrad subways with the often broken-down and inefficient urban mass transit in the United States. On the other hand, the bias against change built into the American system of utility regulation encounters even less opposition in the socialist countries. New technologies, except those with military applications, are not swift in arriving.

The threat of technological change is not unique to regulated public utilities. All businesses face the challenge of finding new products or services to replace those outmoded. One source is research and development, another the acquisition of small and growing concerns. Utilities are as free as other companies to pursue research and development, and some—notably AT&T—have done so with eminent success. They have been far more restricted than other concerns, however, in making acquisitions involving newly emerging technologies in their own fields. Railroads, for instance, may not acquire trucking companies or airlines.

Of late there has been growing demand that regulated utilities also be prevented from acquiring, or being acquired by, concerns outside their area of regulation. Those who make this demand would bar the door, chiefly, against the removal of capital from the regulated industries. It often is argued that the conglomerates should be kept from milking the regulated industries.

One doesn't have to take the opposite position—that the regulated industries should be milked—to observe that if declining industries such as the railroads are prevented from shifting capital from losing to profitable operations, by way of upstream holding companies or other devices, one of three outcomes is certain. Either there will be more bankruptcies, like that of the Penn Central, taxpayer subsidies will be greatly increased, or the industries will be nationalized.

State ownership is no panacea. This is attested to by the fact that, after almost two centuries of public operation, the United States Post Office was the most undercapitalized and least efficient public utility in any industrialized nation. The Post Office was transferred in 1970 to the United States Postal Service, an independent agency under the Executive branch with the right to set its own budget, borrow in its own name and set rates to make itself self-supporting.

It, too, however, had been deprived of competition. As important to postal reform as giving management a free hand and the right to borrow on its own credit is the need to open the postal service to competition.

State ownership doesn't always result from the take-over of losing ventures. Sometimes it represents the exercise of government initiative where private enterprise is reluctant to venture—and that is the topic of the next chapter.

12. Government as Buyer: Defense

In its relations with business, government does not always emerge as a referee seeking to determine and enforce the rules of the competitive game or as a grantor of property rights attempting to regulate the behavior of those it has franchised. There is a large area where the government professes to desire competition but where the result is often something less. This is where the government is a buyer of new technology, where it contracts for something that does not yet exist. It is a region where, increasingly, the line between government and private decision making is blurred.

Defense is the principal area where the government is a major and sometimes the sole buyer of a company's services. The relationship extends to such closely related fields as atomic energy and space and to commercial projects tied closely to the capacity of defense industries, such as the on-again, off-again supersonic transport, or SST. To a lesser degree the role of government as contractor has grown in areas of social concern, such as health care, education, housing, and urban transit.

The common denominator in such undertakings is not merely the fact that government is the principal buyer, but that it is also the venturer, the risk taker. Historically, when the government purchased it bought a standardized product—shoes and blankets for its soldiers, typewriter ribbons and paper clips for its office workers. When it had work to do it did its own, in arsenals and in navy yards and in government bureaus.

Beginning with World War II, however, the government increasingly became a buyer, not of products—most of them did not yet exist—but of research and design capacity and the ability to convert research and design into fully developed weapons and support systems. Previously, wars had been occasioned by great buildups in armament industries, their end marked by similarly great cutbacks. Now, however, a permanent defense industry was to come into existence. The government, as entrepreneur, was to begin a restless search for ever more sophisticated weaponry.

The atom bomb, which gave birth to the new process, also made it a necessity. The United States never would have produced the bomb had President Roosevelt not agreed with Albert Einstein that it was feasible and decided to underwrite the necessary research. To get the "best brains," many of whom were reluctant to become government employees, the project was soon broadened to include participation by private concerns. After the first bomb was dropped it became apparent that never again would there be time to prepare for war. Global weapons, capable of total, instantaneous destruction, created a need for continuous preparedness. The huge lead time needed to design and manufacture more sophisticated means of destruction produced a built-in imperative to further research and development. Or so it seemed.

Interservice rivalry was also a factor. The air force, newly separated from the army, emerged from World War II with no weapons-creating capacity of its own. It was, however, the heir to a vastly overextended private aircraft industry and was also totally dedicated to research and development. The Rand Corporation, whose name is an acronym for Research and Development, was founded under air force auspices as a division of the Douglas Aircraft Corporation. It was the first of the "think tanks," private concerns that use mathematical analysis and other techniques to narrow the error range in governmental decision making.

Such activities have given rise to the charge that private concerns, some operated as profit-making enterprises and others as not-for-profit companies, have abrogated important functions of government, and have also brought criticism that government is seeking to camouflage defense employees who might otherwise appear on its own payrolls.

By way of contrast, in the defense industry the government has taken upon itself many of the managerial prerogatives of private enterprise. It decides what shall be produced, how much shall be produced, and what procedures shall be followed. It rations capital, exercises substantial influence over the selection of subcontractors, and determines pricing. Ultimately it decides the level of profits.

Seymour Melman has likened the defense establishment to a huge, multidivision corporation.* Just as General Motors has its Chevrolet, Pontiac, Oldsmobile, Buick, and Cadillac divisions competing with

* *Pentagon Capitalism, the Political Economy of War,* New York, McGraw-Hill, 1970.

each other as well as with Ford and Chrysler, so the defense establishment has its General Dynamics, Lockheed, McDonnell Douglas, North American Rockwell, Boeing, and others. The issue of ownership, he says, is irrelevant: the only question is control. And most of the decisions, without question, are made by the Pentagon.

Under this hypothesis, profits are not a reward for risk taking, which is a function assumed by government. They are the wages of performance, a useful analogy since it emphasizes the paternal relationship between the Pentagon and its supplier companies. Would a major defense contractor be permitted to succumb? In the past management changes have been engineered and shotgun weddings arranged, but there have been no bankruptcies. For a principal defense supplier to go down the drain seems as unlikely as for GM to permit one of its divisions to expire.

The analogy also suggests that the defense establishment operates under the common imperative of all big business: to perpetuate its ongoing life and to determine, as much as possible, its own future. Here, however, a major flaw in the argument intrudes. For most defense products there is only one consumer, government. This is not true of General Motors. To some degree Chevrolet must lobby at headquarters for capital, manpower, and management talent, but such things are largely determined by an independent judge of its performance, the market. If the division is successful in costing, pricing, and obtaining consumer acceptance for its product, it earns a profit. If profits are good, it gets what it needs from headquarters.

It is possible that Chevrolet may be more independent than, say, General Dynamics, for a book of rules bigger than a Sears, Roebuck catalogue governs the relations between defense "buyer" and "seller," and a companion volume instructs personnel in how to work with the rules. Murray Weidenbaum has cited some of the dos and don'ts that applied to government contractors in one recent period.* In buying rubber for aircraft tires, tubes, and recapping, a contractor had to obtain at least one-half from government stockpiles. He didn't actually have to use the stockpiled rubber in fulfilling the contract, but could keep it for commercial work. Similar although less restrictive rules applied to contractors who supplied products made of aluminum, while contractors who used jewel bearings had to obtain all their requirements from the government-owned Turtle Mountain Bearing Plant at Rolla, North Dakota. Furthermore, help-wanted advertising was permitted in black and white but not in color, and safety rules governing even floor sweepers in a contractor's plant could not be of his own devising

* *The Modern Public Sector, New Ways of Doing the Government's Business,* New York, Basic Books, Inc., 1969, p. 52.

but had to conform to those laid down by the Army Corps of Engineers in the latest edition of its safety manual.

Such matters may seem petty, bureaucratic, and annoying. They are that and much more. Government is a participant in virtually every decision that management makes. It determines what parts of a final assembly a contractor will make and what he will buy, which subcontractors he will use and how they will be paid, how much will be produced domestically and how much imported, what industrial engineering systems and planning programs the contractor will use, what minimum and average wages he will pay, and how much overtime he will authorize. In many respects the contractor's latitude is no greater and possibly less than that of the head of a government agency.

Perhaps the greatest intrusion of government in the private decision-making process occurs in two areas, the allocation of capital and the determination of allowable costs. The degree to which government permits the defense industry to substitute government capital for its own and its judgment of what costs should be permitted and what disallowed greatly influences defense industry profits.

Here some myths must be dispelled. Although some of the nation's largest corporations—General Electric, American Telephone and Telegraph, General Motors, and Ford—rank as major defense suppliers, the giants of American industry do not dominate the defense market. In one recent year, Murray Weidenbaum noted, among the top hundred defense department contractors the twenty-seven corporations with assets of $1 billion or more received only 25 percent of the dollar volume of awards. By way of contrast, the thirty companies with assets ranging from $250 million to $999 million received 58 percent of the awards, the largest share of any group. Similarly, defense orders accounted for less than 25 percent of sales for the twenty-seven corporations with assets of $1 billion or more. Among the medium-sized contractors, most were far more dependent on government orders, and, in the case of ten, government orders exceeded half the total volume of sales for each.

The rankings change from year to year as new contracts are awarded and others are phased out. Nevertheless, the same names keep appearing on the list of companies most heavily dependent on government awards. Among them are the leading aerospace concerns, Lockheed, Hughes, McDonnell Douglas, Boeing, North American Rockwell, Grumman, and Martin Marietta; electronics concerns like Collins Radio and Raytheon; and defense conglomerates like General Dynamics, LTV, and Avco.

Another commonly held notion is that the defense business is highly profitable business, and for some companies, those that supplied ammunition for the Vietnam War, for instance, it is. A study, ordered by Congress and carried out by the General Accounting Office, showed that in the years 1966–69 nine ammunition contractors averaged 10.3 percent profit on sales and 54.4 percent profit on their own invested capital supplying the Defense Department. But making ammunition involves little new technology and almost no research and development. It is a classic example of the possibility of expanding profits by grinding out more units of a standard product at a fixed price for an assured market.

For most defense contractors, however, profit margins on Defense Department contracts run well below those on their commercial business. For seventy-four large contractors, the General Accounting Office found, profits on sales to the Defense Department averaged 2.3 percent in the years 1966–69 compared with 5.3 percent for their commercial business. Profits on total invested capital averaged 6.5 percent, compared with 7.9 percent.

This raises the question of why anyone should put money into a business filling government contracts, with all the red tape, anguish and bureaucratic nonsense they involve, if he can make more money supplying commercial markets. The answer, of course, is that he would not. And, generally speaking, defense contractors do not. Their return on their own equity investment, the General Accounting Office found, averaged only slightly less on Defense Department contracts than on their commercial business in the years 1966–69, 11 percent against 12.2 percent. On work done for other defense-related agencies, the National Aeronautics and Space Administration, the Atomic Energy Commission, and the Coast Guard, the return on their own equity was considerably greater than on their commercial business, 14.2 percent against 12.2 percent.

Let's restate what the General Accounting Office found: profits on Defense Department sales are less than half those on the companies' commercial business, but the return on stockholders' investment is close to if not equal to that obtained on business done in the private market. If this seems a puzzle, the explanation is not hard to find. It lies largely in the extent to which the government supplies capital to defense producers.

This occurs in two ways. The companies' need for long-term capital, for new stock issues and trips to the bond market, is obviated by their use of government-purchased plant and equipment. For large aerospace contractors this customarily amounts to 50 percent or more of their total investment and occasionally to 100 percent. Their need for short-term or working capital is lessened by government progress payments, which do not necessarily mean what they sound like, part payments for projects under way, the usual way government pays for a new highway or a dam. Ordinarily such payments may not exceed 70 percent of total costs or 85 percent of direct labor and material costs. The government, however, also permits "unusual" progress payments, or grants against future contracts—in effect, interest-free working capital loans. It may also make available direct loans from the Treasury or loan guarantees placing the government's credit rating behind that of the contractor. On occasion the government has been known to make credit available to a contractor because of difficulties it has run into producing or marketing a commercial product.

At the same time the government employs an elaborate mechanism for negotiating contract prices and to determine allowable costs. To the extent that a private market exists, what is allowable is what an item would cost if purchased there. But, since most new technology products involve components that cannot be bought on the open market, the government, which eventually pays, has to determine what is reasonable and fair.

Profit is calculated as a cost along with capital, wages, and materials. Procurement officers figure cost components, assigning profit rates to each. The process is akin to the way a state utility commission establishes an allowable rate of return for a power company. There is a difference, however, since seldom are utilities required to make refunds to customers if their profits exceed what has been determined as allowable. On the other hand, if a defense contractor succeeds in achieving a higher profit, the contract is subject to renegotiation. What the government gives with one hand, it takes away with the other.

At last count fifteen thousand men were employed by the government writing defense contracts, another forty thousand attempting to assure compliance. Some thirty-six hundred persons were employed in the New York office of the Defense Contract Administration Services, compared with the three thousand employed by Standard Oil (New Jersey), one of the world's largest corporations, in its New York headquarters. Apart from the Parkinsonian objective of keeping such an army employed, a motive that should not be dismissed casually, why should the government go through the involved charade of supplying plant, equipment, and working capital to defense contractors on the one hand and beating down their prices and profits on the other?

It is intriguing to think that the effort is part of some long-term plan to build up the defense establishment while muting its critics. But the more likely explanation is that it just happened that way. Since every war in American history had been accompanied by notorious profiteering, after World War II Congress attempted to bring the prices and profits of munitions makers under control. At the same time, finding it difficult to attract capital to the feast-and-famine kind of business defense production had shown itself to be, it underwrote the construction and equipping of defense plants, many of which could be used for no other purpose, and it poured working capital into the industry. The military-industrial complex, hammered into the American consciousness by President Eisenhower in his farewell speech, was real enough. But, like Topsy, it just grew.

Certainly the results don't support the notion of a planned conspiracy. The General Accounting Office study showed that through the late 1960s, at least, producing for the Defense Department was a highly risky business, rewarding some contractors but punishing others. It was far more risky than making comparable items for the private market. In three of four years examined, 1966–69, a larger percentage of Defense Department than commercial sales resulted in losses for seventy-four large contractors. At the same time, however, some contractors were able to show profits on their defense work far higher than their return on commercial work. In 1969, for instance, the return on total capital investment on commercial business ranged from a 33 percent loss to a 39 percent profit, while on defense work it ranged from a 12 percent loss to a 96 percent profit. Clearly, the fact that the government was looking continuously over the shoulder of every contractor had failed to stabilize the industry's performance.

The volatility of the business is reflected in the low price/earnings multiple customarily assigned by Wall Street to defense industry stocks, and is reflected as well in the succession of companies that have found themselves at the center of the industry's recurring financial difficulties. The Lockheed rescue is only the most recent example. Congress voted loan guarantees of up to $250 million to Lockheed in July 1971 to keep the aerospace manufacturer from going bankrupt.

If Pentagon management has done little to make defense production a more stable and desirable business, it has also done little to quiet the critics. Some of the more sensational cost overruns have drawn widespread attention. A Navy order for twelve deep submersible rescue vessels, estimated to cost $36.5 million, was cut back to six after the expected cost of the project jumped to $463 million. An army order for the Gama Goat, a new 1¼-ton cargo truck capable of moving across water or being dropped from the air, jumped in cost from $69 million to $373.6 million. An air force order for 115 C-5A transports had jumped from $3.4 billion to $4.8 billion by mid-1969, and there was no assurance whatsoever how much the program eventually would cost or how many planes would be delivered.

These were hardly exceptions to the rule. The General Accounting Office, in information prepared for Senator William Proxmire's Subcommittee on Economy in Government, recorded that of thirty-seven major weapons systems under way in mid-1969, costs were running 50 percent over planning estimates and 28 percent over prices established at the time contracts were defined. Moreover, testimony disclosed that numerous cost items were omitted, making the overruns appear smaller than they actually were.

There were reasons for the overruns, of course. One was the inflation into which escalation of the war in Vietnam had plunged the nation, another was gold-plating—the desire of the military to equip its vehicles, ships, and planes with the latest and most costly gadgetry—and a third was the lack of effective cost controls. Programs had to reach the stage of notoriety before somebody was ready to blow the whistle.

More than any of these things, however, overruns resulted from the inability of planners to estimate the cost of products for which not even prototypes had yet been built. It is significant that of the thirty-seven projects under way in mid-1969, only three produced technological breakthroughs resulting in cost savings. On a number of others—the C-5A wing difficulties are a well-publicized example—design failures resulted in additional costs running into millions of dollars.

The problem is not unique to government managment. Few people in private industry have even dared to propose ways to regularize the costs of research and development, tying year-in, year-out expenses to the profits to be realized later. Moreover, private management has had its share of costly failures, notably Ford's Edsel, as we have already seen, and duPont's Corfam. But these were not design failures—the Edsel worked, and in many ways Corfam was superior to natural leather— but marketing mistakes. The Edsel was another Detroit giant introduced to a market pining for small cars, a need met by importers of foreign cars. Corfam was a high-quality, high-priced shoe material introduced to a market that was learning to wear shoes for a season and throw them away.

Robert S. McNamara, the Kennedy-Johnson Secretary of Defense, sought to hold down costs to the public and increase the research and development product by instituting fixed-price plus incentive contracts, but the chief result of this was to focus the glare of public attention on the cost overruns and to push several defense producers close to bankruptcy. His Nixon administration successor, Melvin R. Laird, retreated quickly to a fly-before-you-buy policy, promising to promote productivity by inducing manufacturers where possible to develop competitive prototypes.

Both approaches, which sought to get more for the defense dollar, were largely irrelevant to the real issue: how much and what kind of defense was needed. In a candid reflection on his years in office, Mr.

McNamara conceded: "If we were to draft every scientist and engineer in the country into weapons-development work, we could still develop only a fraction of the systems that are proposed."*

The judgment, by no means an easy one, rested on an appraisal of who potential enemies might be, their likely intent, the present balance of force, and the "enemy's" capacity for altering that balance. It also rested on how much might have to be sacrificed domestically and internationally to support it. A quick recital can only hint at some of the changes that have occurred in the postwar years in the factors affecting such a judgment: the United States' loss of its atomic monopoly, Russia's development of the sputnik, Europe's and Japan's industrial rebirth, the rise of nationalism within the Soviet bloc, China's development of an atomic bomb, the United States misadventure in Vietnam, and the growing claims in all nations on the resources devoted to war.

Perhaps the only thing that can be said with certainty about the defense establishment is that it tends to change more slowly than the premises upon which it is based. The military-industrial complex only begins to describe the vested interests that have grown up in support of the defense establishment. In addition to the Pentagon itself and the managements of defense producers, both prime contractors and subs, centers of support are lodged in the regions that have benefited most from military contracts; the congressmen elected from those regions; the army, navy, and air force alumni that have found jobs as salesmen for the defense producers; workers in defense plants and the labor unions that represent them; and the great body of highly-trained technical people who find it difficult to market their skills elsewhere.

Arthur F. Burns, who was to become chief domestic counsel to President Nixon and then chairman of the Federal Reserve Board, saw defense expenditures becoming a self-reinforcing process. In the 1967 Moskowitz Lectures at New York University, he said its momentum derived not only from the energy of military planners, contractors, scientists and engineers:

To some degree it is abetted also by the practical interests and anxieties of ordinary citizens. Any announcement that a particular defense installation will be shut down, or that a particular defense contract will be phased out, naturally causes concern among men and women who, however much they abhor war and its trappings, have become dependent for their livelihood on the activity whose continuance is threatened. With a large part of our economy devoted to defense activities, the military-industrial complex has thus acquired a constituency including factory workers, clerks, secretaries, even grocers and barbers.

* *The Essence of Security, Reflections in Office,* New York, Harper & Row, 1968, p. 91.

The other side of the defense coin is what has to be sacrificed to achieve it. Although it was only one-fifth what the nation spent for food, clothing, and other basic necessities, the 8.3 percent of the gross national product that went to war and preparation for war in 1969 was more than twice what the nation—individuals, businesses, and government—spent to replace its aging housing stock. It was a third again as much as it spent on education and manpower development, a third again as much also as it spent on health care.

It is expected that the new F-14 fighter plane, which will replace the Phantom, the workhorse of the Vietnam War, will cost $11.5 million or even more. This compares with an average cost of about $3 million for the Phantom. By way of comparison, administration of the Securities and Exchange Commission cost the nation $21 million in 1971, roughly the cost of two F-14's. Operation of the Food and Drug Administration cost $85 million, or fewer than eight fighters. The federal government's expenditures on air pollution control cost $105 million, or fewer than ten.

The contract cost for modernizing the aircraft carrier *Midway* amounted to $241.3 million, roughly equal to what the federal government spent for maternal and child health care in 1971, and compared with the $280.3 million spent on urban transportation. And the cost overrun so far on the C-5A is $1.5 billion, compared with the $100 million spent in 1971 to operate the Peace Corps, the $400 million to operate the State Department, the $1.7 billion for the Agency for International Development, and the $10 million for the United States Arms Control and Disarmament Agency.

Another way of looking at the cost of defense is in terms of the manpower, capital, and scientific talent diverted from other needs—and the results. The 6 million substandard dwellings, the 10 million people who suffered from hunger, the nation's rank as eighteenth in infant mortality is one kind of evidence. The competitive difficulties of its older industries —steel, railroads, textiles—is another. Still a third is the inflation at home and the dollar's difficulties overseas.

Clearly, arms limitation—whatever its chances for early success— held the promise of significant payoff, and hence was worth substantial investment in government time and effort. Clearly also, in contrast to what long had been confidently assumed, the nation could not have all that it wanted of both guns and butter. Therefore, in view of the standoff between the United States and the Soviet Union in terms of strategic weapons, was the new B-1 bomber necessary? Its estimated cost, $8.8 billion, was more than thirty times the amount President Nixon budgeted for the first year of federal-state revenue sharing. Were the Minuteman II and Minuteman III missile systems, each costing $4.2 billion, essential?

The cost of each was more than the entire 1971 budget for community development and housing.

It is sometimes suggested that the defense industry be nationalized. Since defense production is not private enterprise but little more than state management in disguise, it is argued, why continue the deception? Rearsenalize and end the irrational practice of rewarding shareholders for what essentially is a public business. While this proposal has a super-ficial attractiveness—if anyone should be rewarded, or penalized less, it should be the taxpayers, who put up the defense industry's capital in the first place—it leaves unanswered two more significant questions. Would more or less information become available to the public if the defense industry were nationalized? Would lobbying by the industry be easier or harder to counter?

At present the fiction of private enterprise serves a highly useful purpose. It makes defense producers subject to the same rules of dis-closure the Securities and Exchange Commission applies to other publicly held concerns. Would as much information about cost overruns, manage-ment failures, and other difficulties become available as soon if the companies were run as state enterprises? Experience with other state-owned businesses, the Atomic Energy Commission and the Post Office, suggest that it would not. Even now the General Accounting Office finds it difficult to obtain all the information it wants and needs from the Pentagon.

In much the same vein, it seems unlikely that by burying the manage-ment of the defense industry in the Pentagon bureaucracy its influence would be diminished. Freed of the "merchants of death" stigma, it would undoubtedly become less visible. Its lobbying would continue, but within the walls of government. To an even greater degree than it is today, the electorate would be excluded from the deliberations.

Does this mean that things should be permitted to continue as they have been? Murray Weidenbaum, for one, thinks they should not. The defense producers, he believes, should be encouraged to reduce their dependence on government contracts, by acquisition of consumer-ori-ented companies as well as by the admittedly difficult route of diversifica-tion. Others argue that companies with demonstrated inadequacies should be permitted to go bankrupt. This would do even more than the lure of competitive market rates of return to assure continuing efficiency. The question here is whether the government would permit the aggregation of engineering and scientific talent represented by any of the major defense producers to be dispersed. The space effort, in large measure, was an attempt to keep this from happening, the ill-fated supersonic trans-port another, the Lockheed rescue a third.

What are needed but not as quickly forthcoming are similarly imaginative and bold approaches to more urgent domestic problems. The supersonic transport, upon which close to $1 billion had been spent when work was halted, promised greater convenience for a few and intolerable noise and environmental danger for many. Total rebuilding of the Northeast Corridor rail system, utilizing monorail or air-cushion vehicles, perhaps, was no lesser technological challenge. A huge, unquestioned market stood ready to accept it if it met expectations. Whatever the cost, it would be offset significantly by savings in airport and highway construction. And yet, perhaps because the benefits of such an effort were less than national in scope, the effort was talked about but not begun.

Needs in other areas—housing, health care, and education—are even more urgent. But the possibility of applying the engineering and scientific talent lured to the defense industry from other pursuits seems slim. Moreover, the question of what should be done, say, in reforming education collides directly with the issue of control. If few persons, understandably, have any strong opinion on whether an antiballistic missile system should be built, everyone has some view on school busing.

In the face of demonstrated failings in the area of public product— high school graduates, for instance, who couldn't read—a new trend was seen to be developing. The need for literate workers has forced banks, communications companies, and others to undertake training programs that, utilizing such techniques as programmed instruction, accomplished what the public schools had been unable to do. Middle-class parents, too, in part because of racial bias but also because they recognized the relation of education level to their children's future earning power, have done much the same thing. And owners of fashionable restaurants and office and apartment buildings have hired people to sweep their streets and haul away garbage when these public services, for which they paid, were not performed. Banks and other businesses that depend on the mails have begun to haul more of it themselves.

How far such reprivatization of public services will go is an open question. While the initial result has been duplication, it seems unlikely that taxpayers will willingly continue to pay for public services they aren't receiving. At the least, the growth of private competition for services that have long been a government monopoly has established new yardsticks for measuring the quality of public services and the possibility of infusing new talent into what have often become closed and ingrown systems.

13. The Capital Markets

Ownership of business in the United States is largely private. Since individual citizens supply the funds, or capital, the American economic system is thus spoken of as capitalistic. But even in countries like the Soviet Union, where the state owns the means of production, the accumulation of productive resources, or capital, and their allocation are primary concerns.

In this sense, all modern economies are capitalistic. Only a people who live wholly in the present, making no provision whatsoever for the future, can be thought of otherwise, and such a people is hard to imagine. Even in primitive societies, seed corn is put aside for next year's crop and some cattle is held back from slaughter for breeding purposes.

The big difference between the American economic system and others centers in the way materials, equipment, manpower, and management skills are distributed. In socialist countries productive resources are doled out by agencies of the state, while in the United States capital users compete in the marketplace to obtain funds from capital suppliers.

In times past, capital users were largely of one class and capital suppliers of another. This is still true in parts of the world today, the under-developed countries particularly. In the Western world, however, more and more people wear two hats, one as a capital user, the other as a capital supplier. There are predictable times among individuals when a person is a bigger borrower than saver—the years of career building and family formation—and other times when he is a bigger investor than borrower—the years of high income and declining family obligation. At no time, however, is he likely to be a debtor entirely, for, even when he is mortgaged to the eyebrows and up to his ears in installment debt, he is likely to have some cash savings—if only to provide the down payment for his next credit purchase. He may possibly own stock or mutual fund shares, and, what is more, he is likely to have other savings he may not even be aware of—the cash value of his life insurance, for instance, or the reserves accumulated in his pension plan.

Households, the biggest group of capital suppliers in the economy, own more than 35 percent of all debt, much of which is highly liquid— currency, bank deposits, and savings in thrift institutions. Household borrowings, on the other hand, are principally fixed, long-term obligations, chiefly home mortgages. The strong creditor position of the consumer is reflected in household net worth, which includes in addition to financial assets the unrealized value of homes, automobiles, furnishings, and other durable goods.

Two other major capital users, businesses and governments, are capital suppliers as well. On balance, however, they are consistently bigger borrowers than savers. Only consumers contribute more to the investment stream, year in and year out, than they take out. Financial institutions, as might be expected from middle men, keep their borrowing and lending closely in balance.

Businesses, which save by retaining earnings, own little cash or other highly liquid assets, most of their holdings being in plant, equipment, and inventory. These are offset in part by debt—long-term bonds, mortgages, and bank loans—but to a greater extent by the equity owned by shareholders. Businesses are net debtors, nevertheless.

Governments are a special case. Federal, state, and local governments are the biggest group of debtors by far. Unlike businesses, however, they cannot raise funds by issuing shares. In addition, because they seldom save—state and local governments are often prohibited by law from doing so—they must borrow to bridge the gap between current receipts and expenditures. (When governments do save, they do so by running budget surpluses.)

In addition to individuals, businesses, and governments in the United States, foreigners are important suppliers to and users of capital market funds. On balance, they are usually net users.

To observe that capital flows from suppliers to users is to tell only part of the capital market story. Standing between savers and investors is a host of financial intermediaries, institutions that seek out sources of surplus funds on the one hand and places to invest them on the other. The list is considerable: commercial banks, savings and loan associations, mutual savings banks, credit unions, finance companies, life insurance companies, pension funds, state and local government retirement funds, security brokers, and mutual funds.

Each of these institutions has special sources of savings and special opportunities for investment. Some are determined by history or custom, some by law or regulation. Savings and loan associations and mutual savings banks, for instance, seek small individual savings, which they relend, primarily to mortgage borrowers. Credit unions and mutual funds tap the same source of funds, small individual savings, but each channels the funds into a different use—credit unions into installment loans, mutual funds into the purchase of corporate securities. Commercial banks, the primary supplier of funds to business, draw funds from both businesses and individuals. In addition, as we have noted, they are the only institutions permitted to create lendable funds based on credit advanced by the Federal Reserve System.

Economists speak of *the* interest rate, meaning the rate of return on invested capital, as if there were a single market where the demand for and supplies of savings regularly came together. Actually, of course, there is not one market but many, not one interest rate but a myriad— some advancing, some declining, and some holding steady, all at any point in time. The markets, and the instruments in them, reflect the differing needs of each group of credit suppliers and users. There is a short-term market, a long-term market, a debt market, and an equities market. Within each there are further divisions, within each division still more. The notion of a single capital market and a single interest rate is a useful concept nonetheless, because it emphasizes the links between the parts, the interdependence of each market upon every other.

What is capital? It is the present value of future consumption. The cost of capital is what it would return if put to some alternative use. Spending now, living it up, is usually more pleasurable than spending later. Thus, a dollar of spending a year from now should be worth less in terms of present spending, perhaps eighty-seven cents. If so, the cost of capital is thirteen cents, or 15 percent. (The economist uses the term "interest" to describe this cost of capital, applying it to both debt and equity. In more common usage, interest applies solely to the return on debt capital.) A dollar of spending two years hence, given the same capital cost rate, is worth seventy-six cents now, a dollar of spending three years hence is worth sixty-six cents now, and a dollar of spending twenty years hence is worth six cents now. The longer consumption is put off, then, the lower is its present value and the greater the return on capital. This helps explain why, ordinarily, short-term interest rates are lower than long-term rates.

Spending now not only is more pleasurable than spending later, it is also more certain. A loan to a friend at the office may give promise of "five for four"—five dollars of future spending for four dollars given up now—but the friend may prove to be a deadbeat, or he may quit his job and never be heard from again. Risk, then, is a further factor in determining the cost of capital.

In business one kind of risk is inherent. Frozen enchiladas may have a wide potential market, but this won't be known until considerable sums are invested to determine whether customers will buy them. Another kind of risk is political. An oil discovery in Latin America may offer exceptionally high potential for profit, but the possibility of expropriation may also be great. Capital for both kinds of risks would command high rates of return.

A special kind of risk is the risk of inflation. When prices rise, say, 6 percent a year, any lesser return on investment means that a saver is losing ground. He would be better off spending his income now. Hence, rates of return are sometimes spoken of as nominal and real. A high nominal rate of interest may simply conceal a high rate of rising prices. Subtracting the rate of inflation from nominal rates of return may show real interest rates to be quite low.

Spending now may be more pleasant and less risky than spending later, but it is also less productive. Unless some income is withheld from current consumption and added to productive resources, wealth will fail to grow. The mere fact that a nation, a business concern, or a family isn't spending all it earns may not be enough. For its wealth to grow it first must set aside some savings to cover the cost of replacing things that are wearing out. Then it must channel additional investment into new productive resources.

If an investment goes well, it may be expected to result in a stream of payments extending over a period of time. The added revenues, after expenses, a business may hope to derive from a plant expansion is one example, and the additional wages a college graduate may expect to earn over a lifetime compared with those of a high school graduate is another. Just as it is possible to obtain a present value for a single dollar spent one year or two years from now, so it is possible to determine the present value of a series of payments. For example, at a 15 percent rate of return, one dollar a year for five years would cost $3.35 now, for twenty years $6.23 now, and for fifty years $6.66 now. For only one cent more, $6.67, it would be possible to obtain a dollar a year forever.

This point is so important that it is worth hammering home. It explains how an insurance company can determine with precision the cost of an annuity. In contrast to life insurance, which affords a policyholder's survivors protection if he should die, an annuity provides the policyholder either a fixed number of payments or payments as long as he may live. In effect, the insurance company is protecting the policyholder himself (and his wife, too, possibly) against the financial consequences of living. For a somewhat greater sum it could guarantee him or his heirs a steady stream of payments forever. The fact that no insurance company does so results from the general uncertainty about the future and the fact that there is an alternative way of achieving the same result.

That way, of course, is investment in equities. When an investor purchases a mortgage, bond, or other debt security, he ordinarily buys the right to a fixed number of income payments of known dollar value. Likewise, when he buys a share of stock or other equity, he buys the right to a perpetual stream of income payments of uncertain dollar value. Insurance companies in recent years have begun to sell variable annuities, payments of uncertain dollar value guaranteed for a fixed number of years or for a lifetime. The insurance company invests what the policyholder pays for the annuity in the stock market. The policy holder could, of course, obtain a perpetual stream of payments for himself and his heirs by investing directly in the stock market or in mutual fund shares. Which course would prove to be wiser would depend upon his objectives —how much consideration was he giving his heirs?—and his investment skill, or that of his mutual fund, versus that of the insurance company.

Failure to appreciate the role of productivity in capital investment lies at the root of much misunderstanding about the appropriate uses of credit. No one knows how the first credit came to be extended, but it is known that early moral and legal codes recognized two distinct kinds of loan. The first, of food, clothing, or other necessities of life, was the next thing to charity, and interest was usually forbidden. The other, of animals or seeds, was intended to provide increase. A part of that increase, the first fruits—firstborn young or the crop first harvested—was expected as interest in return.

It is also known that throughout history credit has been a way of transferring resources from haves to have-nots. When an older generation's savings are used to provide tools or training for the young— to finance a college education, for instance—the chances of repayment are usually good. When a rich and prosperous nation lends money to an underdeveloped land to keep its people from starving, on the other hand, the transaction might better be described as a gift. There is often little hope of receiving interest, let alone repayment of the principal.

When the distinction between productive and nonproductive loans has remained clear, little onus has attached to debt. When the line has become blurred, however, abuses have occurred, debtors and creditors have leaped at each others' throats, and all lending has been condemned. By 595 B.C., for instance, half the population of ancient Greece—most of them small farmers—were in practical slavery. Solon, the lawgiver, restored freedom to the population by wiping out most existing debts and forbidding new debts in which a person pledged himself as surety for repayment and limiting those in which he pledged his land.

Solon said nothing about high interest rates.* Others less wise, con-

* The Romans did. Their Five Tables (550 B.C.) set maximum rates of interest but did not limit the right of attachment. Less than three hundred years later,

tinue to this day to try to set maximum rates of inerest above which lending is considered immoral or illegal. The difficulties should be obvious. For a nonproductive loan, any payment of interest is excessive. For example, consumer purchases of small day-to-day items on revolving credit plans at 18 percent interest or more a year often do nothing except reduce the buyer's purchasing power. On the other hand, consumer purchases of big-ticket items on the installment plan are not unproductive. The interest payments, in effect, are a charge for use of the automobile or appliance while funds are accumulated to purchase it. The same is true of mortgage interest and housing. And it should be noted that an even higher rate than 18 percent may not be excessive on a loan made to a business with exceptional earnings prospects.

Liquidity, risk, and productivity are three of the principal factors affecting the cost of capital. Marketability is another. On the basis of balance sheet considerations—their strong creditor position, the liquid nature of their assets—consumers might be expected to command the most favorable interest rates, with businesses obtaining the next most favorable rates, and governments the least favorable. Actually, of course, the situation is exactly the opposite: consumers pay the highest interest rates and governments the lowest, and marketability is the explanation.

Other things being equal, the debt of a big borrower is more marketable than that of a small borrower, which is one reason why big business pays less for credit than small business. The pieces of paper are fewer, the cost of credit investigation is less. Consumer debt comes in small, one-of-a-kind packages, and it is often hard to find a buyer wanting exactly what is offered. By way of contrast, the federal government—the biggest borrower of all—offers something for everyone. For one thing, banks and industrial corporations with temporarily idle cash may earn interest by putting their funds into Treasury bills. Although issued with maturities of three months or more, this "near-money" is so highly marketable that someone with millions of dollars to invest for only a few days can always find bills to buy. Then, savings institutions with a steady inflow of funds that won't be called upon for many years may obtain an assured rate of return by buying bonds issued with maturities as distant as forty years. There are, as well, special obligations tailored to the requirements of commercial banks. Small investors, too, who want a fixed rate of return and don't want to be troubled by market ups and downs may buy savings bonds, while the self-employed may obtain tax advantages by buying a special series of retirement bonds.

---

the descendants of all previously free Roman farmers were slaves. It was not until the dictatorship of Julius Caesar, five centuries after Solon, that the law of debt was abolished in Rome.

Much debt is not readily marketable—the mortgage, installment, and charge-account credit owed by consumers; the advances of businesses to their dealers and suppliers; and the direct loans of banks and other financial institutions, as well as their borrowings from depositors and savers—and although not all such debt continues to be held by the original lender, it tends to seek a lodging and to stay there. As a result, interest rates on less marketable debt move sluggishly. They are not unaffected, however, by what happens to marketable debt.

The credit markets might be thought of as a sea. The waters at the top represent short-term, highly marketable obligations. They move in response to the slightest shift in the wind. The waters deeper down represent longer term, less-marketable obligations. These also move in response to what happens on the surface, but not as much.

Here is a table, setting forth the demand for and supply of credit in recent years:

Supply And Demand For Credit

(Net Annual Increase in Billions of Dollars)

	1965	1966	1967	1968	1969	1970 est.
Net demands:						
Real estate mortgages	24.6	18.2	20.2	23.8	21.8	18.5
Corporate bonds	8.1	11.1	16.0	14.0	13.8	23.5
Municipal bonds	7.4	5.7	9.5	10.8	8.2	11.7
Foreign bonds	1.2	0.9	1.2	1.4	1.0	0.8
Subtotal: Long-term	41.3	35.9	46.9	50.0	44.8	54.5
U.S. government (publicly held)	−2.4	−1.9	3.4	6.1	−6.5	8.8
Federal agencies (publicly held)	2.9	4.8	3.7	5.4	8.1	8.2
Business loans (1)	16.0	8.7	4.3	14.5	19.1	4.8
Consumer & misc. loans (1)	9.2	4.6	6.4	11.5	8.4	2.5
Open market paper	0.7	4.4	3.9	4.1	12.1	2.0
Total demands	67.7	57.5	68.6	91.6	86.0	80.8
Net sources of funds:						
Nonbank institutions	26.3	21.2	25.2	27.9	24.0	29.0
Commercial banks	27.9	17.2	36.6	38.9	16.0	25.0
Finance companies	5.0	2.3	0.6	5.3	7.7	2.5
Business corporations	−0.7	1.4	−2.5	5.7	6.6	−1.5
State and local operating funds	1.9	2.3	0.3	0.1	4.7	0.0
Foreigners	0.0	−1.5	2.0	0.5	0.9	7.0
Subtotal	60.4	42.9	61.6	78.4	59.9	62.0
Residual: Individuals & misc.	7.3	14.6	7.0	13.2	26.1	18.8
Total Sources	67.7	57.5	68.6	91.6	86.0	80.8

(1) By banks and finance companies. Excludes real estate loans.

The table, produced by the investment banking firm of Salomon Brothers, is based on data reported by the Federal Reserve Board. The fact that supply and demand balance shouldn't surprise anyone, because, like other balance sheets, this one is designed to balance.

The most evident observation here is the rather large year-to-year shifts in the overall demand for and supply of credit. In recent years there was a sharp rise following the military buildup in Vietnam in 1965, a slackening during the credit crunch of 1966 and the minirecession that followed, an explosive increase during the inflationary expansion of 1967 and 1968, a moderate decline during the 1969 tight money period and the recession that followed, and renewed growth since.

As interesting as the shifts in the overall flow of funds is the often greater variation between long-term, or investment demand and other demand, mostly short-term. The big 1967–68 bulge in overall demand was satisfied largely through bank-financed borrowing underwritten by the Federal Reserve. Despite the fact that the central banking system slammed on the brakes at the beginning of 1969, it was not until a year later that the flow of short-term funds showed any decline.

The table also shows graphically the failure of interest rate ceilings to limit business borrowings during the same period. When, in 1969, interest rates in the open market soared above the maximum interest rates established under the Federal Reserve Board's Regulation Q, business borrowers deserted the banks for the commercial paper market. If the interest rate ceilings hadn't existed, businesses would have placed their temporarily idle cash into commercial bank time deposits, among other money market instruments. Instead they were forced to lend directly to other businesses in temporary need of funds by way of the commercial paper market. Only after the Penn Central Railroad reneged on some of its commercial paper obligations in June 1970 did the flow reverse. The effect then, however, was that marginal borrowers were entirely denied credit.

The table shows still another result of the 1967–68 inflationary expansion and the efforts to bring it under control, the role of foreigners in meeting domestic credit needs. When, in 1969, the banks found themselves cut off from Federal Reserve credit by the tight money policy and from the market for time deposits by Regulation Q, they turned en masse to the Eurodollar market, bidding up the interest cost of these dollar deposits at their own branches abroad and at other foreign banks, buying money abroad to lend to money-shy companies at home. The big jump in 1970 in funds supplied by foreigners reflects what happened.

Perhaps the most dramatic fluctuation, however, shows up in the item "individuals and miscellaneous." Like similar items in other systems of accounts—statistical discrepancy in the national income accounts, errors and omissions in the balance of payments—this is a balancing item. It means that if the number keepers can't find anyone else to charge an increase or decrease to, they charge it to individuals and miscellaneous. The figures must therefore be regarded with a proper amount of suspicion. Nevertheless, the entry of individuals directly into the market in years of credit restraint, 1966 and 1969, contrasts sharply with their withdrawal in subsequent years. The entry coincides with a big drop-off in the tight money years of new money received by savings institutions and a renewed inflow afterward.

What this reflects is the process of disintermediation. To protect borrowers, mortgage borrowers chiefly, well-meaning governments have imposed maximum interest rates that savings institutions may charge for loans. At the same time, ostensibly to guard the institutions from cutthroat competition, the governments have limited the rates institutions may pay savers.

Life insurance companies face a different kind of problem. Under insurance policies, many of which were written years ago, they are obliged to lend back to policyholders the cash value of their policies at fixed interest rates, now often below the market.

In both cases the rise of open-market rates of interest in 1969 to levels higher even than those experienced during the War of 1812 produced a huge outflow of funds from the savings institutions and insurance companies. In late 1969 high-grade utility bonds were yielding nearly 3 percent more than the average fixed interest rate on savings.

In considering the big changes in the way the credit pie is sliced, it should be evident that in times of sharply rising demands for funds the consumer (housing loans, consumer loans) and state and local governments (municipal bonds) find their sources of funds sharply restricted, while business (corporate bonds, business loans, open-market paper) and the federal government (U.S. government and federal agency borrowings) enjoy greatly increased supplies of funds.

The huge clout of business in the capital markets derives from the productive nature of its investment. So long as opportunities for profit persist, business should be able to look forward to a stream of earnings much more certain than the higher wages anticipated by individuals or the higher taxes anticipated by governments. In addition, governments are often hampered in bidding for funds by interest ceilings. For years a 4.25 percent limit on the maximum interest it might pay on long-term borrowings, now removed, effectively limited the federal government to issues of seven years' maturity or less. In March 1971, Congress lifted the 4.25 percent ceiling to permit the Treasury to borrow up to $10 billion without regard to rate. Similarly, ceilings on state and local government borrowings in times of high and rising interest rates may keep

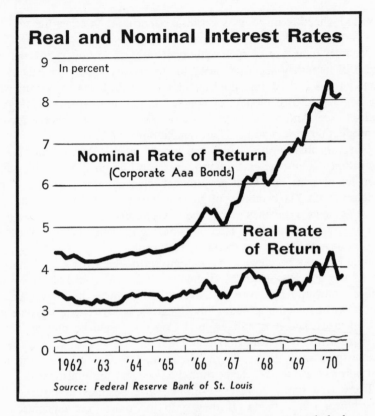

Real and Nominal Interest Rates

In percent

Nominal Rate of Return
(Corporate Aaa Bonds)

Real Rate of Return

1962 '63 '64 '65 '66 '67 '68 '69 '70

Source: Federal Reserve Bank of St. Louis

Economists often view interest rates as a return on capital plus the expected cost of inflation. In recent years, the real rate of return held fairly steady while fears of rising prices caused nominal rates to soar.

some political subdivisions out of the market entirely. If it were not for a special circumstance, business might be able to outbid all other contenders for funds, even the federal government.

The federal government, however, is a special case. It enjoys a singular advantage over all other borrowers in that it is not obligated to compete with other capital users for a limited supply of savings. If it balks at paying too high a price for credit or if its offerings run into rough going, the Federal Reserve can come to its aid by providing additional reserves to its member banks, enabling them to absorb what is offered. Indeed, the central banking system recognizes a duty to keep the market for government securities steady in advance of and during a Treasury financing. When a big budget deficit keeps the investment calendar crowded with frequent Treasury offerings, the Federal Reserve, even if it were inclined to do so, may get little opportunity to offset the additions it is forced to make to member bank reserves.

Member bank use of such additional reserves to underwrite the purchase of Treasury securities adds to the money supply in exactly the same way as if they were used in the creation of loans to consumers or businessmen. More money, of course, means more demand for goods and services. And when the rise in money demand outstrips the increase in production, prices go up. Hence, inflation.

Government securities enjoy the lowest interest cost of any taxable obligations. (Only tax exemption keeps rates on municipals—the generic term for all state and local government issues—lower.) This is in part because of the marketability of governments noted earlier, and also because of the government's taxing and money-creating powers. There never can be any question of the Treasury's paying its debts. If the government doesn't have the money, it can manufacture it.

Inflation may be viewed as an extension of the federal government's taxing powers. Rising prices channel income and resources from consumers and businessmen to the government in much the same way as if a new tax had been imposed. Only Congress, however, can legislate new federal taxes, and it is unlikely that Congress could be prevailed upon to enact a tax as grossly unfair as inflation, a levy that favors the big businessman over the small, the young and productive over the aged and infirm, the rich and clever over the poor and unsophisticated.

There is a limit, however, even to what business and the federal government can demand. If they grab too much, the machine slows down. If consumers are forced to divert an increasing portion of their incomes into savings—either because business and government is taking more or because consumers expect that they will—the amount remaining to buy the things business makes will be reduced. This in turn will mean a reduction in business earnings and a reduction in the wages it can pay. It also means a cut in the taxes government can expect.

The capital markets are resilient—they can accommodate massive shifts in the supply of and demand for funds—but their capacity is not unlimited.

14. Bonds

A bond is a bond is a bond. Like roses, however, bonds come in many varieties. A bond, per se, is a debt obligation backed usually by a specific property—a mortgage on a railroad or an industrial plant, for example. A bond backed by the general earning power of a corporation is called a "debenture." Sometimes, calling a debt obligation a bond means merely that it is issued with a distant maturity. Shorter issues may be called notes and certificates. However, railroad equipment obligations, which are backed by specific collateral—locomotives, freight cars, and other rolling stock—and usually run to maturity in about fifteen years, are called certificates, nonetheless.

Bonds may have coupons attached. These are clipped semiannually or at other payment dates and presented in exchange for interest. Alternatively, bonds may be registered, in which case the issuer keeps a record of who owns the bonds and makes interest payments by check.

Bonds usually come in $1,000 denominations, although, increasingly, $5,000 denominations are taking over. Bond prices, however, continue to be quoted in points and eighths of a point, each point worth $10.00 A quotation of 97⅝ means that a $1,000 bond is priced at $976.25.

Bonds may have a single fixed maturity date or may be issued serially, a different series maturing each year. They may be subject to call by the issuer prior to maturity, or to a sinking fund designed to retire the issue progressively.

Some bonds are hybrids, part bond and part stock. Income bonds, for instance, guarantee the payment of interest, but only if earned. They are closely akin, then, to preferred stock, which trades like—and sometimes is viewed as—bonds without a maturity date. For many years the British government has had such obligations—called "consols," for

147

"consolidated issues"—outstanding. But perhaps the best-known hybrids are convertibles, bonds convertible into common stock, which comprise an important part of the relatively small volume of bonds still traded on stock exchanges.

How important are bonds? In the quarter century since World War II, the nation's gross national product grew from $200 billion to almost $1 trillion. Huge sums were borrowed to underwrite that growth, more than $300 billion by the federal government, $165 billion by state and local governments, $215 billion by industry. Also, all the new money required by the Treasury, federal agencies, and state and local governments and well over half that needed by business corporations—two-thirds of all investment funds—moves through the market for fixed income securities.

Important as it is, however, the volume of new debt obligations sold pales in comparison with the secondary, or resale, market. In 1970 the Treasury sold $14.8 billion of securities and federal agencies $16.2 billion. By way of contrast, trading volume of federal government and agency securities came to $743 billion. In the same year $17.7 billion of new state and local government issues and $30.3 billion of new corporate issues were sold to the public. Trading volume came to many times that amount.

Marketable debt reaches the public in two ways, directly from the issuer or through investment bankers. All federal government debt is sold directly by the Treasury, while most state and local government and corporate debt is marketed by investment bankers.

The Treasury sells three-month, six-month, and other series of bills at regular intervals through tender offers, or auctions. It sells longer-term issues by subscription. Bills are discount obligations—that is, they are sold at a price lower than their value at maturity, the appreciation reflecting the return on the investment. For example, a $10,000 three-month Treasury bill might be auctioned for $9,817.10. The $182.90 increase in value when the bill is presented for redemption three months later would represent an annual yield, or rate of return, of 7.4 percent.

Almost $2 billion of Treasury bills are auctioned every week, and more at other times. Most is outstanding Treasury debt, rolled over as it matures. Some may be new Treasury borrowing. Small buyers—country banks and others wanting no more than $200,000—may enter noncompetitive bids, which means that they will pay the average price at the tender. Others—government securities dealers, large banks, and the biggest international corporations—will attempt to obtain the lowest possible price (highest rate of return) by entering competitive bids.

To determine the results, the Treasury subtracts the sum of the noncompetitive bids from the total amount of bills it is offering. Then it

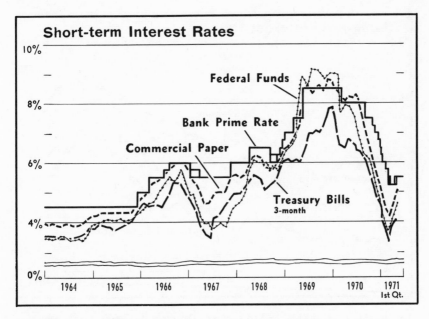

Short-term Interest Rates

Federal Funds

Bank Prime Rate

Commercial Paper

Treasury Bills
3-month

10%

8%

6%

4%

0%

1964 1965 1966 1967 1968 1969 1970 1971
1st Qt.

Short-term interest rates are more volatile than long-term ones, because the Federal Reserve operates chiefly in the Treasury bill market.

awards what is left to the competitive bidders beginning at the highest price. If more than is needed is bid for at the low, or cutoff, price—the usual occurrence—a percentage of what is bid for is accepted.

Tenders are accepted at any of the twelve Federal Reserve Banks or their branches, but most of the activity occurs in New York. Long before the 1:30 P.M. Monday deadline, dealers, banks, and other prospective bidders have been on the telephone, talking to their customers and to each other, attempting to get a feel of the market. In the final half hour this activity reaches fever pitch, most bidders delaying until the final possible moment. A traffic jam or a stalled elevator can mean disaster, so special precautions are taken to assure that the tender will be presented at the Federal Reserve Bank window before the deadline.

Bidders don't enter single, all-or-nothing tenders. They space several bids over a range of prices to make sure they will not be left out even if they miss the low. When the market is steady the range will be narrow, but when it is unpredictable the bids are likely to "tail out" over a wide range of prices.

In offering bills the Treasury permits demand to determine the price it will receive, and thus the rate of interest it will pay. There is never any question of the debt being sold. In offering notes and bonds, longer term debt, it fixes an interest rate and puts a price on the obligations

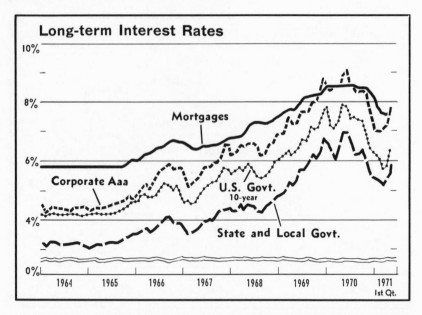

Long-term Interest Rates

Over the long run, yields tend to move in the same direction. For a period of weeks or months, however, one sector may show consistently greater strength than another, causing spreads between them to be altered.

beforehand. Then it invites subscriptions. If it has guessed right, the issue will be neither undersold nor oversubscribed. The Treasury will have marketed its debt at the lowest possible cost.

The Treasury frequently sells notes and bonds through "rights" offerings—that is, by permitting a maturing issue to be exchanged for one or more new ones. The maturing notes and bonds are spoken of as rights because they give a holder the right to make the exchange. If the Treasury has priced the new issue attractively, the rights will go up in price, and only a small percentage of the maturing issue will be redeemed for cash. In other words, the rate of attrition, as it is called, will be low.

While the Treasury does its own pricing and selling, most other debt sellers use investment bankers. These three hundred or so specialized and well-capitalized firms help would-be borrowers decide both on the kinds of obligations and terms likely to win market acceptance and on the proper timing of an offering. They employ salesmen who, well acquainted with this unusual merchandise, talk regularly with likely customers and who, for a fee, will assure a borrower of a guaranteed price for his obligations, lifting from the issuer the fear of a price drop or other market malfunction. This insurance function is spoken of as "underwriting."

Not all debt other than that of the Treasury reaches the market through investment bankers. The growth of large institutional investors capable of absorbing all or a large part of an issue has spurred the direct placement of corporate securities in recent years. Such private placements avoid the necessity for registering the issue with the Securities and Exchange Commission, permit funds to be raised more quickly than through a public offering, and allow financing arrangements more complex than those readily understood by the public.

Of corporate securities sold through public offerings, more than two-thirds are awarded to an investment banking house after negotiation with the issuer. The remainder are awarded through competitive bidding. Virtually all industrial and financial issues are negotiated, while most utility and railroad issues, because of regulatory requirements, are competitive. In the market for state and local government issues, because of the complexity of their design and distribution, perhaps one-third of revenue bonds are negotiated. A much larger volume of general obligation state and local bonds are competitive.

Whether an issue is negotiated or awarded competitively, it is almost certain to be marketed by not one but a syndicate of investment bankers. This permits individual firms to spread their risks over many under-writings, and, in addition, makes the combined sales forces available for the distribution. Long-standing relationships tend to determine the award of the offering and the makeup of the syndicate. A major borrower will turn regularly to the same firm for advice in fashioning new issues and for leadership in organizing a syndicate, and the firm in turn will call upon other firms that have worked well together in the past.

Prestige and power in the closely knit investment banking community are reflected in the organization of a syndicate, as shown in the tombstone advertisements announcing all major offerings. Under the name of the issuer and the amount and terms of the offering, there is a long list of investment banking firms, sometimes more than a hundred, arranged in descending levels, or tiers. The firm at the top is the syndicate manager, the firm that brought the group together. For doing this and for keeping the syndicate books, the manager obtains a special fee. Participants at each level share equally in the offering, the biggest at the top, the smallest at the bottom.

Syndicate members are rewarded for their efforts by being able to buy the issue at one price and reoffer it to the public at a higher one. The difference between the two prices is known as the "underwriting spread" and ranges from less than 1 percent of the proceeds on the offerings of large issuers with excellent credit standing to as much as 10 percent on the nonrated debt of small issuers. In a negotiated offering the syndicate manager and several of the major participants study the capital markets carefully in advance of the selling date to determine the offering price. The day before the registration statement becomes effective, the manager brings the members of the syndicate together. After consulting with them, he negotiates the final terms of the transaction with the issuer. In addition to the public offering price, the price to the issuer, and the underwriting spread, such things as redemption and conversion prices may also be fixed.

Much the same thing goes on in advance of a competitive offering, but instead of a single syndicate there may be as many as six or seven bidding groups, who work together carefully and in great secrecy before turning in their sealed bids. When the bids are opened, the issue is sold to the syndicate with the highest bid and, therefore, the lowest interest cost to the issuer.

If an offering goes well, the securities are sold quickly, their price rises to a small premium, and the underwriting account is quickly terminated. If an offering moves slowly, price concessions may be made or the syndicate may be broken, permitting members to sell their remaining inventory at whatever price they can get.

Not all issues marketed by investment bankers are underwritten. A large number of issues—although a small percentage of total volume—are sold on a "best efforts" basis. The investment banker helps the issuer design, price, and time the offering and to organize a selling group, but no one agrees to purchase any fixed amount of the offering. Instead, the investment banker is paid a fee and members of the selling group are compensated with commissions.

Most bonds are traded in the over-the-counter market. This is not one market, but a network of interlocking markets grouped broadly by issuers, the federal government, state and local governments, and corporations. Bond dealers may operate in all three markets or they may specialize in one. They may limit themselves to money market instruments and shorter maturity bonds or they may operate primarily in longer maturities.

In trading bonds, perhaps the first thing to know is that the rate of interest goes up when the price goes down and the rate of interest goes down when the price goes up. Much more needs to be known, however, before a judgment can be made as to whether a particular issue should be bought or sold. The yield to maturity, or rate of return over the remaining life of the investment, must be determined and compared with those of similar quality obligations. Finally, a decision has to be reached as to whether bond prices as a whole are likely to rise or fall.

In calculating the yield to maturity, the interest payments still due are combined with the discount or premium indicated in the price quotation and prorated over the remaining life of the investment. As an example, consider a bond with a fixed 5 percent interest rate maturing in ten years and selling at 90 ($900 a bond). The bondholder will receive $50 a year in interest and, in addition, $100 in price appreciation when the bond matures. Prorating the $600 total over the ten years produces a yield to maturity of 6.4 percent. The mathematics involves compound interest and is not simple, but since it has all been done beforehand and published in yield tables, determining yields is not difficult.

Comparing issues with others of like quality is not hard either. Independent statistical organizations, like Moody's and Standard and Poor's, attempt to assess the risks involved in a bond investment. They examine an issuer's earning power, resources, and capital structure and review the protection for investors assured in the indenture, or legal agreement between the issuer and the bondholders. Then they assign the issue a rating, ranging from triple-A down to C.

When the yield to maturity and rating of a bond is known, the issue can be plotted on a yield curve chart, a chart in which yields of comparable issues are plotted against time to maturity and on which a curve is drawn through the area of greatest concentration. While the study of yield curves is an art in itself, suffice it to say that an issue far above the curve—with a yield greatly in excess of comparable issues—is a possible candidate for a rise in price while an issue far below the curve—with a yield far below that of comparable issues—is a possible candidate for a drop in price.

Over the long run, yields tend to move in parallel in all sectors of the bond market. On any specific day, however, governments may be up in price, municipals may be down, and corporates may not move at all. Over a period of weeks or months, moreover, one sector may show consistently greater strength than another, causing the spreads between their yields to be altered appreciably.

The reason for this is the unique demand-supply relationship in each sector. Municipals, for instance, are the only securities to enjoy exemption from federal taxation. (At one time, certain Treasury obligations were tax exempt, but no new tax-exempt governments have been issued since 1941.) This makes municipals attractive to people in high income-tax brackets. An individual in the 30 percent bracket, for instance, would have to obtain better than 7 percent on an alternative investment to equal the return on a 5 percent tax-exempt, and an individual in the 65 percent bracket would have to obtain more than 14 percent. Tax exemption also makes municipals attractive to commercial banks. There are other factors—the availability of short maturities, the fact that

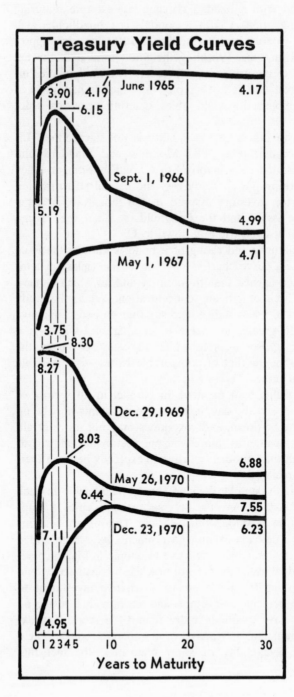

Treasury Yield Curves

3.90 4.19 June 1965 4.17

6.15

Sept. 1, 1966

5.19 4.99

May 1, 1967 4.71

3.75 8.30

8.27

Dec. 29,1969

8.03 6.88

May 26,1970

6.44 7.55

7.11 Dec. 23,1970 6.23

4.95

0 1 2 3 4 5 10 20 30
Years to Maturity

In periods of easy
money, such as June
1965, May 1967, and
December 1970, yields
advance progressively
from the shorter
maturity obligations to
the long. In tight money
periods, September
1966, December 1969,
and May 1970, shorter
maturities command
higher returns than
longer maturities.

banks often underwrite municipals,* and their commitment to the welfare of their communities because of civic sentiment and customer pressures—but tax exemption is important.

Wealthy individuals tend to buy municipals when they become disenchanted with the stock market and to sell them when they become more bullish. Banks tend to buy municipals when money is easy and to limit their purchases and sell when money grows tight. Thus there is a frequent shifting of municipals from wealthy individuals to banks and back again. What is more, because of the lack of interest on the part of life insurance companies, pension funds, and savings institutions—which pay low taxes anyway—there is great difficulty selling municipals with longer maturities.

The institutional investors, on the other hand, are the mainstay of the corporate market. The same forces that may divert funds from the mortgage market—a rise in interest rates that triggers an increase in savings withdrawals and life insurance policy loans, for instance—will be likely to affect the corporate market as well.

Not long ago a major question troubling the capital markets was, will bonds go out of style? Bond buyers had found the value of their holdings eroded by a long-term decline in prices that reached back to the end of World War II. In the five years ending in 1970 the decline had become a rout.

Savings institutions, life insurance companies, and pension funds, the traditional buyers of debt obligations, sought and obtained the right to increase their purchases of equities. Corporations, lured by the favorable tax treatment accorded interest payments on debt, continued to favor debt over equity as a way of raising new money. But they were forced to offer more bonds convertible into shares and more debt with equity kickers, such as leasing arrangements.

By 1970 interest rates had soared well above their post-World War I highs, above their Civil War highs, and finally above the highs established in the War of 1812, the highest interest rates in the history of the American republic. This brought a renewed interest in debt obligations, particularly on the part of individuals.

Much of the interest, however, remained centered in second-class credits, some of which promised astronomical yields. Then the bubble burst. The Penn Central Railroad debacle caused lenders to look to things other than the promise of high return. What was the capacity of

* Banks are important competitors of investment bankers in underwriting general obligation municipals, those backed by the general taxing power of a state or local government. Member banks of the Federal Reserve System are forbidden to underwrite revenue issues, those backed by turnpike tolls, water or utility revenues, or other specific fees or taxes.

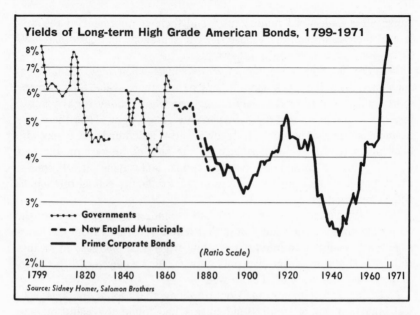

Yields of Long-term High Grade American Bonds, 1799-1971

•••• Governments
--- New England Municipals
——— Prime Corporate Bonds
(Ratio Scale)

Source: Sidney Homer, Salomon Brothers

The historic downtrend of high-grade bond rates in the United States came to an end with World War II and the enactment of the Employment Act of 1946.

a borrower to service its debt? How able was the institutional system, the commercial paper market in particular, to weather prolonged strain? Prompt action by the Federal Reserve kept the liquidity crisis from snowballing, but could the central banking system do the whole job another time? Could a borrower's name be depended upon as the sole measure of its credit standing? Lenders who hadn't made more than a routine credit check in years suddenly found themselves studying income statements, balance sheets, and cash flow reports.

And what of the future? It seemed quite obvious that debt had been saved from extinction. But would its respite be permanent? Much would depend on the ability of governments to halt inflation. On the side of optimism, the withdrawal of American troops from Southeast Asia gave promise of containing defense expenditures, and further cooling of the cold war was seen as a further help. On the side of pessimism, the will to halt inflation—in foreign countries as well as the United States— seemed small against the tendency of political leaders, faced with mounting social demands, to promise everything.

The implications of such a policy—or absence of one—seemed apparent: (1) greater erosion of state and local borrowing power and increased dependency on the federal government; (2) the establishment of direct rationing of capital to such public projects as housing, pollution control, and health services; (3) greater reliance of businesses on equity financing; and (4) social disappointment, as people of every class and status discovered they were being shortchanged.

More than the capital markets would suffer, it seemed certain, unless inflation was contained.

15. The Equity Markets

The stock market is a giant future-earnings rating machine. Imagine a university where a board sits in continuous session from 10:00 to 3:30 each day, offering continuous judgment on the prospects of almost 6,000 graduates, old-timers long out of school and newcomers only recently awarded their diplomas. At stake is the graduates' access to a pool of prize money, funds that offer the opportunity for success but in no way guarantee it. At stake also is current wealth, power, and prestige.

This, by analogy, is what happens every day in the stock market. The 6,000 graduates are those concerns whose shares are regularly traded—sixteen hundred listed on the New York Stock Exchange, thirteen hundred listed on the American Stock Exchange, and 2,800 not listed but most actively traded in the over-the-counter market. The judgment body is made up of the buyers of shares in these companies, who in effect are saying they expect profits to rise; the sellers, who are saying they expect profits to fall; and the holders, too, for they are expressing a third judgment, that of satisfaction with the profit outlook.

Often, people buy or sell shares for reasons that seem to have little to do with how a company will fare in the future. A man may need funds to send his son to college, or he may realize a sum from an inheritance. Even then, however, what he does implies some judgment. When, for instance, he sells his shares instead of cashing in savings bonds or borrowing money, he reveals his lack of hope for any substantial rise in future earnings, and when he buys the shares of one company instead of some other, he gives it a secret vote of confidence.

Continuing the analogy, the prize money is the companies' access to new capital, the funds they will need to undertake research and development, market new products, expand their plant and equipment, and attract superior management. How a concern's shares are regarded by share buyers and sellers has an important bearing on the price it must pay for and the availability of bank loans, as well as on what it can expect to obtain by marketing bonds or selling new shares.

Finally, the wealth of a company's shareowners is determined—at least insofar as their holdings in the company are concerned—by the price judgment of the marketplace. And this will affect the prestige and power they may attempt to enjoy. The judgment of share buyers and sellers may be in error, sometimes grievously so, either as to the prospects of particular companies or to the economy in general, but it is subject to constant amendment—and the surest thing that can be said about the stock market is that stocks that go up too fast today are certain to come down tomorrow. The corollary is, happiness is owning a stock whose performance turns out to be greater than the market had expected. Finding such opportunities is the eternal quest of all investors.

The actual performance of companies confirms or denies the earlier judgments of share buyers and sellers. Investing in stocks, then, involves speculation, the assumption of risk. This is not the same thing as gambling. The laws of chance determine that a gambler will do no better than break even, and after the house or the track takes its cut, he may do considerably worse. A stock market speculator, on the other hand, can expect to do considerably better than break even. His results will be affected by the stocks he selects, when he buys and sells, by tax considerations, and by other factors. On average, however, he should show a return on capital roughly in line with his selections' profit performance.

Likening the stock market to a university prize committee is not as tenuous an analogy as it might seem. Some universities, Yale, for instance, are considering the well-founded idea of tying their own wealth to the earning power of their graduates. They would lend endowment funds to promising students, expecting to be repaid not in fixed dollars but in a share of the graduates' lifetime earnings, reasoning that if a college education increases the earnings of its graduates, the university should not be restricted in its ability to serve future generations of students by the present generation's limited ability to pay or past generations' sometimes grudging charity.

It would be only a step beyond the creation of such claims on future earning power—brainpower shares, they perhaps will be dubbed—to the institution of a market for trading them. Indeed, Wall Street may have anticipated such a development. Increasingly mindful of the value of brain capital, investment bankers have reached into university faculties and graduate schools to obtain talent with marketable ideas as the nuclei of new enterprises to be brought to the market through public offering of shares.

Ownership of shares, particularly of concerns listed on major exchanges or enjoying active over-the-counter market trading, has the advantage of ready markets, easy transferability, and low unit prices. But shares of stock are not the only form of equity investment. The ownership value of a home—what the house will bring on the market less what is still owed the mortgage holder—is another. So is the paid-for value of an automobile, boat, or home furnishings. Some equities benefit chiefly from their scarcity value. Land in general but beach-front property in particular, art, antiques, stamps, coins, and rare wines are examples. This makes them desirable as hedges against inflation.

For most of the postwar era the value of shareownership, like that of the other equities just mentioned, has also represented a hedge against inflation. In part this has reflected the profitability of American business, in part a scarcity of shares relative to other kinds of securities. Whether shareownership will continue to fulfill this role in the way it has for the last several decades is a matter of growing debate.

It might be useful here to dwell for a moment on the nature of wealth. How wealthy is anyone? Ask a man of some means and he almost certainly would be unable to say. Given a moment or two with the stock pages, or on the telephone with his broker, he might produce a figure. But unless a house next door to his own and exactly like his was sold within the last month or two, he would have to say that his estimate of the value of his home was only a rough guess And he would have to add that he had little idea of what he might be earning a year from now, let alone five years or ten years from now, so that any attempt to assign a present value to his future earnings would be an exercise in the ridiculous.

The point is that a man is as wealthy as the market says he is. If the value of the things he owns—stocks, a home, marketable skills—goes up, selling them permits him to convert them into a greater volume of current consumption. If their value goes down, selling them forces him to give up some volume of current consumption. Even if he keeps every cent he owns in cash, only money value of his wealth will stay the same. Rising prices will chip away steadily at the volume of current consumption into which his wealth could be converted.

If the wealth of a nation can be thought of as the sum of the wealth of its citizens, this, too, would be rising and falling, depending on the market's valuation of its many components. How is this possible? How did the loss of $300 billion in New York Stock Exchange paper values in the 1969–70 market decline, for instance, affect the worth of the nation's resources? Weren't its plant, equipment, men, and management just as productive afterward as they were before the market drop?

The answer lies largely in the stream of earnings resources will generate. If earnings fail to drop off as a decline in market values indicates, a market break will be short lived and people will be able to fulfill their plans. They may convert some of their wealth to new homes, perhaps, to new cars, or to Caribbean vacations. If earnings do fall off, people will be well advised to tighten their belts and trim their expectations.

A share of stock represents a specific kind of wealth, part ownership in a corporation. Someone who buys twenty-five shares of a chemical company with 5 million shares outstanding, for instance, obtains a proportionate fractional interest in everything the company owns—its plants, its laboratories, its materials, its inventories, its trademarks, its patents, its sales organization, and its management. He obtains a like share in what the company earns. A single stock certificate may represent any number of shares, from one to many thousands, registered in the name of the owner typed on its face. When shares are sold the owner endorses the certificate on its back and gives it to his broker. The broker gives it to a transfer agent, who records the number of shares and the new owners, cancels the old certificate, and issues a new one. (Shares are sometimes kept in the name of a shareholder's broker. This is known as a "street name" registration.)

Common stock has the last claim on a company's earnings. This increases the risk, but it also increases the possibility of reward. Everything left after other, mostly fixed, claims are satisfied goes to the holders of common stock. Holders of bonds, for instance, are entitled to regular payments of fixed amounts of interest. The dividends paid to common stockholders, on the other hand, vary according to the level of profits, the capital needs of the company, and other considerations.

Owners of common stock enjoy the right to vote for the directors of the corporation, and for major changes in the nature of the concern, such as merger or dissolution, casting one vote for each share they hold. When the corporation offers additional shares or bonds by way of privileged subscription, if preemptive rights exist they enjoy the right to subscribe, receiving one right for each share they own. Alternatively, they may sell or give away subscription rights.

Each right offers a shareholder the privilege of subscribing for new shares at a fixed price and at a fixed rate of exchange—say, one new share at twenty-five dollars, a figure well below the market level, for each five shares held. A right expires in a fairly short period of time. A warrant is much the same thing, but it is good for years, sometimes forever.

A holder of common stock enjoys the right to dividends when de-

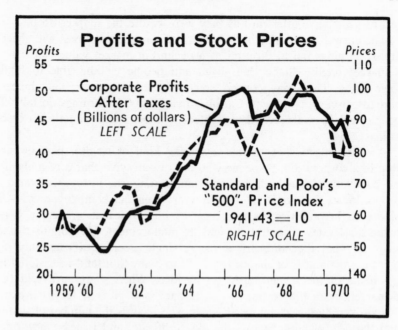

Profits and Stock Prices

Profits   *Prices*

Corporate Profits After Taxes (Billions of dollars) *LEFT SCALE*

Standard and Poor's "500"- Price Index 1941-43 = 10 *RIGHT SCALE*

1959 '60   '62   '64   '66   '68   1970

Stock price movements tend to anticipate trends of corporate earnings. The stock market is highly regarded as a leading economic indicator.

clared by the directors. Sometimes he receives additional shares by way of a stock dividend or stock split, neither of which adds to his share in the company's assets and earnings. The holder of one hundred shares in a company with 1 million shares outstanding, for example, ends up with two hundred shares after a two-for-one split. But the outstanding stock increases to 2 million shares, so his percentage of ownership remains the same. By issuing more pieces of paper, management usually hopes to increase the number of shareholders by lowering the price per share. Occasionally, a company may sweeten a stock split by increasing the dividend.

A stock's dividend for the previous year divided by its current price is known as the "current yield." A fifty-dollar stock with a dividend of $2,000, for instance, yields 4 percent. Its price divided by its earnings per share is described as its "price/earnings multiple," perhaps more often as its "price/earnings ratio." A fifty-dollar stock with share earnings of $2.50 has a p/e multiple of 20. Earnings per share divided by the price is called the "earnings yield."

Because the stock market is a market of expectations, information is vital to its functioning. This includes information from the world outside that may affect the price of shares, and the return flow of information from the market to the world outside. These are some of the external things the market wants to know: news about company sales, earnings, dividends and other evidences of past performance; news of promising new developments, a research breakthrough, a new mineral find, a new process, a new appointment; news of past mistakes, the write-off of major losses, the abandonment of profit-draining experiments, the departure of unsuccessful managers; news about the cost of money, of politics, of developments that may affect the company alone or of others that may affect the profitability of business generally.

These are only some of the things which may affect the price of shares. The alert investor is reading constantly, listening constantly, attempting to appraise the effect of the news on the prospects of his shareholdings. He also listens attentively for news from the market itself. What does it mean, for instance, when the shares of a pharmaceutical company begin to rise, apparently for no specific reason? Nothing, possibly. Or it may mean that the company has been test marketing a new cold remedy, that druggists have seen it move off their shelves rapidly, and that purchases of the company's shares have been building up in the test market areas. And what does it mean when the mutual funds begin to get out of the market, building up their cash reserves? Or when odd-lot (fewer than a hundred shares) buyers begin to outnumber odd-lot sellers? The same thing possibly, an anticipated break in the market—a conclusion based on the theory, not always borne out in fact, that the institutional investor behaves correctly but that the small investor usually does the right thing at the wrong time.

What does it mean when the volume of margin debt begins to rise? It means that speculative interest in the market is increasing, something that usually goes along with a rise in stock prices, although credit may also be used to sell short or to pay for securities borrowed in hope of a market decline. Margin is the percentage of equity a customer has in his trading account with a broker. When establishing an account, the New York Stock Exchange requires a customer to put up a minimum of one thousand dollars. Then, if the stock goes up in price, he can use the increase in market value to buy additional shares. But if the stock goes down below certain levels, he must put up more cash.

To limit excessive speculation, the Federal Reserve controls initial margin requirements, which have varied between 50 and 90 percent of the purchase price in recent years. Exchange rules govern maintenance margin requirements. The New York Stock Exchange sets a 25 percent minimum, but some brokerage houses may require more.

Looking outside the market for clues to future stock price behavior is known as "fundamental analysis." Fundamental analysis focuses on trying to forecast such things as gross national product, industrial production, growth and inflation rates, and profits, as well as on trying to forecast the outlook for specific industries and companies. Looking to the market itself for clues to future stock price behavior is known as "technical analysis." Technical analysis concentrates on such things as the number of issues that have advanced in price in relation to the number that have declined, or on the short interest, the number of shares that have been borrowed and sold in the hope of purchasing them at a lower price. A rise in the advance/decline ratio on growing volume is thought to foretell a rise in prices, as, usually, does a rise in the short interest in relation to the average volume in any month.

A subsection of technical analysis is charting, which regards moves in individual stocks and in the averages as an indicator of their future moves. A whole cult has grown up around the Dow theory, which seeks to forecast the future course of the market by interpretation of the Dow-Jones industrial and transportation averages. The averages forecast continuing rising (bull) or declining (bear) markets only when one average confirms the signals of the other. Although once widely followed, the Dow theory signals are watched today primarily because of how investors suspect others may behave because of them.

The averages themselves are watched constantly, for they are the yard-sticks of stock market behavior. Before discussing the averages, however, it may be useful to mention how share prices are quoted. Most of the items are self-explanatory: the high and low price for the year through the previous day (the switch to a new year is made in March); the company name; a notation if the issue is something other than common stock; the previous year's dividend in dollars and cents per share; the volume for the day in hundreds of shares; the opening, high, low, and closing prices for the day; and the net change in the closing price from that of the previous day.

The footnotes are similarly self-explanatory, with one exception, perhaps—the designations "ex dividend" and "ex rights." Ordinarily, when a purchaser buys a share of stock the seller agrees to deliver it on the fifth full business day (Saturdays, Sundays, and holidays are excluded) after the transaction. This means that a buyer who purchases an issue for which a dividend or a rights offering had been declared would not get the right in the four business days before the record date. During that time the stock is said to be "ex dividend" or "ex rights," and the price is marked down accordingly. But back to the averages.

Two averages, the Dow-Jones and the *New York Times,* chart the movement of the so-called blue chips, a few large, well-established companies that alone comprise a major portion of the market value of all New York Stock Exchange issues. The Dow-Jones averages include industrial, transportation (including eleven rails, six airlines, and three truckers), and utility components, but the one most closely watched is that based on the movement of thirty large industrial companies. The *New York Times* average balances twenty-five industrial and twenty-five rail stocks in a fifty-stock combined average.

A more inclusive yardstick is Standard and Poor's 500-stock index, which includes a 425-stock industrial component. Still more inclusive is the New York Stock Exchange index, which records the movement of all shares listed on the Big Board. There is an American Stock Exchange index as well, plus a series of indexes for the over-the-counter stocks displayed in the National Association of Securities Dealers automated quotations system (Nasdaq). There are also other, less well-known averages and indexes.

Most of the averages are weighted. That is to say, a big company with hundreds of millions of shares outstanding is given much more prominence in the averages than a smaller one with fewer shares outstanding. The movement of a point or two in General Motors or duPont, then, will have a much greater effect than a bigger movement in a smaller issue.

Most of the averages are calculated in points, but, except for the New York Stock Exchange index, no effort is made to relate the price movements of the averages directly to the value of an average share. Because of the way it handles stock splits, the Dow-Jones industrial average has grown to more than twenty times the value of an average share. A five-point decline in the D-J, therefore, should not be regarded as a five-point (five-dollar) decline in the value of an average share. It is more like a quarter-point drop. The other averages are closer to the value of an average share.

Volume, or the number of shares traded, is another important yardstick. Rising prices on growing volume means much more to the market than a similar rise with only feeble or scattered support. Volume figures on the exchange are tabulated five times each day, at the end of each of the first four hours of trading and at the close. Volume for issues included in the Nasdaq quotations system in the over-the-counter market are tabulated once each day, after the close.

Stock price indexes are watched closely as an indicator of general business ups and downs. Indeed, the National Bureau of Economic Research, the private economic fact finders who have assumed the awesome burden of saying when the nation is in a recession and how long it has lasted, gives stock prices the highest rating of a large number of economic indicators. Stock prices score high for several reasons—the frequency of the data and the speed with which it becomes available, the absence of big erratic movements, and the fact that stock prices tend to lead major turning points in the economy by about four months. In a study of fifty-two business turning points, the bureau showed that the Standard and

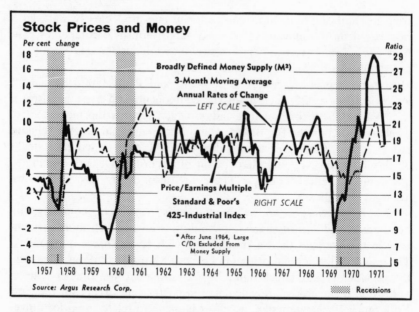

Stock Prices and Money

Per cent change / Ratio

Broadly Defined Money Supply (M²)
3-Month Moving Average
Annual Rates of Change
— LEFT SCALE →

Price/Earnings Multiple
Standard & Poor's   RIGHT SCALE
425-Industrial Index

* After June 1964, Large
C/Ds Excluded From
Money Supply

1957 1958 1959 1960 1961 1962 1963 1964 1965 1966 1967 1968 1969 1970 1971

Source: Argus Research Corp.   ▒▒▒▒ Recessions

Changes in the money supply tend to lead turning points in the stock market, more closely when the turn is upward than when it is downward.

Poor's 500-stock index led thirty-three turns, roughly coincided with fourteen turns, and lagged only five times.

If the market ranks high as a leading indicator of business cycle turning points, it sometimes does too well. The indexes clearly signaled the 1960–61 recession and the one ten years later. In between, however, it indicated, by major stock price adjustments in 1962 and 1966 and lesser ones in 1965 and 1968, that there would be at least two other recessions and possibly four which never materialized.

Stock price movements seem to correspond even more closely to two things other than general turning points in the economy, changes in the rate of growth of the money supply and changes in popular sentiment, particularly that of businessmen. A calculation of changes in the broadly based money supply (private commercial bank demand and time deposits plus currency outside banks) against the price/earnings multiple of the Standard and Poor's index of 425 industrial stocks show that changes in the money supply tend to lead turns in the stock market sooner when prices turn up than when they turn down. And regular polling of business managers, professionals, and executives—the people most likely to buy shares—by the Sindlinger organization shows the leading influence of changes in business sentiment.

A matter of debate is how much the money supply and business sentiment should be viewed as causes of stock market movements and how much shifts in the stock market should be viewed as causes of change in the demand for money and of changes in business sentiment.

Psychology is always a factor in the behavior of stock prices. In the late stages of a bull market, for example, the mood is one of almost blind euphoria, with people thinking there is no way for the market to go but up. In the late stages of a bear market, the mood is exactly the reverse, with everyone believing the worst is yet to come. The best indicator of psychology, both for the market as a whole and for individual stocks, is price/earnings multiples. The p/e for the Dow industrial average usually gets as high as twenty in bull markets and as low as fifteen or less in bear markets, and individual stocks show much the same pattern. IBM, for example, has ranged over the years from a p/e high of fifty or more to a low of thirty.

Apart from cyclical influences that may operate upon stock prices and the counterinfluence that stock prices themselves may have upon the economy, stock prices have enjoyed a long-term rise for more than a quarter century. For most of this period the demand for shares greatly outdistanced the supply of new issues. Institutions—the pension funds, state and local government retirement funds, life insurance companies, mutual funds, and savings banks—stepped up their buying sharply, their annual purchases rising from $3.5 billion in 1960 to more than $10 billion before the end of the decade, the buying by private noninsured pension funds alone rising from $2 billion to well over $5 billion.

At the same time, because of a high level of retained earnings and because of favorable credit conditions, corporations were able to meet their long-term capital needs by issuing a minimum amount of new stock. In 1963, for instance, corporations were required to reach beyond their doors for only $12.4 billion of their $58.2 billion total fund requirements, and of this only $3.6 billion represented the proceeds of new long-term securities issued. What is more, the corporations were totally independent of equity financing. They obtained $3.9 billion from the bond market, but they were able to retire $300 million more stock than they issued.

By the late 1960s, however, as the squeeze on their profits and liquidity grew, the corporations were forced to go outside for a greater portion of their total fund requirements and to look increasingly to convertible bonds and stocks. At the same time the rise in bond yields to record levels at the end of the decade was beginning to woo the institutions back to the bond market—or at the least was causing them to engage in soul-searching about the wisdom of deserting it.

There were broad implications in what was happening. With the supply of stocks coming into better balance with the long-term demand, a major force powering the quarter-century bull market was losing some of its steam. Did this mean the bull market was over? In part this was simply the other side of the question raised in the last chapter, are bonds going out of style?

At first glance it might seem that the principal factor threatening the bonds, a continuation or aggravation of inflation, might favor stocks, but this is quickly seen to be specious reasoning. Rising inflation makes all savings less attractive, all capital investment more precarious. It increases the squeeze on corporate profits and results in a proliferation of debt with equity kickers, or debt that permits its holders to share in the benefits of ownership, which alone may contribute to some easing of supply-demand pressures in the stock market. If the life insurance companies, for instance, are able to meet their needs for hedges against inflation by purchasing commercial mortgages that permit them to share in the earnings of, say, a hotel, office building, or shopping center, they may become less active bidders for shares.

So long as inflation does not extinguish the profit-generating capacity of business entirely, share prices should continue to rise. But the certainty that the stock market will outperform other kinds of equity investment is far less today than it was a decade ago.

16. The Exchanges

Although there are many stock exchanges in the United States and abroad, the New York Stock Exchange is the biggest, both in terms of the total value of shares traded and the number of large companies represented. Trading shares on both this and other exchanges in the United States involves the auction system, and the key man in this system is the specialist.

Looking down on the floor of the New York Stock Exchange from the visitors' gallery, one finds it difficult to find purpose in the apparent confusion. In an arena two-thirds the size of a football field, hundreds of men huddle in booths along the walls, stroll about without apparent purpose, or cluster in and around horseshoe-shaped structures spaced around the room. A large red-bulbed sign tells the passing hour, minute by minute. A jumble of letters and numbers streams across several wide, thin screens.

This, one is told, is the nation's marketplace, but what does that mean? The huge, cavernous hall looks more like a railroad station than most markets. Certainly it bears little resemblance to a neighborhood super-market, or even an ordinary auction—of jewelry or antiques, for instance.

To gain some notion of what the activity is all about, let's move down on the floor to Post 12, one of the horseshoe-shaped structures, and meet William Meehan, specialist in the shares of RCA Corporation. He received a commendation from the Securities and Exchange Commission for his performance on November 22, 1963, the day President Kennedy was assassinated.

Here's the way he describes what happened: "Somebody came by and told me there was an unconfirmed report that President Kennedy had been shot, but there was no indication how seriously. Two minutes later the selling began. It started gradually but accelerated very rapidly. Radio [RCA] had been selling at ninety and I ate [bought for his own account] perhaps ten thousand. Very often this will stop the excitement, but it didn't stop anyone that day. Finally, after letting it slip an eighth, I had to let it drop a quarter of a point at a time. I had no idea how many orders I had on the book. I knew I had bought a substantial amount of stock. Finally, I just had to stop trading, something I had never done in twenty-eight years on the floor."

Many traders called the activity that day the most frenzied since the 1929 crash. Mr. Meehan, said the SEC, made "especially large purchases all during the decline," fulfilling his obligation to maintain fair and orderly markets in the issues assigned to him.

At the heart of similar dramas, repeated each day in less spectacular fashion, is the specialist. He operates at a particular location at one of the eighteen trading posts on the floor of the exchange—the only place where the stocks in which he specializes may be traded. To appreciate his role, let's follow a transaction.

In something less than half of all transactions the specialist plays no active role. A customer in, say, Milwaukee telephones his broker to buy a hundred shares of United States Steel "at the market." By wiring his New York office for a "quote," the broker determines that the market is "fifty-six to a quarter." That means, at the moment, that the highest bid to buy "Steel" is $56.00 a share and the lowest offer to sell is $56.25. The customer tells his broker to go ahead.

About the same time another customer, this one in San Francisco, tells his broker to sell a hundred shares of "Steel." Both orders, the one to buy and the one to sell, are wired to the floor of the exchange, where order clerks, in the booths along the walls, signal the representatives of each firm, known as "commission house brokers," on the floor. Each picks up his order and hurries to the post where United States Steel is traded. As they enter the "crowd" around the post, one of them asks, "How's Steel?" Someone—usually the specialist—answers, "Fifty-six to a quarter."

Right then, without further effort, each man could complete his trade, the Milwaukee firm buying for $56.25 or the San Francisco firm selling for $56.00 but since each broker—like all others—is charged with getting the best possible price for his customer, the broker for the San Francisco customer might try to sell at an eighth of a point more and the one for the Milwaukee customer might try to buy at an eighth of a point less. So when the latter bids 56⅛ for 100 shares the broker for the San Francisco customer responds, "Sold 100 at 56⅛." Then the two write down each other's firm name and report the transaction back to the telephone clerks so that the customers may be notified.

At the same time a reporter at the trading post pencil-marks details of the transaction on a special card and feeds it into an optional scanning device. The electronic device "reads" the card and transmits the data on it to the exchange computer center. In the form of coded electrical impulses, the information goes to the exchange's nine hundred character-a-minute ticker, or printing quotations telegraph network. Thus, within seconds the transaction will appear on thirty-six hundred tickers in more than a thousand cities in the United States, including the big ones that overlook the floor of the exchange. It will appear like this: X 56⅛.

The number of shares is specified only when multiples of one hundred shares are involved. Otherwise, only the stock's symbol(X for United States Steel) and price are printed. (Only "round lots," or units of one hundred shares are traded. "Odd lots," ordinarily less than hundred-share units, are bought and sold through odd-lot dealers, who obtain the shares they need and get rid of surplus shares by selling in the round-lot market.)

This is the auction system in its simplest form. Not everyone, however, is willing to buy or sell at the market. In our example the quote represents only the highest bid, 56, and the lowest offer, 56¼. Other people may be willing to buy at 55⅞, 55¾, 55⅜, and so on down the scale. Others may be willing to sell at 56⅜, 56½, 56⅝ and so on up. They enter "limit" orders rather than orders "at the market," which means that the orders come into force when the price reaches that level.

This is where the specialist comes in. Because commission brokers can't wait all day at a single post for the price to go up or down, the specialist accepts "limit" orders from other brokers, promising to execute them if and when the market reaches the specified levels. He puts each order in his "book" under each price in the order received, noting the number of shares and the broker from whom the order was taken. As the market moves up or down he executes the orders, often bidding against other brokers in behalf of the orders on his book. When an order is executed or when one is canceled, he crosses it off his book, notifying the broker for whom he has acted.

No one knows exactly how the specialist function came into being. According to a popular account, about a hundred years ago, soon after the exchange shifted from twice-a-day* to continuous auctions, a commission broker suffered a serious disability, keeping him from moving from post to post. Making an asset out of his adversity, he began to "specialize" in the stocks traded at a single post. Serving as a broker's broker, however, is only one important function of the specialist, one for which he earns a floor broker's commission. In recent years he has come to perform an even more important function, buying or selling against

---

* The twice-a-day sessions were known as call auctions, where brokers entered bids as clerks droned through a roll call of all listed issues.

the trend of the market to keep prices from moving down or up too rapidly, which he does by buying or selling from his own holdings, selling "short" if necessary to maintain a market. This means he borrows shares and sells them, hoping to buy them back at a lower price later, and in so doing he must observe all the rules of the Securities and Exchange Commission governing short selling.

An important attribute of a specialist is his ability to establish and keep order in a crowd. Some men have done this with physical size, others with a booming voice, still others with sheer force of personality. Some years ago the role of specialist fell to an armless member of the exchange, who impressed his fellows in difficult moments by waving aloft a large hook, like the pirate captain in *Peter Pan*.

In recent years the exchange has made great strides in automating its procedures. A computerized depository for stock certificates, in which ownership changes are accomplished by bookkeeping entries should eventually eliminate up to 75 percent of listed stock certificate handling for member firms. Other developments include a centralized "back-office" accounting service for member firms and the automated handling of odd-lot orders—which last raises the question, why can't the specialist's function be given to a computer and the specialist retired to the sidelines?

The question reveals a fundamental misunderstanding of odd-lot automation. While the flow of orders to the odd-lot dealers are handled by a computer, the dealer himself—as he always has—is required to exercise judgment about whether to add to his inventory or to deplete it. Similarly, only the specialist himself can exercise the judgment needed to fulfill his function and still make a profit.

"Like all other dealers," the New York Stock Exchange says in its official explanation of the specialist's role, "the specialist's success in making a profit is largely determined by his own judgment and astuteness as well as by the general market conditions. However, the specialist alone has the unique responsibility for maintaining markets, and this often makes it necessary for him to take risks not required of other dealers."

In addition to specialists, commission house brokers, and odd-lot dealers, two other kinds of members do business on the floor of the exchange, floor brokers and registered traders. Both are independents, free-lancers as it were. The floor broker—still called a "two-dollar broker," although the commission he receives for executing a trade for another broker long has exceeded that amount—assists the commission house broker during peak trading periods. The registered trader, formerly known as a floor trader, buys and sells for his own account, adding liquidity to the markets of the stocks in which he trades and being under obligation to help the specialist in his stabilizing efforts.

It is the specialist, however, who stands at the hub of the market process. And it is the specialist who has borne the brunt of the criticism of the exchanges, which has included charges that specialists tend to deal in the more active stocks, in which there are the greatest opportunities for profit and least opportunities for acquiring unwanted inventory; that less active issues may be neglected; that there is an inherent conflict of interest in the specialist's combined role as broker and dealer; and that specialists vary greatly in their capital and in their ability to handle certain transactions, particularly large blocks.

The exchanges have done much to answer such criticism. They have stepped up their self-policing, given greater attention to the adequacy of capital and to the surveillance of specialists' performance, largely through use of the computer, and used capital adequacy and performance as prime tests in the assignment of new listings to specialist units. Nevertheless, the specialist's role as a privileged participant in the market process, the sole person except for registered traders able to buy and sell for his own account on an exchange floor, has come under increasing competitive challenge. And exchange rules that tend to enforce the monopolistic character of the specialist's position—and to bolster the value of exchange membership—have come under similar fire.

An increasing challenge to the specialist system has been the growth of trading in large blocks, principally on behalf of institutions. As recently as 1965, 2,171 block transactions accounted for only 48.3 million shares valued at $1.8 billion, or 3.1 percent of reported volume on the New York Stock Exchange. By 1970, the number of transactions had grown to 17,217 accounting for 451 million shares valued at $13.4 billion, or 15.4 percent of reported volume. On an average market day in 1970, there were sixty-eight large block transactions of 21,190 shares each at $30 a share or an average value of $775,628.

Large blocks are defined by the New York Stock Exchange as transactions in which 10,000 shares or more are traded on the Big Board floor. Included are crosses, or executions where one member firm is at least partially on both the purchase and sale side of the same transaction, and exchange distributions where the necessary orders are accumulated and the block filled by executing a cross in the auction market between the current bid and asked quotations. Excluded are secondary distributions, sell orders for extremely large blocks of stock executed after market hours at a fixed price, the bunching of orders at the opening of trading or the reopening after trading has been suspended, and large orders broken into multiple executions of fewer than 10,000 shares.

In addition to exchange distributions and secondary distributions, two other special methods of distribution have been developed to facilitate block transactions on the floor of the exchange. One is the specialist block purchase or sale, in which the specialist negotiates a direct purchase or sale of a large block outside the regular auction market. The other is the special bid or offering, in which the offering or bid price is printed on the ticker, open to all members and their customers, again outside the regular auction market.

Most large block transactions, however, originate in the "upstairs" offices of brokerage firms and are brought to the floor only for execution. One reason block trading often bypasses the specialist is that he frequently doesn't have the capital to absorb the flow of very large and very frequent large-block offerings. Brokerage houses with substantial capital and considerable skill in executing large-block orders may buy part of a large offering for their own account, hopefully selling the shares later at a profit. Such "block positioning" is akin to the dealer function of the specialist and puts brokerage houses that practice it in direct competition with him.

Even when a member firm acts merely to assemble the orders on the opposite side of a large block transaction, the trade often means bypassing the specialist and the auction system. Typically, a firm will arrange the pricing of a block transaction, within market limits, before the trade goes to the floor. If it can't find a buyer on its own, it may know of another broker who has a customer and the two firms will go to the floor together with the trade.

Even then, some dexterity is required of the broker who executes the transaction. He must make an offer to buy or sell, in accordance with the auction rules, and then pick up his own block before anyone else can intervene. Usually, the size of the block prevents someone else in the "crowd" from making an immediate response. The talk goes something like this: "Selling 50,000 Xerox at 115½. Taken."

In a competitive economy there are always new technologies waiting to gain acceptance, new companies crowding to be born. The innovators aren't always successful—far from it—but there are always nibblers at the Establishment. And sometimes they succeed in taking fairly big bites.

In the world of business, listing on the New York Stock Exchange long has represented acceptance into the Establishment. The Big Board is not misnamed; it still accounts for the lion's share of all stocks sold on national exchanges. A look down the list of Big Board companies, however, reveals change. Mainly through mergers, acquisitions, and consolidations but occasionally through delisting or bankruptcy, names once famous are no longer found. Consider this: of the leading issues of

1920—American Car and Foundry, American Locomotive, American Woolen, Baldwin Locomotive, Crucible Steel, and General Motors—only General Motors remains.

The newcomers are even more interesting. The glamour issues of today represent whole new industries: computers, electronics, photocopying machines. Other newcomers, some of them wholly unknown today, are likely to be joining the Big Board ranks in the years to come.

From the time a company comes of age until it arrives at full maturity—from the date of its going public until its listing on the Big Board—many companies seek listing on the American Stock Exchange. Although the Amex includes large, long-established companies, blue chips no less than similar concerns listed on the New York Stock Exchange, it represents itself primarily as a nationwide market for younger companies seeking to acquire a wider investor following.

That it has been successful in this ambition is attested to by the names of some of its listings that have graduated to the Big Board: Computer Sciences and Leasco Corporation (computers), Skyline Corporation (mobile homes), Microdot and Conrac (aerospace and electronics), Signal Companies and Monogram Industries (conglomerates), and Flying Tiger (airfreight).

The history of the Amex, formerly known as the Curb Exchange, is rooted deeply in New York. The exchange came into being about the time of the 1849 gold rush, when curbstone markets developed in the shares of such infant industries as telegraphy, then five years old; steamships, ten years old; and railroads, twenty years old. The outdoor market, situated originally at Wall and Hanover Streets, was moved several times, reaching its heyday shortly after the turn of the century on Broad Street, just below Wall Street. The scene was one not likely to be seen again. Hundreds of brokers milled about in the street, buying and selling stocks and bonds. Above them, perched in windows of an office building, telephone clerks waved and shouted orders to the brokers who, to be recognized more readily by their clerks, wore yellow Homburgs, green derbies, or other brightly colored hats or loud-striped jackets.

Although the exchange moved indoors after World War I, remnants of the scene persist to this day. The telephone clerks, no longer in windows but sitting at desks on tiers overlooking the trading floor, shout and signal to brokers at posts below, using an unusual set of hand signals developed during the exchange's outdoor days—a one-handed version of the deaf-mute's sign language, which speeds communications and saves brokers' shoe leather.

The American Stock Exchange is growing rapidly. Its volume in 1970 was 843 million shares, down from the boom level of 1.4 billion in its record year, 1968, but still almost three times its 1963 volume of 300 million. The three largest regional exchanges—the Midwest, the Pacific Coast, and the Philadelphia-Baltimore-Washington—and at least two smaller regional exchanges—Detroit and Boston—have also enjoyed growth no less than that of the Big Board.

On all exchanges each member must own a "seat," or membership. (Actually, there are no seats—the term survives from the early days when there were—and members remain on their feet throughout the trading session.) Seats are bought and sold at auction, much as shares. Since 1950 the price of Big Board seats has ranged from $38,000 to $425,000, with members paying an initiation fee of $7,500 and annual dues of $1,500. Lesser sums are required on the Amex and the regionals. At one time only individuals or partnerships could hold memberships on the exchange, but today corporations may also be members.

A complex set of rules governs members' behavior. In the long history of the exchanges, these have sometimes been more often flouted than observed. Nevertheless, self-regulation remains the cornerstone of federal regulation of the securities markets.

Securities may be bought and sold only at prices openly and fairly determined, and all bids and offers must be spoken aloud. The highest bid, or seller's price, and the lowest offer, or buyer's price, take precedence. All transactions are reported at once, publicly, over the exchange's ticker system, and no trades are permitted on the exchange floor before or after trading hours, 10:00 A.M. to 3:30 P.M. Monday through Friday. Member firms carrying customer accounts must have adequate capital and must answer at least three financial questionnaires each year, including one based upon a surprise audit by the firm's independent public accountants. They must open their books and records to spot checks by exchange examiners, report weekly on their position as underwriters of securities, and disclose loans or borrowings by the firm, its partners, or voting shareholders.

Employees of member firms who do business with the public—known as "registered representatives"—must meet the exchanges' standards of training, and newcomers who hold seats must pass qualifying examinations. New allied members, the partners in member firms plus the voting shareholders in member corporations, must also pass qualifying examinations, and although they may not do business on the trading floor, they are expected nevertheless to live up to the same standards set for members. In addition, the office management and sales activities of member firms must pass inspection by the exchanges, and member firms doing business with the public must carry fidelity insurance against possible loss due to fraud or dishonest acts on the part of their personnel. They must also contribute to the Federal Securities Investors

Protective Corporation (Sipic) to protect customers against losses because of their own or another member firm's insolvency.

Listing requirements on the American Stock Exchange emphasize its role as a place where the shares of new and growing industries season and mature. For initial listing, the New York Stock Exchange requires demonstrated earning power of $1.2 million after taxes, while the Amex requires $150,000. The Big Board requires net tangible assets of $10 million and the Amex, $1 million. Finally, the Big Board requires that 700,000 shares be publicly held by 2,000 shareholders, of whom 1,700 must be round-lot holders; the Amex requires 250,000 shares publicly held by 750 shareholders, of whom 500 must be round-lot holders.

Both exchanges insist that listed companies publish quarterly sales and earnings statements, solicit proxies, and make timely disclosure of important information that might affect share prices. For many years the Big Board has refused to list nonvoting common stocks. Recently the Amex began requiring additional information to assure that its listings hold more than local investor interest and to determine the extent to which institutional holdings limit the breadth of the market for an issue.

The ultimate weapon in the hands of the exchanges is delisting. A company must continue to operate at a profit, show continued market value in its shares, and retain wide shareholder distribution to stay on the Big Board or the Amex.

17.   The Over-the-Counter Market

Buying and selling shares through the New York Stock Exchange and other exchanges is only one of two ways of trading in equity securities. The other is to trade in the over-the-counter market.

In contrast to the New York Stock Exchange, the American Stock Exchange, and the regional exchanges, the over-the-counter market has no central selling place, no trading posts where stocks offered for sale are knocked down to the highest bidders in a continuous two-way auction, and no ticker tape to record the price and volume of each transaction. Instead the over-the-counter market exists through a network of thousands of dealers in large cities and small linked by telephone, teletype, and increasingly by data communications. These dealers stand ready to "make markets"—to buy or sell at least one hundred shares—in a list of issues they advertise to other market makers and to securities retailers. Prices depend on negotiation between the buyer and seller. In a less active issue only one or two dealers may make a market, so prices are apt to change infrequently, and the spreads between bid and asked prices—the prices at which a dealer will buy or sell—are apt to be wide. In a more active issue there may be fifteen or twenty market makers, so prices are apt to move often, the spreads will be narrow, and the prices quoted by any one dealer will be no more than an eighth or a quarter point from what most of the other dealers are quoting.

The over-the-counter market—or over-the-telephone market, more accurately—could perhaps be dubbed the market that nobody knows. Probably not one investor in a hundred would know that the OTC, as it is known familiarly in Wall Street, is the oldest securities market in the world. Interdealer trading was common in England and in this country before the first stock exchanges were founded. It is also the largest securities market in the world, accounting for at least three-fourths the gross value of all securities sold in the United States. Issues traded over-the-counter include almost all federal, state, and municipal bonds, many bank and insurance company issues, a big percentage of industrial and utility stocks, all mutual fund shares, and the shares of any company going public for the first time.

Stocks traded over-the-counter range from hot new issues, the speculative offerings of small unproven companies, to the blue-chip shares of long-established corporations. Such well-known and highly respected names as Anheuser-Busch, Cannon Mills, Kaiser Steel, Brink's, Inc., Mohawk Rubber, The Hoover Company, and American Express have long been identified with the over-the-counter market. Among banks the United States Trust Company, New York; the Cleveland Trust Company; the Manufacturers National Bank of Detroit; the Mellon National Bank, Pittsburgh; and the BankAmerica Corporation, holding company for the Bank of America, San Francisco, the nation's largest bank, are traded over-the-counter. Insurance companies traded over-the-counter include Connecticut General, Great Western Life, General Reinsurance, and the Kemper Companies.

There are no more than 4,000 issues traded daily on all major stock exchanges throughout the United States. By way of contrast, over-the-counter markets are advertised at least once a year for some 20,000 issues, of which 5,000 are quoted or traded each business day. Some twenty-eight hundred of these are big enough and widely enough held to be traded nationally, and the remainder are traded primarily in regional markets.

A look at the trading room of a large over-the-counter dealer would reveal a scene of considerable confusion. A telephone operator, seated at a switchboard, directs calls to thirty or so people at three long desks, and a clerk hovers over three constantly chattering teletype machines.

The key man in the scene is the trader, the man seated at the desk. With phone in one hand and order pad in the other, he engages in a staccato conversation with dozens of people exactly like himself at other over-the-counter houses across the nation. Perhaps nowhere else in the world do people get to know other people so well—their habits, their patterns of thought, their likely reactions to a news announcement—and yet know them so little. A man may trade for thirty years in the over-the-counter market and never get to meet his counterparts at the other end of the line.

The conversation itself is cryptic:

"How's Bud?"

"Seventy to a quarter."

"I'll take two hundred."

"You bought two hundred Bud at seventy and a quarter."

Translated, the conversation would be:

"How are you quoting Anheuser-Busch?"

"Seventy bid, seventy and a quarter asked."

"I'll buy two hundred shares."

"You bought two hundred shares of Anheuser-Busch at seventy and a quarter."

The conversation uses as few words as possible. The trader knows who is talking when the customer identifies himself at the beginning of a conversation. Well-known customers won't even give their names but are identified through their private wire numbers, and they may not even mention price if they are well acquainted with the latest quote.

Thus: "Clinton Oil, five hundred, Merrill Lynch" (or simply 95, Merrill Lynch's private wire number).

The trader, however, responds precisely. "You bought five hundred Clinton Oil."

Advent of the Nasdaq system has clipped the conversation even more. Nasdaq, as has already been mentioned, stands for National Association of Securities Dealers automated quotations. NASD is the quasi-official self-policing organization of the over-the-counter industry, and its new quotations system provides up-to-the-minute bid and asked prices for twenty-eight hundred more actively traded issues, eliminating the need for telephone inquiry. Since nine out of ten calls to a dealer's trading room before inauguration of the system were for quotes, Nasdaq has cut down considerably on the decibel level and confusion.

Words like "okay" or "all right" are never heard in the conversations of over-the-counter traders. They may be costly. Some years ago, when First National City Bank shares were selling at 240, the story goes, a customer came in with an order for a thousand shares. The next day he came back for a thousand more at 241. The trader's response was, "Okay." Overnight the issue dropped seven points, and the customer reneged. He just wanted a quote, he said. The house's loss on the transaction was $7,000. The trader subsequently was careful to say, "You bought," "You sold."

The number "fifty" is also forbidden, since it sounds too much like "fifteen." In trader conversation, fifty is "half a hundred."

Traders are obliged to buy or sell at least one hundred shares at their latest quotation. But when larger purchases or offerings are made, they may respond, "I hear you," or, "Subject," meaning the quotation isn't firm for that amount, or, "I pass," meaning that they do not choose to trade that amount at that price.

In addition to pads of differently colored buy and sell orders, a trader keeps in front of him at all times a running account of his transactions in every issue he trades. A newcomer to the business may trade no more than half a dozen issues, while a fully experienced trader may handle up to fifty or sixty stocks.

The running account lists the name of the issue traded, the final bid of the day before, and the trader's overnight long or short position in the stock. Each trade is identified by the account number of the customer, the number of shares bought or sold, and the price. In addition, as each trade is made the cumulative position is adjusted and the trader may alter his quotations. As he acquires shares he may drop his buying price, and as he sells them he may raise his selling price. Price adjustments are usually made in eighths, although in fast-moving markets or markets in stocks that are thinly traded they may be greater.

An over-the-counter house that makes markets in a large number of issues—there are perhaps two hundred fifty houses trading fifty or more issues—attempts to keep its position at a minimum. Thus, one house has a rule that whenever a trader goes long or short by five hundred shares or more he must get permission from a partner. A trader ends his day by circling the final quote for each issue he trades and by totting up his profit or loss in the issue.

There are days, in rapidly declining markets, when a house will have to "eat" stock—that is, to take losses in most of the issues it trades. Doing business in bad markets as well as good is part of its obligation as a market maker. But most of the time, obviously, it has to show a profit or it would no longer remain in business. The profit comes from the "spread," the difference between the dealer's buying price and his selling price. When a dealer quotes forty-nine bid, forty-nine and a half asked, he is willing to buy at $49 and sell at $49.50. The half point difference represents a fifty cent profit on each share sold. Retail customers, in addition, are usually charged the equivalent of a stock exchange commission.

There are two essentially different kinds of transactions in the over-the-counter market, agency transactions where the broker is buying or selling for someone else and dealer transactions where he is buying for his own account.

The large over-the-counter houses doing business in fifty or more stocks, the so-called wholesale houses, ordinarily do little or no retail business. For years, brokerage houses doing business with the public have come to the wholesalers to obtain OTC merchandise to fill customer orders. Recently, however, the largest wire houses—nationwide brokerage firms with retail offices in many cities linked by telephone and teletype wires—have entered the market directly as wholesalers. Although heavily capitalized, both the wholesalers and the integrated houses—those doing both a wholesale and a retail business—put little of their capital behind any one issue. Both, however, are quite catholic in their interests, and will do business in any issue that meets their standards of quality and activity.

Other firms are more selective. The bank and insurance stock markets are separate markets, as are the local issues of each region and each major city. There is an over-the-counter market in foreign securities, new issues, inactive bank stocks, and unlisted convertible bonds. There is a market in penny stocks, shares selling for one dollar or less, and even a market in the shares of bankrupt companies. The over-the-counter market is wholly geared to opportunity. Let speculative or investment interest crop up anywhere, and someone is certain to make a market.

Not all market makers spread their capital thinly over many issues. Underwriters traditionally support the issues they bring to market for several months or a year, and retail firms frequently make markets only in the shares they are recommending. Of late, a new kind of market maker, the special situations firm, has been growing fast. Heavily capitalized, it seeks out and carefully researches companies—young companies in new industries of great growth potential or older companies with turnaround possibilities—whose shares it thinks will appreciate rapidly. In contrast to the wholesale house, the special situations firm handles only a few issues and will take large positions, if necessary. Its object is to become the primary market maker in the issues it trades, to guide prices steadily to higher levels by absorbing stock when there are more sellers than buyers and by supplying stock when there are more buyers than sellers, and to have sufficient merchandise to supply the block demands—often thousands of shares—of the institutional customers it solicits.

For all its ingenuity and potential capability, the over-the-counter market has not always enjoyed the highest reputation. The negotiated character of the market, the lack of a central selling place, and the absence of current price and volume information have offered opportunity for self-dealing and fraud and have made policing difficult. It is the great variety of securities bought and sold, of sizes and kinds of market makers, and of ways of doing business that have attracted the inevitable sharp operator, and the rapid growth of the market and the limited powers of the National Association of Securities Dealers that have made control difficult.

A market as vast and as varied as the over-the-counter market could not operate without a high standard of commercial ethics. No other selling place in the world functions with as little formality. Billions of dollars of securities change hands without as much as a handshake, merely the spoken words, "you bought," "you sold," on the telephone. There is real meaning, then, to the motto of the Security Traders Association of New York, "My Word Is My Bond." Nevertheless, despite the high performance of many, a few have traded the industry's ethical obligations at deep discount. Advertising fictitious quotations, sometimes for nonexistent companies; backing away from firm quotations; "hand-holding," or the creation of an appearance of interdealer competition when in fact there is none—these are only a few of the practices that have occasionally troubled the industry.

Without the over-the-counter market, shareholders in thousands of companies too small, too narrowly held, or too unseasoned to merit exchange listing would lack ready markets for their shares. But, on the other hand, such shareholders often have to do business at the mercy of a single man, determined to obtain all the traffic will bear. While it may be too much to expect the same performance from a single dealer who dominates the market for an obscure recent issue as from that sector of the market where many dealers make close, competitive markets in the shares of well-known established companies, it is a fact that over the years, most investors lacked the information to distinguish between active and inactive issues. Only professionals were permitted to know the number of dealers making a market in any one issue, and there were no indications of volume.

Even where active, competitive markets existed, a buyer had no assurance that his broker would fulfill his obligation to shop the market to get him the best possible price. Because of incompetence, indifference, or too much business, the broker might simply fail to check. On occasion, however, brokers channeled orders to firms—not necessarily at the most competitive prices—in the hope of obtaining reciprocal business, order clerks directed business in return for expected favors, and unjustified payments were made to third firms that performed no service but positioned themselves between the broker and the market maker.

The difficulties of the over-the-counter market centered importantly in its information system. For years the industry relied chiefly on a system—for its time a marvel of ingenuity—of pink, green, and white mimeographed quotations sheets, published in New York, Chicago, and San Francisco. Subscribers—thirteen hundred market makers across the nation—would pay to advertise the issues in which they made markets and their quotations in the sheets. At or near the close of the market, market makers would enter their latest quotations on forms. Messengers would be standing by to run the forms to a central location, where typists would be waiting to type the quotations on stencils and high school boys, operating souped-up mimeograph machines, to grind out more than two hundred pages of updated sheets in time to have a new list in the hands of most subscribers at the start of business the next day. From the sheets and other information, the National Association of Securities Dealers would prepare a selected list of quotations for newspaper publication.

While the system represented great cleverness, it had serious short-comings nevertheless. The quotations were current only at the start of the day, and there was no indication of volume. Qualification for inclusion of a market maker or his quotations in the sheets was determined by the publisher. And while he sought determinedly to protect the integrity and value of his property, he lacked investigatory powers and the system was occasionally susceptible to abuse.

Apart from the quotations published in the newspapers, an investor had no information about an over-the-counter issue—price, spread, number of market makers, or activity—except what he could obtain from his broker. This meant he had no independent criteria for judging whether his broker was doing his job in getting him the best possible markets. At the same time, the lack of up-to-the-minute information made policing by the NASD difficult.

Automation offers great hope for overcoming these difficulties. Eventually, it is hoped, the Nasdaq system now in operation will be extended to perhaps twenty thousand issues, all over-the-counter stocks in which there is a continuing market.

The Nasdaq system operates at three levels: of brokerage house salesman or registered representative, retail order taker, and market maker. By punching a few keys on his deskside electronic visual display stock quotation machine—the familiar Quotron, Telequote, or Stockmaster device—a customer's man obtains the middle-range, or median, bid and asked price prevailing at the moment for an over-the counter stock, much as punching other keys would produce the last sale price for a listed issue.

From a somewhat different visual display device, a retail order taker obtains the same representative bid and asked price prevailing at the moment. In addition, however, if he is buying for a customer, market makers and their quotations are set before him on the screen, ranked in ascending order of asked prices from lowest to highest. If he is selling, market makers are ranked in descending order of bid prices from highest to lowest.*

A market maker uses a device similar to that of a retail order taker. But in addition, by pressing a key, he is able to raise or lower his quota-

* In mid-1971, there were 500 Nasdaq market makers with 16,500 market positions, or an average of six for each issue. A typical Nasdaq-displayed issue had no fewer than three market makers.

tions instantaneously by one-eighth of a point, automatically repositioning himself in the electronic display.

The system, reputed to be the largest private information retrieval system ever built, has many advantages. Market makers don't have to answer the nine calls in ten intended solely to obtain information, and retail order takers don't have to make several calls to obtain the best market every time they execute a routine order for a hundred shares. Registered representatives have at their fingertips, for the first time, instantaneous representative bid and asked prices on a large list of over-the-counter securities, and investors aren't plagued with delays in obtaining current price information on over-the-counter stocks.

While the number and identity of market makers remains information available only to the trade, newspaper lists of over-the-counter stocks for the first time carry volume information as well as representative bid and asked prices. And in the future an over-the-counter tape, showing changes in quotations as they occur, may even be instituted.

The system is subject to careful regulation by the NASD. Member firms must meet certain capital requirements and must apply to and be approved for each security in which they wish to make a market. A registered market maker must continually maintain a net capital position of $50,000 or a net capital position of $5,000 for each security in which it is registered as a market maker, whichever is less. A registered market maker must maintain a two-sided market, both on the bid side and the asked side, at all times in all securities in which he makes a market, except that he may withdraw under unusual circumstances. Quotations are expected to be firm for at least one hundred shares, and a pattern of continued backing away is grounds for NASD disciplinary action.

Several conclusions are obvious. More and better information should increase the possibilities of over-the-counter market surveillance and policing, better information and better supervision should improve the market's reputation, and these in turn should add to the growth and acceptance of the OTC.

18. Intermarket Competition

Competition has grown greatly among the exchanges, and between the exchanges and the over-the-counter market, largely because of the rapid rise of institutional shareholding and trading. At the same time brokerage houses—a number of which operate in all markets —have been plagued with problems. Rising retail volume outdistanced some firms' ability to service their customers, creating a paperwork tangle and sapping their profits, and inadequate capital made it difficult for them to weather downturns in share prices and volume. The result has been a massive restructuring of the securities industry, one that may not be over.

The two matters are not unconnected. The structural form the market is permitted to take will affect greatly the value, say, of a membership on the Big Board against one on the Midwest or Pacific Coast exchanges, or of operating in the over-the-counter market with no exchange franchise whatsoever. On the other hand, demonstration of greater efficiency by one market than another should have much to say about the competitive outcome.

Not too many years ago, the Big Board in effect had the only game in town. The regional exchanges, limited largely to local issues of minor investor interest, were losing the small share of the market they then held. The Amex and the over-the-counter market enjoyed a questionable reputation as places where hot issues were traded, where oversight was minimal, and where the guardians of the public interest occasionally dealt themselves in on the action.

In those halcyon days for the New York Stock Exchange, if a share buyer wanted a sound investment—the kind of stock he could rely on to put a son through college—he was required to look to a Big

Board-listed issue, and to get it he had to deal with a Big Board member firm.

There were exceptions, of course. The Amex and the over-the-counter market traded a few blue-chip industrials which, largely because of the more restrictive listing requirements there, remained off the Big Board. The markets for insurance stocks and bank shares, which attracted little interest among individual investors, stayed over-the-counter.

All this, however, was before the great growth of institutional shareholding and trading, and before the development of sophisticated communications made it possible to link one market readily to another. At the beginning of the 1960s institutional trading amounted to no more than one-quarter of the dollar value of all public trading on the New York Stock Exchange. A decade later, it had risen to well over one-half.

Today the Big Board still accounts for two-thirds of all the shares sold on national exchanges and for more than four-fifths of the dollar value of trading. But it is encountering growing competition from regional exchanges, which have merged into stronger units, admitted Big Board and Amex issues to their own lists, and through rebates and institutional membership offered cut-rate access to Big Board and Amex markets. It is encountering competition also from the over-the-counter market, where a small fraternity of dealers has arisen to compete for institutional orders in the shares of Big Board- and Amex-listed companies.

How significant this trend has become is attested to in figures produced by the New York Stock Exchange. As recently as 1967 the regional exchanges and the third market—the name given to over-the-counter trading in listed stocks—accounted for just over 10 percent of all trading in Big Board issues. Three years later they accounted for almost 20 percent. One of the regional exchanges had trebled its market share in two years, principally because of large institutional transactions. And the Big Board estimated that it had lost a significant share of institutional block trades, perhaps 35 to 45 percent of those orders of ten thousand shares or more being traded away from its floor.

There was no question that the growth of institutional trading had created a challenge not only to the New York Stock Exchange but to the specialist-centered system of trading shares in continuous auction markets. The institutions deal in large blocks, thousands of shares at a time, and demand fast service, prompt execution or orders to buy and orders to sell. This has put an increasing strain on the specialist system. Huge offerings without correspondingly large bids, and vice versa, create giant mismatches, ones no single specialist might be expected to absorb.

The Big Board made mighty efforts to overcome the inadequacies of the system, permitting member firms other than the specialist to take positions in large blocks when he is unable to do so, utilizing their capital and risk capacity to support those block positions. It also encouraged firms specializing in institutional orders to develop expertise in lining up both sides of a trade, utilizing their intimate knowledge of the portfolio holdings and interests of institutions to effect such two-sided transactions, or crosses, quickly, confidentially, and with minimum upset to the market. It even developed a computer network to facilitate such transactions.

It acceded in 1968 to a volume discount in its commission rate structure, hoping to end reciprocal practices Robert Haack, Big Board president, later was to term "mazes of blatant gimmickry" and a threat not only to the central marketplace but to the "entire moral fabric" of the securities industry. The volume discount, plus a Securities and Exchange Commission regulation, eliminated the customer-directed give-up, which was a practice whereby member firms, in executing orders on the New York Stock Exchange, gave up part of their commissions to other broker-dealers to pay for such things as research or mutual fund sales.

Reciprocity, however, quickly took other forms. Big Board member firms stepped up the practice of splitting commissions with members of regional exchanges, while the institutions themselves hurried to stake out memberships on the regional exchanges. Big Board members with no direct stake in the survival of the exchange as an institution found themselves enjoying the best of both worlds. They were able to exact the fixed minimum Big Board commission from customers who brought business to them, while at the same time they were able to meet the competition for institutional business by negotiating deals on regional exchanges, either directly with institutional members or indirectly through other regional members. They were protected from third-market competition, however, by Big Board rules (394 and 394[b]) that restricted members from making price inquiries freely outside the exchange. They were protected also by a ruling of the National Association of Securities Dealers, which eliminated third-market quotations on listed stocks from display in its automated quotations system, until NASD, under pressure of a court suit, approved the experimental display of thirty Big Board issues on Nasdaq, then extended the experiment to include all third-market issues.

Third-market dealers, naturally, saw such exclusion in none too kindly a light. Some were large and heavily capitalized firms that had effectively been barred from exchange membership because of the Big Board prohibition against publicly owned firms becoming members. Others, like the bank stock dealers, had enjoyed the entire market for a group of issues until Big Board listings cut into their domain. Now they found themselves cut off, in effect, from exchange members with whom they used to deal. An antitrust challenge to the NASD action, alleging Big Board domination, was begun in the courts.

The case seemed likely to open the door to other issues. In 1941 the Securities and Exchange Commission had affirmed the right of Big Board members to trade on regional exchanges, asserting that it was the intent of Congress to foster intermarket competition "to allow each type of market to develop in accordance with its natural genius and consistent with the public interest." In 1970 the Justice Department submitted a brief to the SEC asserting its belief that the same principle dictated that members should be free to obtain price information and execute trades off the board.

For its part, the New York Stock Exchange cited other legal chapter and verse in support of its claim that under the Securities Act of 1934 it was under mandate of Congress to set commission rates and that its fixed minimum commission schedule was a proper exercise of that responsibility.

Apart from legality, the Big Board finds no ethical reason to back away from its stand. The exchange's rules make the Big Board what it is. And, in the words of Robert Haack:

There is no other market which is so highly regulated, which discloses its activities so promptly, which oversees its members so closely, which sets such high standards on the calibre of issues traded, which monitors not only its members but its listed companies, which promptly disseminates price data and which provides depth, liquidity and continuity to the same extent to buyers and sellers of securities.*

In fact, in the Big Board's view one of the ways the "natural genius" of competing markets has been permitted to reveal itself is in competition over standards of regulation, although this is scarcely in the public interest. In Mr. Haack's words again:

It makes little sense for the New York Stock Exchange to enforce rules against short sales in a declining market when there is no such prohibition in the third market. It is self-defeating regulation to permit customers to short stock in the third market without so stating and then to permit that stock to be resold as long stock in our marketplace. Additionally, the rules of the New York Stock Exchange governing the trading of specialists and floor traders have no parallel in the over-the-counter market. Off-board trades are permitted by regional exchanges under less restrictive rules than ours. Unhappily, we have found that our prompt disclosure of price and volume data, which has no counterpart in any other market, redounds to our detriment. Some traders deliberately instruct brokers to execute orders on regional

* Speech to the Economic Club of New York, Nov. 17, 1970.

exchanges or take their business to the third market in order to conceal their activity from the public view.*

Be that as it may, to avoid unfavorable antitrust implications the Big Board may be forced to give nonmember broker-dealers—regional and third-market traders equally—access to its facilities at a discount from the full public commission. And it may be forced to abandon fixed minimum commissions, permitting member firms to negotiate commissions directly at least with institutional customers, and permitting customers who do not require such services as investment advice and research to avoid paying for them.

The problem of intermarket competition would be more readily susceptible to solution if there were not a continuing conflict between the exchange's floor members, who have a vested interest in continuing things as they are, and its "upstairs" members, who have felt the pinch of rising costs of doing a public business against less rapidly rising revenues. This conflict results in paradoxes. It would be demeaning and inaccurate to say that floor members are unaware of their interest in preserving the exchange system and the role that efficiency plays in preserving it. Not unnaturally, however, some are reluctant to vote for greater efficiency if it means elimination of their own functions. At the moment, for instance, the technology exists to automate much of what now goes on on the exchange floor. The specialist would still be needed to exercise judgment, to put his money where his mouth is, but commission brokers and most of the other people now working so hard on the exchange floor could be called redundant.† But since these people exercise a sizable number of votes in exchange deliberations, it is questionable whether the number needed for approval could be obtained—if the matter could be brought to a vote.

By the same token, the large brokerage houses that pay for exchange services—but who don't necessarily control the votes of their floor members—must be aware of the fact that rising commission rates induce customers to sit on their shares, reducing the volume of active trading. Thus, if commissions are reduced for large-block transactions but increased for smaller ones, the public will probably be driven further from direct participation in the market and the effects of institutionalization should be felt even more. Nevertheless, the need for revenues being what it is, the big member firms often see no way out except to plump

* Ibid.
† If anyone could buy 100 shares of American Telephone at 45, for example, who would need a broker to make what is essentially a routine trade? The situation would be different, of course, if the trade involved 10,000 or 100,000 shares and either a buyer or a seller had to be found.

for increased commissions in the only segment of their market that can be forced to accept them, notably small transactions.

The bloodbath the securities industry went through in 1969 and 1970 did much to color its thinking. In two years the industry was pushed through a financial wringer exceeding in some respects the distress of the 1930s. More than a hundred Big Board member firms disappeared either through merger, dissolution, or outright liquidation, and hundreds of brokerage house offices across the United States were shut down or consolidated with other facilities. Unknown amounts of capital fled the industry in search of greater safety and more certain return.

The immediate cause of Wall Street's difficulties was the decline in share prices that began in December 1968 and by May 1970 had carried the market to its lowest level in eight years. In contrast to earlier postwar declines, in which the market had declined for fairly short periods of time and then bounced back, the drop was the most severe and, more important, the most prolonged since the 1930s. The extent of the decline was important because it meant a drying up of transactions, the turnover out of which brokerage houses generate commission revenues and profits.

If the proximate cause of the securities industry's trauma was the eighteen-month decline in share prices, the root cause lay in the long bull market that began immediately after World War II. After the long drought of the depression and war years, the industry embarked on an extensive advertising and promotional program to bring an estranged public back into the market, a campaign epitomized by a slogan made popular by G. Keith Funston, former Big Board president, "Own Your Share of American Business." As a result, the number of member firms, brokerage house offices, and salesmen—or "registered representatives," as they came to be called—mushroomed.

With the great emphasis on sales, back-office operations, or the paperwork processing, tended to be neglected. One study showed that between 1950 and 1968 the number of registered representatives rose 335 percent, compared with an overall personnel increase of 223 percent. This would have been acceptable, indeed desirable, had the decline in back-office personnel the study indicated reflected the growing use of automated processes. But in many brokerage houses back-office procedures, seldom seen by the public, remained reminiscent of Dickens. Clerks in shirtsleeves or smocks sat at desks, thumbing manually through stacks of stock certificates, performing many functions with pencil or pen.

The efficiency of the system, or its lack, was revealed dramatically in the rate of "fails," or failures to complete transactions through the delivery of certificates. By December 1968, on the eve of the market's lengthy downturn, fails had risen to an astronomical $4.1 billion. There was irony in the fact that many of the fails resulted from over-the-counter trades, but the simple fact was that the industry had sold more services than it had been able to deliver. One source, not challenged, estimated that it was costing the industry $100 million a year to correct its mistakes.

This was a price, it soon became evident, that Wall Street could not afford to pay. The decline in share prices and volume brought temporary respite from the paperwork tangle, but it did nothing to improve profitability. In fact, the decline in revenues was swifter than the decline in costs, forcing most firms, even the more profitable, to operate for a time in the red.

If the lengthy market decline created difficulties for the more efficient firms, it spelled disaster for the others. First one brokerage house, then another, then a whole string of houses were forced to close their doors, some through liquidation, others through merger with houses less sorely pressed. The anguish exhausted the exchange's $75 million emergency fund, which had been created to guarantee investors against losses in case of brokerage-house failures, and forced the industry to turn to Congress for aid. The result was the creation of the Securities Investor Protection Corporation, through which the industry will receive assistance from the Treasury if it again exhausts its own funds and additional funds the Treasury tap will permit it to borrow from banks and other lenders.

The industry's problems centered in profitability and remain there, but they were greatly exacerbated by New York Stock Exchange rules governing the capital of member firms. For years the Big Board insisted that only individual proprietors or partners of brokerage houses be permitted to hold seats on the exchange. Corporations were barred from membership.

Even after corporations were permitted to become Big Board members, those whose shares were traded publicly were still kept outside until a small but influential member firm, Donaldson, Lufkin and Jenrette, Inc., threatened to quit unless it was permitted to raise capital through a public offering of shares. Faced with this loss, the exchange once again altered its rules, opening the door to public share offerings by many of the large member firms.

For years the industry had no need for public financing. So long as its customers were mainly small, there was no pressure on it to hold down commission rates and, so long as the Big Board was, in effect, the only game in town, there was no necessity. But while Big Board rules prevented brokerage houses from raising capital through the public sale of securities, the kind of financing the houses helped make available in vast amounts to most other businesses, they did permit other, highly questionable, practices. Member firms were allowed to use borrowed money up to twenty times their capital and were permitted to use marketable securities as part of their capital base as well.

When stock prices went down, then, some firms found themselves in a two-way capital squeeze. The decline in share values reduced their capital base, and this in turn pulled down the amount of borrowed funds they were able to utilize. Exchange rules required that securities included as part of a firm's capital be given a "haircut," or discounted, from face value. But the decline in share value often was greater than the amount of the haircut, and, when this was so, the multiplier effects could be considerable.

One large concern that was subsequently forced into a shotgun wedding with a more stable house entered the steepest part of the 1970 market decline with a portfolio of securities valued at $17.5 million for use as capital. It was required to apply a 30 percent haircut, trimming the allowable value of the securities to $12.3 million. Within two months the value of the securities for capital purposes had shrunk to $6.7 million, and soon thereafter shares that had contributed $3 million to the original total were suspended from trading, later to be declared worthless. For each one-dollar shrinkage in its capital base, moreover, the brokerage house suffered a shrinkage of several dollars in the borrowed funds it was permitted to use as capital, multiplying its problems. This was a situation not unlike that of one of the house's own margin account customers in a declining market, the difference being that no customer would have been permitted to borrow on so thin an equity.

If this were not enough, much of the industry's capital other than securities was transient, that is, it was borrowed from wealthy individuals under subordinated loan agreements that permitted it to be withdrawn on as little as thirty days' notice. Clearly, the New York Stock Exchange, which had concerned itself so much with the strength of the companies in its listing, had not concerned itself enough with the strength of its own members. Reform of the exchange's capital rules seemed certain. The pressure on costs seemed likely to continue, especially if negotiated commissions became widespread. One possibility that suggested itself to members of the industry was merger of all the exchanges into a single national exchange, the same advances in computer technology that made it possible to eliminate most people other than the specialist from the exchange floor making it possible for specialists in different physical locations to compete actively with each other. A prototype of such a system even existed, in the Pacific Coast Exchange's Comex system.

Through Comex, the dozen or more oral and manual steps previously required to transmit, execute, and report on an order were reduced to a single teletype entry by a trained order clerk. Member firms utilizing the system were able to direct orders to either of the Pacific Coast Exchange's two trading floors, in San Francisco and Los Angeles. Specialists in the two cities already competed with each other.

The creation of a giant nationwide stock exchange with separate trading floors in various cities had an obvious advantage, the elimination of duplicative overhead, which applied particularly to areas of regulation, oversight, and surveillance. It had a less obvious disadvantage, the creation once again of a single game in town, possibly to the public's disadvantage.

Revival of the stock market after its eighteen-month decline seemed likely to remove some of the urgency for solving the industry's problems. But it did not seem likely to make them go away.

19. Regulating Securities
Markets: the SEC

Regulation of the securities industry is split between the federal government and the industry itself. Before the 1929 market crash there was no federal regulation. The public interest, to the degree that anyone paid attention to it all, was the ward of the industry and of the several states. And it was treated as an orphan.

The history of the stock market had been synonymous with manipulation. Wash sales, corners, bull and bear raids, rumor, deceit, and fraud were commonplace from the days of Vanderbilt, Drew, Fisk, and Gould. But the great bull market of the 1920s, associated with jazz, bathtub gin, and F. Scott Fitzgerald, would not have been possible except for two things: the public involvement in the market and the noninvolvement of government.

The huge demand for capital produced by World War I brought the general public into the securities markets for the first time. Inducing people to surrender their savings for marketable securities, the Liberty Bonds that fell in price soon after the war, was a giant step. Putting them into a rising stock market in the years that followed was much less of one.

The creation of the Federal Reserve System had shifted the money-creating power from Wall Street to Washington, but it was to be twenty years or more before the significance of this fact was appreciated. Washington made no move to control the speculative bubble that was rising in New York. And the Federal Reserve, which could have acted on its own, found international demands more pressing. So it first eased, then tightened money, giving force to the boom and to the depression that followed.

In the Street itself, the scene was almost bacchanalian. The lure of available credit—margin requirements customarily were only 20 percent —brought clerks, stenographers, and taxicab drivers into the market. Acting on tips or snatches of overheard conversation, they were able to jump in on a shoestring and, occasionally, run up fortunes. The successes were frequent enough and big enough to bring others running after them. Businessmen and the banks that financed them found the attractions of the call money market—overnight loans to brokers—more seductive than the profits to be made manufacturing and selling products.

The successes resulted in part from the great holding companies and trusts into which Samuel Insull, the Van Sweringen brothers, Ivar Kreuger and others pyramided electric utilities, railroads, and industrial and financial concerns. The pyramiders owned a controlling block of shares in the top company, which in turn held control of the company immediately below it, and so on down. At the operating company level, their ownership often was infinitesimal. The holding companies employed generous infusions of debt capital at every level, causing earnings per share at the top to multiply, but only so long as sales and earnings at the bottom continued to rise. Like all such schemes that rely heavily on leverage, the difficulties grew as much or more when business began to sag.

In the anything-goes atmosphere of the era, Wall Street trotted out all the old kinds of chicanery and added a few more. The pool, perhaps, was the most notable of the new additions. In 1929, 107 issues listed on the New York Stock Exchange were subject to pool operations. The names read like a Who's Who: American Tobacco, Chrysler, Curtiss-Wright, Goodrich, Montgomery Ward, National Cash Register, Packard, Radio Corporation of America, Standard Oil (California), Studebaker, and Union Carbide, among others. The RCA pool, the biggest, netted for its seventy participants a profit of $4,900,000. The Sinclair Oil pool, although smaller in numbers, turned in a profit of $12,618,000.

The pool was simply a group effort to manipulate prices, much as individuals had done in the past. Its inspiration may have come from the underwriting syndicates, which had emerged early in the decade because of the inability or unwillingness of individual underwriters to tackle the much larger capital offerings of the postwar era. Some pools were put together informally, while others involved complex and detailed contracts. Typically, a pool sought to stabilize or bring down prices while members of the syndicate climbed aboard. Then, in a coordinated program of purchases and sales, it sought to drive prices up in a manner calculated to bring in the public. Getting out took great skill, but this was usually accomplished with simultaneous short sales, with the result that the pool profited both from the rise in prices it induced and the collapse that followed after it unloaded.

A pool depended on the collusion of corporate insiders. Their cooperation was essential because opposition from the officers or directors of a corporation would have exposed the pool for what it was, an attempt to defraud the public. The insiders also supplied information to start and keep the rumor mills grinding, and they often provided options to pool members to buy shares at prices set before the operation began.

The specialist in the issue on the floor of the exchange was also a key man. Because of his privileged position, he could help push the price of the issue in the direction the pool wanted. No less important were the paid publicity experts, and the friendly newspaper men and broadcasters whose help they enlisted. These and the market-letter writers for the firms that participated in the pool helped generate the public enthusiasm necessary to the undertaking. Their reward, usually, was a piece of the action.

By far the most important means of bringing in the public, however, was "painting the tape," the pool's own buying and selling, which gave an impression of busy and steadily rising market activity. Thousands of transactions, at different prices and for varying amounts of stock, would move back and forth through the market in quantities even a not unsophisticated public might find hard to comprehend. In five days of operation, for instance, the RCA pool bought almost 1 million shares and sold 1.2 million.

Such things would be no more than a chapter in America's colorful past were it not for the influence they exerted on Congress in the years that followed. Soon after Franklin Roosevelt's election as President, Ferdinand Pecora was appointed counsel to a Senate Banking subcommittee that had begun looking into what had gone on. For two years, in testimony that filled twelve hundred pages, the story was told. And it was not pretty at all.

The first result, less than three months after the new President was inaugurated, was enactment of the Securities Act of 1933, which was quickly dubbed the "truth in securities" law. Stating that underwriters of new securities issues would henceforth be obliged to disclose all material information to would-be subscribers, the act was founded in the belief that if the facts were known investors would no longer rush to buy the flotations of profitless companies or offerings in which the underwriters skimmed off all the cream.

The 1933 act, however, was only the beginning. Soon afterward Congress passed the Glass-Steagall Act, establishing the Federal Deposit Insurance Corporation and divorcing investment banking from commercial banking. And a little over a year later it added the Securities and Exchange Act of 1934, extending the "truth in securities" notion to outstanding as well as newly issued securities, and placing the nation's securities markets as well as their brokers and dealers under federal regulation.

The 1934 act also established a new independent agency, the Securities and Exchange Commission, with five members appointed by the President. It had been expected that James Landis of the Federal Trade Commission, who had been administering the 1933 act, or possibly Judge Pecora would be named the first chairman. But Roosevelt surprised Wall Street and confounded some of his liberal followers by appointing Joseph P. Kennedy, later the father of a President. Kennedy was remembered in Wall Street as a bold and ruthless plunger whose activities in RKO Pictures and Libbey-Owens-Ford won him the respect if not the endearment of his fellows. Kennedy did what was expected of him. He got the SEC launched. And he obtained the Street's participation, if not its active cooperation, in the process of regulation that was to evolve. Others were to follow, notably Landis and William O. Douglas, who would advance the reach of administrative law. But it was Kennedy who ended the threat of an industry boycott, paving the way for the pattern of government-industry sharing of regulatory responsibility that continues to this day.

The two acts bear examination in greater detail. They require that all publicly issued securities, except certain exempt ones, be registered. The acts and later amendments automatically exempt government securities; federal agency securities; the securities of state and local governments; bank, insurance company, and mutual fund shares, and certain other securities. In addition, they give power to the SEC to exercise its discretion in granting exemption to small issues.

Registered securities can be sold only after a prospective buyer has received an approved prospectus. In it, the issuer has to set forth the terms of the offering and detailed information concerning the company's history and plans, including balance sheets and income statements for three previous years, the effect of the new offering on the company's capital structure, the names of insiders (officers, directors, and holders of 10 percent or more of the company's stock), their remuneration from all company sources, their holdings of the company shares, financial opportunities and privileges they may enjoy, and other material information. Although the SEC will not permit an issue to be sold without its approving the prospectus, the burden of determining what is material remains with the issuer, and any omission may give the SEC cause for action.

An issuer must observe a waiting period—no fewer than twenty days, unless the SEC permits the process to be accelerated—between the time he files for registration and approval, and he must avoid any public communication that goes beyond what appears in the prospectus. In newspaper advertising he is limited to a bare announcement setting forth the nature of the offering, its terms, and the fact that a prospectus is available. (Because of its resemblance to the inscription on a grave marker, such an advertisement is known as a "tombstone.") Upon request, however, he may provide a preliminary prospectus containing all the information set forth in the document filed with the SEC except the final terms and things, like underwriters' discounts, affected by them. (Because of a cautionary warning printed in red, this is known as a "red herring.")

Information similar to that required in a new offering prospectus is required every time an exchange-listed or over-the-counter registered company makes a proxy solicitation. In addition, among other things such companies are required to file annual financial statements with the SEC and monthly reports concerning changes in insider shareholdings.

All national securities exchanges and recognized associations of over-the-counter dealers similarly must file registration statements, setting forth their constitutions, bylaws, rules, and membership, all of which must meet SEC approval. An exchange is thus obliged to initiate changes in its rules, such, for instance, as the code of ethics governing members' behavior. But the SEC may disapprove if it finds the changes unacceptable.

Wash sales, matched orders, and other kinds of artificial market activity are specifically barred, as is the dissemination of news about manipulative activities and rumor spreading to aid them. Certain other activities, not specifically prohibited but brought under SEC control, include price stabilization; trading in puts, calls, and other options; short sales; and stop orders.

Exchange members and registered over-the-counter dealers may not perform as broker, or customer's agent, and dealer, selling from his own inventory, in the same transaction. The SEC is given the right to prevent excessive trading on or off the floor, and it may require specific registration of certain floor members, such as specialists, odd-lot dealers, and registered traders (formerly floor traders). Specialists, for instance, are restricted to maintaining a fair and orderly market. They may disclose their books only under certain conditions, and, when acting as brokers, they may accept limit orders only.

Insiders may not profit from short-term trades, or trades of less than six months, in their company's stock. They are also barred from selling their company's stock short.

The SEC may make rules, undertake investigations, and help judicial proceedings. It may require that books and records be provided, and request a change in rules of an exchange or recognized over-the-counter dealers association. It may suspend trading in a particular security and suspend or withdraw the registration of an exchange or off-board association or of one of its officers or members. It may also seek an injunction or obtain a writ of mandamus to obtain compliance with its orders.

The 1933 and 1934 acts said nothing about the over-the-counter market, mutual funds, or investment advisers. A 1936 amendment extended the jurisdiction of the SEC to the over-the-counter market, and two years later the so-called Maloney Act gave quasi-official status to the National Association of Securities Dealers, the self-policing organization for the over-the-counter market. The Investment Company Act of 1940 outlawed investment company pyramiding and set detailed standards governing the creation and operation of mutual funds, and the Investment Advisers Act of the same year established rules of behavior for people who accept fees for market advice.

These basic laws, and later amendments, gave primary responsibility to the exchanges and the NASD for the qualification and behavior of listed and OTC-registered companies and for the qualification and behavior of their members as well. How has this government-industry sharing of responsibility worked?

Initially, it didn't work at all. Wall Street had been prepared to accept a "truth in securities" law, but it didn't think regulation of the exchanges was desirable or necessary. Even the appointment of the elder Kennedy as the first head of the SEC didn't end the antagonism—but then something wholly unexpected did change things. Richard Whitney, a blue blood and six times president of the exchange, was caught with his hand in the till, and Wall Street was forced to surrender. For the remainder of the thirties the SEC kept occupied helping Congress flesh out the new laws and building a staff and a body of administrative law. In New Deal Washington the agency came to be recognized by bright young lawyers as one of the desirable places to launch a career.

The basic purpose of the securities acts, restoring confidence in the capital markets and winning back the disenchanted, however, was not to be fulfilled until after World War II—and then, possibly, it was fulfilled too well. In sending up the 1933 act to Congress, Franklin Roosevelt had said it was his purpose to substitute for *caveat emptor,* "Let the buyer beware," the adage that had ruled the securities markets since their founding, a new motto, "Let the seller beware." As postwar incomes and savings fattened, the public trooped back to the market, lulled by the belief that the promise had become reality. Under the stimulus of rising share prices, public ownership broadened and mutual fund sales rose.

Some of those who returned to the market were sympathetic undoubtedly to the promotional urging of the New York Stock Exchange to "own a share in America." But others saw the end of the long drought on Wall Street as an opportunity to profit again as they had in bygone days, and, as the early glow of the Eisenhower years faded, the action seekers moved from the blue chips to the low-priced issues. Volume on the Amex and in the over-the-counter market swelled. In the bull market revival that followed the election as President of Joseph Kennedy's son John, the interest turned to hot new issues. As they had for almost thirty years, the prospectuses for every new offering carried the familiar words: "These securities have not been approved or disapproved by the Securities and Exchange Commission nor has the commission passed upon the accuracy or adequacy of this prospectus. Any representation to the contrary is a criminal offense." Nevertheless, buyers rushed to snap up offerings of companies whose assets were little more than names suggesting technology or electronics. Often these companies had no earnings or even a string of losses. In a favorite joke, a hard-pressed businessman queried his partner: "Should we go bankrupt or should we go public?"

For most of the forties and fifties, the SEC had been starved for funds and forced to operate on past momentum. It had been assumed, however, that the exchanges had been filling the gap, an assumption that soon proved false. Not long after the new President took office, SEC investigators discovered that for six years a firm of specialists on the Amex, headed by the father-son team of Gerard A. and Gerard F. Re, had systematically unloaded thousands of shares of stock on the public at rigged prices. Much of the stock had not even been registered. The scandal brought an SEC investigation of the Amex and a shake-up of its top management. This in turn led Congress to order a full-scale special study by the SEC staff of the adequacy of securities industry regulation, the first since the federal government had asumed the responsibility almost thirty years before.

For almost two years a team of lawyers, economists, and financial analysts, some from the SEC and some from outside, labored. Their product was a fifteen-volume, fifteen-pound report containing 2 million words and many charts, tables, and appendixes. It found, among many other things, that often the principals of members firms were inexperienced, securities salesmen were unqualified, supervision of salesmen was lax, research was deceptive or nonexistent, and customers' funds were poorly protected. In all, the report made 175 recommendations.

The results were not inconsequential. Congress in 1964 extended to companies with shares publicly traded in the over-the-counter market the disclosure and other requirements that had previously applied only to listed concerns. The SEC required floor traders to register, to observe minimal capital requirements, and to assist in helping to stabilize the market. It prodded the exchanges and the NASD to improve the training and examination of newcomers to the industry, both principals and their salesmen.

Much of the improvement was undertaken voluntarily by the exchanges and the NASD. Listing requirements were upped, disclosure rules tightened, and surveillance improved. The Amex, in particular, sought to assure itself that its listings held more than local interest and were not unduly affected by institutional holdings. The computer was enlisted to detect and pinpoint unusual speculative activity. Special margin requirements, ranging up to 100 percent, were slapped on issues suspected of being used in speculative manipulations.

More recently, the SEC has taken giant steps to increase the risk of profiting from inside information. The Texas Gulf Sulphur case made it clear that getting caught could be costly to company officers and directors, and the Merrill Lynch case emphasized that the dangers extended beyond the company executive suite to Wall Street professionals with access to privileged information. Texas Gulf officials passed news of a Canadian mining discovery by the company to associates, permitting them to buy shares before the news reached the public, while Merrill Lynch gave unfavorable information about the Douglas Aircraft Company to selected institutional customers, permitting them to sell their shares before the news became public. The SEC has also gone far in stressing the responsibility of executives of member firms for the failings of their subordinates.

If the SEC gets good marks on some tests, it gets bad marks on others. The Ira Haupt case caught it and the Big Board flat-footed. Ira Haupt, a Big Board member firm, went bankrupt in 1963 after extending credit to a big commodities customer who defaulted, largely as a result of fraudulent acts. Apparently no one had considered the possibility that a member firm's activities in the commodity markets could endanger the funds of its securities customers. Despite the warnings of its own special study, however, the SEC did nothing to require exchange members to strengthen their capital positions, create reserves, and segregate customer cash, with the result that, half a dozen years later, under somewhat different conditions, the SEC and the Big Board were facing the same problem again. It should also be noted here that the SEC did little to help the Commodity Exchange Authority gain increased power from Congress to cope with problems like those leading to the demise of Ira Haupt and Company.

In the runaway market of 1967 and 1968, the SEC was unable to come up with any feasible solution to the problems caused by the conglomerates, the performance funds, and—once again—by hot new issues. Even more important, it semed to approach the whole issue of intermarket competition—with its related questions of negotiated commissions, institutional membership, and public ownership—as if it were a bad dream. The world of the thirties, with all of its difficulties, was the way the SEC seemed to like it. If there was only one game in town then, there were many participants, none of them big enough to exercise any significant control, and little need, therefore, to worry much about utility-type regulation. Indeed, as late as 1965 William L. Cary, the former SEC chairman who presided over the special study, could exult in the fact that the "SEC does not bestow grants of immense value: airline routes or television licenses."

But this was changing. Giant buyers and giant sellers were emerging, and this was disturbing the comfortable patterns of the past. Wall Street was moving out of a Seventh Avenue kind of world into a General Motors–Ford–Chrysler kind of existence, so whatever the SEC did was likely to affect the competitive balance. Like it or not, the SEC seemed headed for a new kind of regulatory role.

20. Mutual Funds

Mutual funds have grown rapidly, posing questions for their operators and customers, for the markets they trade in, and for their regulators.

Mutual funds are open-end investment companies that accept the savings of people with similar investment goals—growth, income, or safety of principal—and, under professional investment management, channel them into a wide variety of securities. In contrast to closed-end investment companies, they have no fixed number of shares. And because a mutual fund issues and redeems its shares continuously, the shares have no independent value of their own but reflect entirely the underlying value of the securities in the fund's portfolio.

The great bulk of mutual fund holdings are in common stocks. For most buyers, therefore, mutual funds answer the question, "What stocks should I buy?" They also help avoid the risk that arises from putting too many eggs in one basket. A fund may spread its holding over fifty or a hundred different issues, all calculated to produce a similar investment result.

Mutual funds, of course, do nothing to lessen the risk of share investment in general, the fact that stock prices go down as well as up, and do little to help investors answer a question equally as important as what shares to buy: "When should I buy?" Some people use funds, much as they might the stocks of individual companies, as a vehicle for dollar averaging. That is, they invest fixed sums at regular intervals, say, a hundred dollars once a month, obtaining more shares when prices go down and fewer shares when prices go up. In this way they avoid deciding when stock prices are too high to buy or too low to sell. Most funds offer investors the opportunity to reinvest dividends automatically, helping them to avoid another kind of timing decision. And through programs permitting the withdrawal of fixed sums at regular intervals, they help investors dollar-average out if they choose, avoiding still another.

There is little, however, to prevent people of a more adventuresome nature from using funds as a speculative vehicle, buying low and selling high, or even for realizing short-term trading profits. This is especially true for funds that place a low sales charge, or load, on large new investments and those that make no sales charge at all, the so-called no-load funds.

If mutual fund investment helps a share buyer diversify his holdings and avoid the question of stock selection, it raises a new question of comparable perplexity, "Which fund should I choose?" No one, of course, should buy securities at all unless he has enough cash savings to cover his most pressing needs and sufficient insurance to guard his family against the unexpected. Then his investment program should be tailored to his age, his obligations, and his temperament. A retired couple, for instance, is usually far more interested in income and safety of principal than in growth of an investment. A young couple just starting their married life, on the other hand, is usually interested in exactly the opposite. Funds offering a portfolio of lesser-risk stocks, and possibly of some fixed-interest obligations, would meet the objective of income and safety. Those offering a portfolio of higher-risk stocks would meet the objective of growth.

Among funds with the same investment objective, however, performance may vary greatly. Performance is measured usually by change in net asset value per share. After the close of the stock market each day, a fund obtains the closing price of each of the issues in its portfolio, multiples the price by the number of shares of each issue it holds, then divides the total by the number of its own shares outstanding. This is its net asset value per share. (New funds received during the day are divided by this net asset value per share to determine the number of additional shares and share fractions each buyer will receive. Share redemptions are handled in the same way. When the total of new shares bought or redeemed is known, it is combined with the total outstanding to create a new figure for use in the following day's calculation of net asset value per share.)

From an investor's point of view, successful performance means the ability of a fund to show growth in net asset value equal to or better than that of funds of similar risk and investment objectives. Statistical organizations, such as Weisenberger Services Inc., and Arthur J. Lipper, and publications such as *Fundscope* and *Forbes* magazines, measure mutual fund performance regularly, some at frequent intervals, others less frequently. Knowledgeable investors look for consistency of performance over three, five, or even ten years, and look as well for average performance or better in down markets as well as up.

But since all this is merely past performance, and no assurance that what happens in the future will match what has happened before, sophisticated investors give attention to a number of other things, in their attempt to determine whether a fund will equal or exceed in the future what it has done in the past. How big is it? How great is its portfolio turnover? How steady is the flow of funds into the fund? These are only a few of the questions that bear on the matter. There is an opinion that the larger the fund, the greater the difficulty it will have achieving its objectives, especially growth. This results, in part, from the difficulty a large fund experiences in investing in smaller issues,* and also from the difficulty a large fund may experience in obtaining prompt execution of its investment decisions in the stock market. On the other hand, no study has proved that a relation between fund size and performance exists, and several have come close to disproving such a relation. Moreover, there is no denying that smaller funds may have great difficulty attracting and keeping portfolio managers and covering other costs.

Portfolio turnover is a similar matter. The past history of the relation between a fund's trading activity—the average of share purchases and sales—and its total assets may be found in the prospectus the Securities and Exchange Commission requires that every mutual fund buyer get. What the information means, however, isn't as easy to ascertain. High turnover has sometimes been associated with "churning," or the purchase and sale of securities simply to generate brokerage house commissions, and the growth of funds affiliated with stock exchange member firms has done little to put this suspicion to rest. On the other hand, high turnover has also been shown to be a characteristic of funds with above-average growth. To the query, Is the high turnover necessary to achieve this performance? no satisfactory answer has been forthcoming yet.

Cash flow is still another matter requiring careful consideration. One of the great advantages of managing a mutual fund portfolio, in contrast to that of a closed-end fund, say, is that there is always tomorrow. An old investment doesn't have to be sold to make room for a new one, and, if there is steady inflow of funds, past mistakes don't have to be corrected at once. Stocks can be held until a more propitious moment for selling. Meanwhile, simply by channeling new money into better buys, the fund can improve its overall performance. New funds with large cash

---

* The Investment Company Act of 1940 limits the unrestricted holdings of any one fund to fewer than 10 percent of the shares of a single portfolio company. For a large fund to invest in smaller issues, it would have to include an unmanageable number in its portfolio.

inflows relative to their existing holdings, then, find it difficult not to perform well. Established funds that experience a sudden choking off of new money or net redemptions, on the other hand, may experience great difficulty, and even a superior portfolio manager may find it impossible to turn in something other than a mediocre performance.

Because they enjoy a steady cash flow, load funds and especially contractual plans—which require that investors forfeit a part of the sales charge if they discontinue regular monthly payments—have an opportunity to show above-average performance. But there has been no demonstrated link between the size of the sales charge and the performance actually achieved. In fact, the performance funds—those which emphasize performance to encourage sales—have often been no-loads, or funds that make no sales charge.

Other not-inconsequential matters involve the kinds of services a fund offers, the ability of a fund to handle properly and account for purchases and redemptions, and continuity of investment management. Sometimes a special service may be more valuable than performance. For older persons and uninsurables, for instance, the possibility of obtaining group life insurance as part of a fund purchase package may outweigh other features. Equally important is the assurance that a back-office foul-up won't cause the SEC to halt redemptions, impinging upon the liquidity that has come to be expected from ownership of mutual fund shares. Finally, the departure of a portfolio manager with above-average performance from one fund and his arrival at another can make a great difference to each.

Investors with the time, energy, talent, and inclination to pursue such matters are apt customers for no-load funds. Because such funds are bought directly from the fund, not sold, there is no sales charge to pay. Others, who prefer the counsel of an adviser, may feel that the commission is a fair price to pay for the comfort of knowing the answers, not guessing. Because most funds are sold, not bought, the load funds also offer a wider choice than the no-loads. Load funds are sold in two ways, through direct selling organizations that employ their own salesmen or through wholesalers who sell to retailers who employ salesmen. The most common sales charge is 8.5 percent of the offering price, which amounts to 9.3 percent of the funds actually invested. Of this amount, the salesman usually gets one-half or more.

The load applies only to selling costs. Most mutual funds are managed by separate investment advisory organizations controlled by the fund's organizers or their successors. These charge a percentage of the fund's assets for portfolio management and other services. A fairly frequent percentage is .05 percent per year, with some advisory companies scaling down their fees as a fund's assets grow. Criticism of fund performance has led some funds to tie their management fees to the ability of their advisers to outperform a stock market yardstick, the New York Stock Exchange index, for instance.

So long as they pass on to shareholders 90 percent of their dividends received and capital gains realized, mutual funds pay no separate income taxes, a privilege based on the theory that the funds act merely as conduits in making investments for and passing along tax liabilities to shareholders. Shareholders, of course, must include in their tax returns any income from a fund when it is received.

How well a specific fund performs has competitive importance for fund buyers and for fund sellers, while how well funds perform in general has a different kind of importance for the markets funds operate in and for their regulators. Do funds give the superior performance their advisers are paid to assure? If they do, is it because they have exercised better predictive ability than other investors in finding the growth companies of tomorrow? Or, unwittingly perhaps, like the pool operators of the twenties, have they achieved performance merely by bulling up one group of stocks after another? The first question has an important bearing on how much management fees should be and the way they should be paid, the second on whether fund activities in the market should be controlled and, if so, how.

Both matters are linked to the way mutual funds have grown. The long-term growth of mutual fund ownership and trading has been little less than phenomenal. From less than $500 million in 1940, total fund assets had grown to $52.7 billion by the end of 1968, about half, $25.7 billion, coming from net new money—purchases less redemptions—and the remainder from share price appreciation. (Because total assets depend so importantly upon market action, they fluctuate considerably. By the end of 1970, after the 1969–70 decline, for example, they had dropped back to $47.6 billion.) In the three decades, the number of shareholder accounts had grown comparably, swelling from 296,000 in 1940 to 9.1 million at the end of 1968. The industry estimated that each owner on average held two accounts, putting the number of individuals, families or institutions owning mutual fund shares at 4.6 million. The figure jibes roughly with a 1970 survey that showed that a little over 7.6 percent of all American households owned at least one mutual fund, compared with perhaps 4.5 percent ten years earlier.

But, if mutual fund ownership has grown rapidly, it still has a long way to go. In view of the expected rise in personal incomes and the industry's demonstrated ability to break down sales resistance, the low level of market penetration seems certain to be challenged, a conclusion that gains force from the flow of capital into management companies

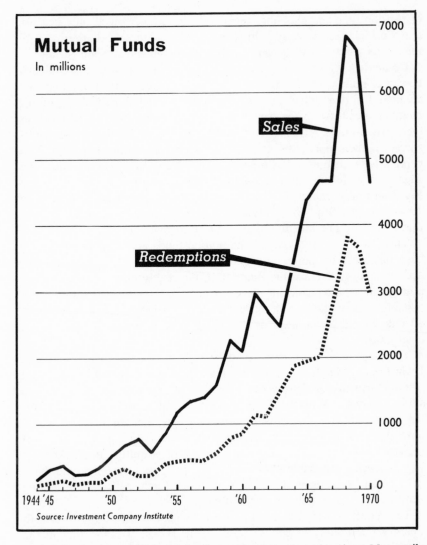

Mutual Funds

In millions

Sales

Redemptions

7000

6000

5000

4000

3000

2000

1000

0

1944 '45   '50   '55   '60   '65   1970

Source: Investment Company Institute

Mutual fund sales parallel closely the movement of stock prices. Not until the big 1969-70 break did the industry suffer a serious reversal.

from the insurance industry and other sources. Selling mutual funds is big business and is likely to become much bigger.

Mutual funds aren't the biggest institutional shareowners. Private noninsured pension funds, which in the 1960s stepped up their share purchases substantially, are. At the end of 1968, mutual funds held 6.8 percent of all stock outstanding, pension funds 7.8 percent. But growth of pension fund shareholdings seemed likely to taper off, if only because the pension funds already held so much stock—three dollars of five of their total assets—and because of the improvement in bond yields.

Compared with pension funds and other institutional shareholders, however, mutual funds are far more active traders. In 1968 they accounted for one dollar in six of all shares traded publicly (not for member accounts) on the New York Stock Exchange, twice as much as the pension funds. And for the first nine months of 1969 the turnover of shares in their portfolios came to 50.8 percent, compared with 21.6 percent for pension funds, 26.8 percent for life insurance companies, and 21.2 percent for fire and casualty companies. Turnover overall on the Big Board grew rapidly in the late 1960s, rising about 50 percent from 1964 through 1969. But mutual fund activity grew three times as fast, that of most other institutions only twice as fast.

There is no doubt about it. The mutual funds and their brokers have been busy moving shares into and out of portfolios. But what has this activity achieved? Have the funds been noticeably more successful than other investors in achieving performance? Even more important from a public policy standpoint, have they done a better job in helping to allocate capital to the most deserving—that is, future most profitable—enterprises?

The most serious attempt to answer these questions is a study by Irwin Friend, Marshall Blume, and Jean Crockett of the Wharton School of the University of Pennsylvania for the Twentieth Century Fund. The study updates a Wharton School effort of half a dozen years earlier, the most publicized conclusion of which was that an investor would have done as well selecting stocks at random—by throwing darts at the stock tables—as by using the facilities of a mutual fund. Another way of saying the same thing is to say that an investor would have done better investing in the New York Stock Exchange index of all Big Board listed shares than in mutual funds.

The Wharton study looked at performance in the 1950s, the Twentieth Century Fund study at performance in the 1960s. It found that in the period 1960–68 the funds outperformed the New York Stock Exchange index. High-risk funds clearly outperformed a portfolio of similar risk stocks chosen at random from the index. Medium-risk funds came out somewhat ahead, while low-risk funds did worse. (The index gives weight to the number of shares a company has outstanding as well as to their price. The stocks randomly selected for the study were weighted in the same way.) In the market decline of 1968–70, the funds did worse.

Another way of comparing performance is to pay no attention to the number of shares a company has outstanding but to invest equal sums in comparable issues. On this basis, the Twentieth Century Fund study found, a random selection of high-risk, medium-risk, and low-risk Big Board stocks outperformed each of their fund counterparts in 1960–68. The authors' conclusion? That it is hard to declare a certain winner.

Ever since publication of the original Wharton study, the industry has quarreled with people who have compared its performance with the stock market indexes, even one with so few issues as the Dow-Jones average of thirty industrial stocks. The head of an important midwestern fund has called the idea that it would be simple for an investor to duplicate the performance of a stock market average a "myth," observing:

The Dow-Jones industrials, and other well-known averages, are mathematical devices designed to show the approximate general trend of stock prices. As such, they enjoy a protected status, free of the complications of real investment life, such as brokerage commissions, odd lot differentials, taxes, fees, fractional shares, difficulties of execution of orders, ready availability of new money, etc. In fact, the one practically foolproof way of starting out worse than the Dow-Jones industrials, and then . . . progressively doing worse than the Dow-Jones industrials, is to buy the 30 stocks which on any given date make up that average.*

The authors of the Twentieth Century Fund study acknowledge such criticism implicitly. Even if the funds have performed no better than the market in general, they say, they have served a useful economic function by providing small investors with a convenient, low-cost way of spreading the risk of common stock investment. The funds have given them the opportunity to realize an average rate of return greater than they might obtain from savings deposits or bonds.

The more formidable question, however, remains. To what extent does mutual fund performance, when it can be demonstrated, result from a superior ability to forecast a company's future earnings? The Twentieth Century Fund study attempted to answer this question by comparing the earnings of stocks in fund portfolios one to eleven years after purchase with the prices paid when they were bought. The authors' conclusion? The funds seemed just as likely to invest in a stock that proves to be overvalued in the light of its later earnings than one that appears to be undervalued. If anything, the funds bought more overvalued than undervalued issues.

In the short run, the study found, prices of issues the funds bought tended to go up for a while, then to fall off as much as they had gone up. This destabilizing influence—the funds' first pushing prices up, then

* Quoted in The Investment Company Institute, *The Money Managers, Professional Investment Through Mutual Funds,* New York, McGraw-Hill, 1967, p. 62.

depressing them—was most marked for small, high-risk issues. In all, the study came to a fairly damning set of conclusions, conclusions tempered, however, by the observation that the funds were probably no more guilty of faddism or excessive speculation than anyone else in the market.

Mutual funds operate under a heavy regulatory mantle. In contrast to the insurance industry and the trust departments of banks, with which they compete directly, they must perform under the glare of total disclosure. Like other sellers of securities, the funds are subject to the Securities Act of 1933 and the Securities Exchange Act of 1934, and, in addition, every phase of their operations is detailed carefully in the Investment Company Act of 1940. These provisions are supplemented by rules of the National Association of Securities Dealers and state "blue sky" laws.

The 1933 act has special application to mutual funds because they are constantly issuing shares to the public and hence are in continuous registration. The 1934 act affects them through its requirements that they solicit proxies, make regular reports, and observe standards for the conduct and training of salesmen. The Investment Company Act of 1940 lays down forty-seven pages of "thou shalts" and "thou shalt nots," among which is a requirement that funds spell out their investment objectives and how they intend to carry them out, their policies with regard to borrowing, for instance, their issuance of senior securities, concentration of investments in certain industries, and the like. Once registered, these policies cannot be changed except with the approval of shareholders.

The significance of this requirement is obvious. A fund can't switch suddenly out of a portfolio of blue chips and fixed-interest obligations, designed to assure safety of principal and some modest income, into high-risk growth stocks. Nor, if it claims to be a diversified fund, can it invest a third or a half of its assets in a single industry. A fund must pursue the policies set forth in its prospectus, unless it gets shareholder approval to change them.

The 1940 act also lays down the following provisions, designed to prevent the abuses and pyramiding that characterized investment company activity in the twenties. At least 40 percent of a fund's directors must be independent—that is, not connected with the fund's advisory company—and no fund may sell its shares at a price less than net asset value per share. Insiders are not permitted to sell shares to or buy shares from a fund, and a fund may not acquire a substantial block of stock of another investment company.

Everyone with a role in selling mutual fund shares is subject to the rules of the SEC. In addition, the NASD governs the behavior of its member dealers and the salesmen they employ. It has the right to expel from membership any firm or individual found guilty of unfair or unethical conduct.

The reach of the law and regulation affects the way a fund may advertise and promote its product. A fund may say nothing about its activities except what it includes in its prospectus and in regular reports to shareholders, and it may not imply in any way that it can guarantee future success, or even duplication of past performance. In advertising it may state only its name, address, logotype, and investment objective— although never let it be thought that even such a hammerlock restriction would daunt an advertising copywriter. The Oppenheimer hands clasping in geometric pattern and the familiar Dreyfus lion emerging from a subway station on television commercials are representations simply of fund logotypes.

Two matters, sales charges and advisory fees, have been the subjects of long-standing regulatory concern. The 1940 act, as amended in 1961, said sales charges should not be unconscionable or grossly excessive. It also said that in selling a fund's shares no retail dealer should charge less than any other. Sales charges themselves were not prescribed. Funds were free to determine competitively what load, if any, they would apply.

The Wharton report and the special study by the SEC staff each concluded that such competition was insufficient to assure fund shareholders of the benefits of selling efficiencies, where they might occur. They recommended removal of the retail price maintenance provisions of the 1940 act, permitting dealers to compete with each other in selling a fund's shares. The industry complained that this would mean the elimination of many small independent dealers and would foster the growth of large selling organizations.

As a result, the SEC rejected repeal of retail price maintenance. Instead, it recommended to Congress that sales charges be limited to 5 percent of a fund's offering price. The industry balked at this idea, too, convincing Congress in 1970 to give the NASD the power to fix sales charges, subject to SEC review. Loads, Congress said, should be reasonable, from the standpoint of brokers, dealers, underwriters, and salesmen as well as investors. In regard to this, one NASD official noted that since 1940 the organization had been required to prevent highway robbery. Now, he said, if highway robbery was to occur all parties had to be pleased with the outcome.

The industry also succeeded in getting Congress to water down a provision that would have eliminated the front-end load, the practice in selling contractual plans of deducting the entire sales charge from the first year's payments. As the law stands now, an investor who redeems shares during the first three years of a contractual plan is entitled to a refund of any sales charge in excess of his total payments. Alternatively, a fund may elect to stretch out the front-end load so that it does not exceed 20 percent of any payment or average more than 16 percent over the first four years.

The regulatory concern about advisory fees results from the way the industry is structured. With only a very few exceptions, mutual funds are managed by outside investment advisory concerns. Funds didn't just spring into existence. Every one was started by entrepreneurs seeking to make a profit, and their desire to maximize this profit is in the tradition of American enterprise. The Investment Company Act of 1940, on the other hand, puts a fund's directors and advisers in a fiduciary relationship with its shareholders. The directors and advisers are required to do everything possible to further shareholder interests even when they differ from the adviser's.

After its special study the SEC interpreted this to mean that advisory concerns should charge no more than they would if the funds were dealing with them on an arm's-length basis and asked Congress to make such a standard the law. For some time it had been apparent that the funds were charging considerably more, a conclusion made evident both by the fact that the fees advisers charged their clients other than funds were invariably lower and by the fact that the few internally managed funds paid lower fees.

Once again, however, the industry succeeded in getting Congress to water down the SEC proposal. The 1970 amendment to the 1940 act reasserted the obligation of an advisory company to observe a fiduciary relationship to a fund it managed, but it also directed the courts to give appropriate weight to director approval and shareholder ratification of advisory contracts. This meant that shareholders who might sue over excessive fees would have to continue to bear the expense of litigation, a position the courts had arrived at before passage of the amendment.

Another regulatory matter that had occupied attention in years past, the distribution of brokerage commissions generated by mutual fund purchases and sales—the extensive practice of give-ups—seemed likely to fade as volume discounts first and negotiated commissions eventually supplanted the exchanges' fixed minimum commission schedule.

Delays in achieving a truly competitive commission schedule and the retention of such things as the prohibition against retail price cutting gave the small mutual fund distributor a new lease on life. But the respite seemed likely to be temporary. The profit-protecting measures also caused the big money—in the form of insurance companies and other major capital sources—to move in, confident in the knowledge that if they came under legislative or regulatory attack they could switch to direct selling or some other merchandising method less costly than the present.

The industry as it is presently constituted had an ace up its sleeve, however, the ignorance of most mutual fund buyers. Surveys of share buyers showed that most had no notion at all about what they were buying or how it compared with other funds. (In this regard, fund buyers are not unusual. Not one insurance buyer in a thousand can tell how to figure the net cost of life insurance—premium, minus dividend, minus addition to cash value—or how his company's performance compares with that of other insurers.) Ironically, the SEC's "truth in securities" policies may add to this ignorance. For all its emphasis on internal disclosure, the SEC does nothing to encourage awareness among fund buyers of the relative merits of one fund against another, or of relative costs. The information is all there, but the only person to interpret it is usually a fund salesman. Is it reasonable to expect him to recommend someone else's product?

The SEC might permit the NASD, which already has responsibility for gathering and disseminating fund quotations, to compile regular performance and cost statistics, and it might permit the funds themselves to repeat such information, in a manner determined by the SEC, in their advertising. Even then, however, there is no assurance that buyers would behave rationally. Surveys of consumer credit users show that many are still unaware of the high cost of installment loans, despite the full disclosure lenders now are required to make of annual rates of interest under the "truth in lending" law.

21. Commodities: Futures

The commodities futures markets offer businessmen who are unable or unwilling to bear the risks of price fluctuations insurance against such hazards, and they offer others who have no objection to undertaking such risks the opportunity to profit from them.

Tomorrow morning, as you butter your breakfast toast, pause for a moment to consider the people who have had a part in bringing the bread to you. As long as a year ago, fleets of combines moved across a Nebraska ranch harvesting wheat sown before the snows of the previous winter. The rancher trucked the wheat to a nearby country grain elevator, one of twenty thousand that rise out of the horizon interminably across the plains. The country elevator operator sold the wheat to a Chicago terminal warehouseman, and he sold it to a Buffalo miller. The miller, in turn, sold the flour to a New York City baker, and the baker sold the bread to your neighborhood supermarket.

At each step in the farm-to-market chain, people were assuming risks, many of these involving the risk of a fall in the price of wheat. The rancher risked time, labor, and capital in the hope that he would have a crop to harvest and would obtain a price sufficient to recover his costs and earn a profit. The country elevator operator hoped that the price would remain high enough for him to earn back storage and transportation costs, plus a return on his investment. The terminal warehouseman held the same hope. The miller, on the other hand, ran an opposite risk. Since he held contracts to supply flour to the New York and other bakers for several months ahead, his hope for profit faded if the price of wheat should rise.

The rancher can buy private insurance to protect his crop against damage from hail and buy government insurance to protect it against

216

insect infestation and other risks. He can also put his crop into government loan, limiting the risk of a decline in price. Neither the farmer, the country elevator operator, or the terminal warehouseman, however, has any assurance that a price that seems favorable early in the season won't drop later, nor does a livestock or poultry grower, a miller, or an exporter have any assurance that it won't rise.

Fortunately for all—producers, storers, transporters, processors and exporters of wheat and dozens of other commodities—have ready access to insurance against fluctuating prices. Obtaining such insurance doesn't involve purchasing any policies or paying any premiums. It doesn't even involve any insurance company or mutual risk-sharing arrangement. Rather, it involves a process called "hedging"—the sale of a futures contract whenever a cash commodity is purchased or the purchase of a futures contract whenever a cash commodity is sold.

A futures contract may sound mysterious, but it isn't at all. It is a contract to deliver or receive a stated quantity of certain traded commodities at a future date. A July wheat contract on the Chicago Board of Trade, for example, calls for the delivery or receipt of five thousand bushels of any twelve grades of wheat during the last seven days of July, July being the first delivery month of a new harvest. Other deliveries are spaced throughout the crop year, in September, December, March, and May.

Futures contracts aren't unique to the grain trade. Anyone who buys an automobile or a new home enters into a contract for future delivery of a specified item at a roughly specified time. What is unique about futures trading on a national commodities exchange is the nature of the commodity and its market. Unlike a new car or a new home, a traded commodity should be homogeneous and capable of standardization. Styling, fashion, brand preference, and specially tailored characteristics can play no part. A traded commodity should be readily storable; produced seasonally, requiring storage and marketing over a period of time; produced by a large number of producers; and used by a large number of consumers. Supply and demand must be broad and uncertain and the movement of goods to market unrestricted.

In economic terms a market like the Chicago Board of Trade is the nearest thing in our world today to a perfectly competitive market. As such, it is also something of a rarity.

How, then, does hedging insure a producer, storer, exporter, or processor against price fluctuation? The basic principle is that cash and futures prices tend to rise and fall together. Since the hedger's position is equal and opposite—a purchase in one market and a sale in the other —a loss in the cash market offsets a gain in the futures market, and vice versa, no matter which way prices move.

Take this example. A country elevator operator wants to hedge against a decline in price. On September 1 he buys five thousand bushels of wheat from the rancher at $2.00 a bushel. At the same time, he sells a December futures contract at $2.00 a bushel. On October 20 he delivers the wheat to Chicago. By then, however, the price has fallen to $1.85, resulting in a loss of 15 cents a bushel. But he is able to buy in the futures contract at $1.85 a bushel, resulting in a profit of 15 cents a bushel. Profit on the futures contract purchase offsets the loss on the cash wheat sale. Result: insurance against price decline.

To insure against a price advance, the miller does exactly the same thing—in reverse. On September 1 he takes an order for flour based on the wheat equivalent of five thousand bushels priced at $2.00 a bushel. At the same time he buys a December futures contract at $2.00 a bushel. By October 20, when he must buy the wheat to fill the order he has taken, the price has advanced to $2.15, resulting in a loss of 15 cents a bushel. But he is able to sell the futures contract at $2.15, producing an offsetting profit of 15 cents a bushel.

In actual practice a hedge is not that simple. Cash prices tend to move up and down with futures prices, but seldom by the same amount. Futures prices reflect all the forces operating at the moment in the pricing of wheat: rain in Nebraska, a shortage of boxcars in Illinois, the release of government stocks from surplus, growing famine in India, a threat of war in the Middle East. Cash prices, on the other hand, tend to reflect local storage conditions. In the first months of a new harvest, when the market is glutted with newly arriving grain and storage is short, cash prices tend to fall sharply below futures prices. Then, as the marketing season advances, this relationship—known as "basis"— moves to a narrower discount and possibly even to a premium. This narrowing of basis, normal to a marketing season, tends to reflect the cost of storage.

Things, however, may not move normally. A shortage of moisture in the final months of the new crop-growing season may produce a harvest smaller than expected. An early winter and ice on the Great Lakes may prevent the movement of wheat from Duluth and other upper lake ports. A large export order after the turn of the year may draw down existing supplies. Finally, late in the season, the release of government wheat from stockpile may add to them. Instead of widening at harvest and then narrowing, the basis may remain narrow and fairly flat throughout the marketing season.

Hedging, then, does not eliminate all risks for the producer and marketer, no more than liability or even collision insurance eliminates all risks for an automobile owner. But it does limit them and keep them manageable. As a result, the rancher, grain elevator operator, processor, or exporter can borrow larger sums of money, adding to his working capital. Moreover, the various middlemen who stand between the farmer and the consumer can operate on narrower margins of profit. They can pay more to the producer and charge less to the consumer.

Although the retail price of bread has risen over the years, the increase in price has occurred largely at the wholesale and retail level. Here is a comparison of the costs entering into the production of a one-pound loaf of bread, based on Department of Agriculture figures:

	1947–49 Average	1961	1971 First Quarter
Retail Price	13.5	20.2	25.0
Retailer	2.2	4.1	5.7
Baker-Wholesaler	6.3	10.9	13.4
Flour Miller	0.6	0.8	0.7
Other*	1.1	1.4	1.6
All Farm Ingredients	3.3	3.0	3.6
(Wheat Farmer)	(2.6)	(2.4)	(2.7)

* Transporting, handling and storing all ingredients, or processing ingredients other than flour, and costs of raw material from which non-farm ingredients are processed.

So far, the explanation of futures trading and hedging may have seemed to make sense. But, you may ask, who buys the futures contract when a hedger wants to sell? Who sells when he wants to buy? It must be fairly rare to have two hedgers enter the market at the same time, one offering to sell and the other offering to buy a like quantity of the same commodity for delivery in the same month.

The answer is the speculator, a likely winner in any competition for the most misunderstood man of all time. In 1890 Rep. Frederick Funston of Kansas observed:

Those who deal in . . . futures contracts, which is mere gambling no matter what less offensive name such transactions may be designated, neither add to the supply nor increase the demand for consumption, nor do they accomplish any useful purpose by their calling; but on the contrary, they speculate in fictitious products. The wheat they buy and sell is known as "wind wheat," and doubtless for the reason that it is invisible, intangible, and felt or realized only in the terrible force it exerts in destroying the farming industry of the country.

Forty years later, Senator James T. Heflin of Alabama felt called upon to comment on a big trading day when, it was estimated, futures contracts involving 300 million bushels of grain changed hands on the Chicago Board of Trade. He observed:

Mr. President, I want to remind the Senate that 300 million bushels is more than a third of the wheat crop of the United States. . . . These gamblers did not have any wheat; they were selling fictitious stuff called wheat. They were not dealing in grain; they were dealing in chalk marks on the blackboard. . . .

Critics of the futures markets generally haven't objected when the price of commodities have been rising. But speculators, the short sellers in particular, have come under repeated attack whenever prices have gone into a tailspin.

Markets, it is said, talk. The movement of prices up and down helps producers decide what to sell and consumers what to buy. With so many more speculators than hedgers operating in futures markets, however, how can we be sure that what the markets are saying isn't false? How can we be sure that price movements don't reflect the combined judgment of gamblers who are betting on the wrong horse?

The answer is that futures prices and cash prices are interacting at all times. Futures prices can't go one way and cash prices the other, or not for long. If one or the other gets out of line, speculators who make a profit from arbitraging such relationships can be expected to step in and halt the divergence.

The basic reason is that the financial consequences of holding a futures contract become more and more like those of owning the cash commodity itself as the maturity date for the futures contract approaches. A futures contract isn't an option; there is nothing take-it-or-leave-it about it. A holder must take or make delivery of the physical commodity, or he must offset, even up, or close out his position by making an equal and opposite transaction in the same contract before the final day of trading.

(That is the essential difference between commodities futures contracts and stock market puts and calls. Puts are options to sell and calls are options to buy specified stocks at specified prices at specified future dates. But they do not reflect the meeting of supply and demand for the actual commodity, in this case shares. They are, in effect, side bets on market fluctuations and, as such, are prohibited from taking place on the exchange floor.)

In either case, the financial consequences are approximately the same. The contract holder has completed a transaction realizing a profit or a loss. Or he owns a commodity, the value of which reflects a similar profit or loss. A futures speculator, thus, is no more—or less—a gambler than the holder of a cash commodity.

A speculator, actually, is someone willing to say that the price of a commodity now is wrong—that it is too high or too low—and is ready to put his money where his mouth is. A speculator who believes that the price of soybeans, say, is too low buys a futures contract, hoping to sell it later at a higher price. He is said to be "long" the market. A speculator who believes that the price is too high sells a futures contract, hoping to buy it back later at a lower price. He is said to be "short" the market.

A speculator, however, doesn't have to operate in a futures market. Anyone who stands to gain or lose from a rise or fall of prices is a speculator. Thus, to some degree everyone is a speculator, some people much more than others. It may come as a surprise to farmers, who have been among the more persistent critics of futures trading, that as a group they have speculated more often than not. Over the years they have had the same opportunities as storers, forwarders, and processors to avail themselves of the insurance against price fluctuation obtainable from hedging. But if hedging limits the risk attendant to a decline in prices, it also limits the gain resulting from a rise in prices. And farmers, by and large, have chosen to ignore the risk in the hope of gain.

This situation may be changing. Farmers have sharply stepped up their use of fertilizers, pesticides, and new equipment, greatly increasing their ability to produce crops, livestock, and livestock products and drastically cutting back the number of people needed to produce them. Total farm acreage has declined but the number of farms has dropped even faster, which has meant a substantial increase in the average farm size, in the value of its acreage and equipment, and in farmers' annual production expenses. It has also meant a big increase in agricultural credit requirements.

As the Federal Reserve Bank of Chicago has observed, farmers' equity in their products at the time of marketing has declined: "Therefore, even a modest change in price has a large effect on net income. To the extent this has occurred, farmers have a greater interest in the possibility of shifting the risk of price declines." Hence the possibility that farmers may give up their historic preference for the chance of windfall profits to avoid the risk of sizable losses.

Who are the commodity market speculators? They may be business or professional men, farmers, commodity handlers, or even housewives. All, however, must have capital over and above their ordinary requirements to put at risk. Some speculators, called "scalpers," operate principally on the floor of an exchange, like the Chicago Board of Trade. They trade on the thinnest of margins, going long to extract a profit from an eighth- or quarter-point rise, then swinging short before the market turns about to extract another eighth or quarter point on the way down. The function of the scalper is to add liquidity to the market, thus helping to maintain an orderly succession of prices. Because he operates on so thin a margin, the scalper seldom carries a position overnight.

There is another group of professional speculators who spend their time arbitraging, or "spreading." The spreaders may buy March wheat and sell May wheat, or sell soybeans and buy soybean oil and meal, or buy rye in Chicago and sell rye in Winnipeg. Their function is to keep the prices of related products or markets in line with one another. In the process they, too, help to maintain an orderly, fluid market by furnishing contracts to offset the contracts of other speculators and hedgers.

To get some idea how a commodity market operates, it might be worthwhile to look in on the Chicago Board of Trade. Not all commodity markets operate in exactly the same way, but the Board of Trade—which accounts for about 90 percent of the world's grain futures trading —is sufficiently typical to give a good idea of how it is done.

From the fifth floor visitors' gallery, you look down on a huge room five stories high, a block long, and a quarter of a block wide. Spaced around the floor are a number of octagonal amphitheaters, some large, others smaller. Men in suit coats or tan or gray jackets cluster in groups on the steps that line these so-called pits, gesticulating to each other with an elaborate system of hand signals and shouting back and forth. They are the traders. Other men, in blue jackets, stand on high platforms over-looking each of the pits, watching and listening to the traders, making notations on pieces of paper, and operating keyboards. They are ex-change employees called "quotation reporters." Still other men, in green jackets, move between the pits and banks of telephones and teletypes arrayed in the far corners of the room. They are messengers who relay orders from commission, or brokerage, houses to the traders.

The trading day begins, precisely at 9:30 A.M., with the clanging of a loud gong, and trading continues through 1:15 P.M. each business day, Monday through Friday. The traders stand in the pits according to the futures contract in which they trade, the more active months around the rim, the less active months in the center. No secret trades are per-mitted, so each order must be shouted aloud. Every change in price is re-corded by the men in the "pulpit," and relayed by them to the exchange's computer. This in turn operates the exchange's commodity ticker and the big electronic quotation boards at either end of the trading room.

The hand signals supplement the public outcry. The palm of the hand held upward and inward is a bid to buy. The palm held outward is an offer to sell. Fingers held vertically indicate the quantities traded, each finger representing five thousand bushels of grain or one contract of other commodities. Prices are indicated by fingers held horizontally, each finger representing one-eighth cent. The full cent price at which trading is taking place is shown on the quotation boards above the trading floor.

Each trader lists all of his completed transactions on a trading card. These are printed in blue on one side for futures contracts bought and in red on the opposite for contracts sold. The amount of the commodity, the grain, the month of the contract, the price, the name of the firm on the opposite side of the transaction, and the initials of the other broker go down on the card. The other broker in turn puts the same kind of information on his trading card, but on the opposite side. Throughout the session each trader turns his cards over to his clearing firm, one of some ninety members of the Clearing Corporation of the Chicago Board of Trade. At the end of the day the Clearing Corporation tallies the account of each member firm, offsetting purchases against sales. By exchange rule, all members must settle their accounts in cash on the day the trade is made. Traders are financially responsible to their clearing firms, who in turn guarantee the performance of all contracts traded.

Speculation in commodities futures contracts performs a useful economic function, but how much speculation is necessary to offset hedging? Fewer than 1 percent of all futures contracts are settled by delivery, and, allowing for the fact that many hedges are lifted without delivery, speculative transactions often outnumber hedges a dozen or more to one.

The question is irrelevant, most commodities men will argue. Every additional dollar put in by the speculator means a broader, deeper, and more resilient market for the hedger. Thus, nothing should be done to discourage speculation lest some of the market's liquidity be lost. Margin buying should not be impeded, government policing of the exchanges should be held to a minimum, and the right of traders largely to determine their own standards and practices should be maintained. The commodities exchanges have been much more successful than the securities markets in defending these goals.

The result is, still, the fastest game in the Midwest—or, for that matter, anywhere else in the financial world. It is a game in which fortunes can be made or lost overnight, in which luck plays an important part, and in which the foolhardy soon are eliminated. It is not a game for the necessitous, the timid, or the emotional. Commodities brokers like young bachelors as well as successful businessmen as customers, since both can afford to lose. They abjure customers who become nervous when prices begin to go down. Most won't accept the accounts of women, although some of them consistently outperform men in this hazardous undertaking.

How the rules of the game have evolved and what is being done to keep the game honest is the subject of the next chapter.

22. Commodities: Regulation

Speculation in commodities futures is not only the fastest game in town, it is also far less regulated than trading in securities. Some commodities markets—such as sugar, coffee, cocoa, plywood, silver, and platinum—aren't regulated at all. Others—grains, textile fibers, cattle, meat, dairy products, and other farm crops—are under the jurisdiction of the Commodity Exchange Authority, an agency of the Department of Agriculture. But the CEA has one-tenth the staff and budget of the Securities and Exchange Commission, itself an agency seldom overwhelmed with resources, and it lacks the power enjoyed by the SEC to obtain a court injunction when it finds its authority violated. And it also has no statutory authority to sue in behalf of the injured public when it determines large-scale fraud, as the SEC did successfully in the Texas Gulf Sulphur case.

What is more, some of the principal means of protecting the public that have evolved in securities regulation simply don't exist in the commodities area. There is no requirement, for instance, that salesmen for commodities brokers observe ethical standards of conduct. Outright fraud and deceit are barred, but although commodities futures trading is far more risky than buying and selling stocks, there is nothing to prevent salesmen from using pressure tactics to put people into commodities who shouldn't be there and from recommending actions that may result in losses a customer can ill afford. In addition, no obligation is placed on commodities advisory services to disclose whether or not they held positions in the commodities they recommended, just as no obligation is placed on persons with access to inside information affecting the price of commodities—knowledge, for instance, concerning the discovery of a major new source of a commodity—to make that knowledge available equally to all other market participants.

The plain fact is that protection of the investing public is a latter-day concern of regulation and probably still not its most important. Federal regulation of commodities trading, which antedated similar regulation of the securities markets by a dozen years, grew out of a tug-of-war between farmers who viewed the entire futures trade as an immense evil and big-time speculators who neither needed nor wanted government protection.

The farmers had reason for their strong views. For years after futures trading sprang up in the Chicago grain market in the mid-nineteenth century, questionable practices abounded. Corners, squeezes, wash sales, bucketing, and trading in options or privileges were only some of the things later outlawed. A corner results when a speculator contracts to buy a commodity and makes it impossible for the seller to deliver. In 1868 there was a corner a month—three in wheat, two in corn, one in oats, one attempted in rye, and as the year ended one was developing in pork products. As a result, the Chicago Board of Trade passed a resolution condemning corners, and six years later the Illinois Legislature made cornering a criminal offense. But neither the resolution nor the statute did much to prevent the practice. In 1874, after passage of the prohibition, there was a corner a month for the rest of the year.

A corner may occur in many ways. It invariably involves an attempt to force the shorts—speculators who have sold futures contracts and promised to deliver the cash commodity at a later date—to settle their contracts with the cornerer at a manipulated price. Most often the cornerer builds up a big futures position in a specific contract month, usually one in which supplies of the cash commodity are low. He then acquires control over part of the cash commodity, either by buying in the cash market or by taking delivery on his long futures contracts. When the shorts discover that supplies of the cash commodity are insufficient to make deliveries, they must either make offsetting futures transactions with the cornerer on the exchange or buy the cash commodity from him. Either way they must pay his price.

One of the problems any cornerer must face is the difficulty of "burying the corpse"—that is, of disposing of the cash commodity without serious loss. The great Leiter corner of 1897, the episode upon which the Frank Norris novel, *The Pit,* may have been based, tells why.

Joseph Leiter, "the boldest and strongest cornerer of all," held the biggest position in wheat ever known on the Chicago Board of Trade. He had the market cornered—or so he thought, until the shorts revolted. Instead of paying the price Leiter demanded, they began to deliver actual wheat. A magazine writer of the time described the situation: "The Northwest scraped its granaries. Russia ate rye and emptied its mill-bins of wheat. Argentina swept the floor. . . . Armour kept steel-prowed tugs plowing up the ice at the head of the Lakes, and by lake and rail moved 6-million bushels from Minnesota and the Dakotas to Chicago in midwinter." The corner was broken. Joseph Leiter's paper profits dissolved, then turned to losses.

Cornering is only one of a number of questionable practices that have plagued commodities exchanges since futures trading sprang up in the mid-nineteenth century. Other forms of price manipulation have included "squeezes," or brief, less-than-total corners; concentrated buying or selling designed to drive prices up or down; and the spreading of rumors and false reports. All are now outlawed, as are wash sales, cross trades, ac-commodation trades and other fictitious transactions, and all attempts to cheat and defraud. So are "bucketing" and trading in privileges or in-demnities.

Bucketing was the practice of matching offsetting buy and sell orders in a broker's office without bringing them to the floor of an exchange. Most often, a bucket shop was a small, fly-by-night operation with a blackboard on the wall listing current prices, some chairs, market infor-mation circulars, and a cashier's cage. It was often referred to as the "poor man's Board of Trade," inasmuch as it offered an opportunity to small speculators to get rich quick. Operations could be financed on small amounts of cash, but, since the speculator obtained no contract made on the floor of an exchange, defaults were numerous. Attempts to make a killing more often than not ended in financial ruin.

The exchanges, of course, had a direct financial stake in eliminating bucketing. Volume that went to the bucketers meant commissions lost to exchange members, and this undercut the value of a seat on the ex-change. On the Chicago Board of Trade an important part of the effort to close down the bucketers involved attempts to deny these competitors use of the board's telegraphed market quotations.

In the late 1870s one Board of Trade president, A. M. Wright, re-moved all telegraph tickers from the Board of Trade building, soaped the trading room windows to prevent signaling by persons on the floor to people outside, and prosecuted the bucket shops without letup. But Mr. Wright proved a bit too zealous. Suspecting that information was still leaking from the building, he led a party into the basement, where he ordered a cable cut with an axe. The cable, it turned out, contained the fire and police alarm systems. Mr. Wright's presidency sank in a torrent of ridicule, and the bucketers obtained a new lease on life.

The bucket shop controversy might be set down simply as an interest-ing footnote to history except for two things. The Board of Trade's at-tempt to restrict dissemination of its market quotations led directly to the Christie Grain case, in which the United States Supreme Court affirmed the legality of futures trading and offsetting settlements. The effort to stamp out bucketing, accomplished by the end of the first decade of the twentieth century with generous help from federal authorities, also lent some credence to the industry's argument—which persists today— that self-regulation is the most efficient form of commodities trading regulation in the public interest.

For years some farm groups had contended that buying and selling futures contracts was nothing more than wagering, and they had persuaded several state legislatures to enact statutes incorporating this idea. In the Board of Trade's attempt to keep the Christie Grain and Stock Company from using its market quotations, the issue narrowed to whether the accepted Board of Trade practice of settling futures contracts by offsetting transactions did not, in fact, constitute gambling. An appeals court said yes, but a majority of the Supreme Court said no. The opinion of Justice Oliver Wendell Holmes is often cited:

> In a modern market contracts are not confined to sales for immediate delivery. People will endeavor to forecast the future and to make agreements according to their prophecy. Speculation of this kind by competent men is the self-adjustment of society to the probable. Its value is well known as a means of avoiding or mitigating catastrophes, equalizing prices and providing for periods of want.

The fight against bucketing proved a greater triumph for legitimacy than for self-regulation. After all, the fight would never have been so long or so difficult had not members of the Board of Trade themselves cooperated with the bucket shops and in numerous instances bucketed on their own.

The difficulties of self-regulation were even more evident in the efforts to end trading in privileges or indemnities. Like stock market puts and calls, these give the buyer the option to sell or buy a futures contract at a specified price within a fixed period of time. Here the analogy to wagering was entirely relevant. The seller of a put gambled that a price would go down, the buyer of a call that it would go up. There was no obligation to deliver anything, the cash commodity or an offsetting futures contract. But although officials of the Board of Trade inveighed regularly against privileges and indemnities and succeeded several times in limiting the traffic in options, the practice was suppressed only to come back stronger. This was the case, notwithstanding the fact that trading in privileges clearly endangered legitimate forms of futures trading—hedging and offsetting speculation. Not until passage of the Commodity Exchange Act in 1936 was the practice finally eliminated.

The first bill providing for regulation of futures trading in agricultural commodities was introduced in Congress in 1884, and by 1922 more than two hundred bills had been put in the hopper to regulate or prohibit futures trading. The first comprehensive statute to be enacted, coming on the heels of congressional investigations into the sharp drop in farm prices following World War I, when futures trading in most commodities had been suspended, was the Futures Trading Act, which became law in 1921. The Supreme Court, however, declared the Futures Trading Act invalid on grounds that it attempted to regulate by means of the taxing power. Soon afterward Congress passed the Grain Futures Act of 1922, based on the commerce clause of the Constitution. Thus, more than a decade before passage of laws establishing federal regulation of securities markets, Washington assumed regulatory control over commodities futures trading.

The Grain Futures Act established the basic pattern for commodities market regulation that persists to this day. Futures trading in wheat, corn, oats, barley, rye, flaxseed, and grain sorghums was restricted to owners and growers of the physical commodity and to persons trading through exchanges designated by the Secretary of Agriculture as "contract markets." The principal requirement for such designation was that the exchange take responsibility for preventing price manipulation by its members. In addition, the Secretary of Agriculture was authorized to make investigations relating to futures trading and conditions affecting the grain markets and to publish the results. The Grain Futures Act also established a commission comprised of the Secretary of Agriculture, the Secretary of Commerce, and the Attorney General, with authority to suspend or revoke the designation of a contract market.

The Grain Futures Act was strengthened substantially by amendment in 1936 and renamed the Commodity Exchange Act. Its coverage was extended to cotton, butter, eggs, and potatoes, and subsequently wool and wool tops, soybeans, soybean oil and soybean meal, cottonseed oil, livestock and livestock products, and frozen concentrated orange juice, in addition to some commodities no longer traded, were also added.

The Commodity Exchange Act divided regulation of futures markets among the Secretary of Agriculture, the Commodity Exchange Commission—comprising also the Secretary of Commerce and the Attorney General—and the exchanges themselves. The Secretary of Agriculture was authorized to license boards of trade, futures commission merchants, and floor brokers. The Commission was authorized to fix trading limits, to suspend or revoke the licenses of boards of trade, and to serve as a court of appeals from actions of the Secretary of Agriculture. In administering the law, both the Secretary of Agriculture and the Commission operate through the Commodity Exchange Authority, an agency of the Department of Agriculture. In the fiscal year ended June 30, 1970, the authority's supervision covered twenty-one commodities traded on twenty contract markets.

The Commodity Exchange Act prohibits price manipulation and illegal trading and requires that commission merchants put each customer's funds in an account separate from his own and those of other customers. The act limits the maximum amount of futures that speculators may buy or sell on one business day and sets limits as well on the maximum net long or net short position that may be carried overnight. The limits do not apply, however, to bona fide hedging transactions as defined by the law.

Self-regulation by the exchanges themselves is a kingpin of the system. The Commodity Exchange Act let the exchanges remain free to admit new members and elect officers, to discipline offenders and expel members, and to fix brokerage fees, price fluctuation limits, and margin requirements.

The matter of margins has been a particularly controversial subject. Margin, as we have already mentioned, is the cash or collateral deposited by a trader with his broker to secure the broker from loss on any contracts he makes for his trader client. The exchanges like to think of margin as a performance bond rather than as a down payment. Here it would be well to discuss the difference, an important one, between buying a share of stock and buying a commodities futures contract. In buying stock an investor obtains title to the shares, getting certain rights—the right to receive declared dividends, for instance—into the bargain. At the same time, he contracts to repay his broker the percentage of purchase price the broker has advanced at a determined rate of interest.

In purchasing a futures contract, on the other hand, a buyer does not receive title to a commodity. He makes a contract to buy or sell a fixed quantity of a commodity at a future date at the price then prevailing. Since he owns nothing, the cash he puts up can't be thought of as a down payment. And since he pays no interest, the remainder of the contract price can't be thought of as credit. If there were any doubt remaining as to the nature of the funds he is putting up—guarantee money that he will fulfill his contract—they are required to be kept by his broker in cash or Treasury bills in the buyer's name and not mixed in with the brokers' other funds.

It is axiomatic that an increase in margin requirements—meaning that speculators have to put up more cash to finance a given volume of transactions—slows speculation. A decrease in margin requirements, on the other hand, tends to increase speculation. The commodities exchanges, then, have been careful to keep margin requirements at levels that would not impede speculation. Initial margin requirements in one recent period ranged from 3 to 18 percent of the current market value of futures contracts.

Economists and legislators have often expressed the belief that the power to determine margin requirements should be vested in the federal government to prevent speculative excesses. But through the years the exchanges have successfully resisted all attempts to relieve them of this power.

For three decades the exchanges successfully resisted other changes in the law, despite the fact that they did not always utilize the self-regulatory powers they enjoyed. Then, the same weekend that President Kennedy's death resulted in feverish activity on the stock market, a scandal of great dimension rocked the commodities markets, sending tremors throughout the financial world.

A previously obscure vegetable oil processor had attempted, and almost succeeded, in cornering the market for soybean oil. Operating on the New York Produce Exchange and the Chicago Board of Trade, he pyramided his purchases of futures contracts by use of credit obtained against warehouse receipts for nonexistent inventory and forged warehouse receipts and through an elaborate check-kiting scheme. When he was unable to meet more than $30 million in margin calls when prices went down instead of up as he had expected, he went into bankruptcy, bringing down with him two old and respected Wall Street brokerage houses, causing extreme embarrassment and endless litigation for one of the country's best-known international financial organizations, creating losses of more than $150 million for a score of innocent and trusting lenders, and raising doubt whether the stock market would reopen after the Kennedy funeral.

The swindle could never have reached the size that it did without a number of unhappy coincidences. The field warehousing company that certified to the existence of the phantom oil was about to be sold off by its parent company. The head of the commodity department at the largest of the two Wall Street brokerage houses that went down was in the hospital. The banks that lent against worthless warehouse receipts never questioned for a moment whether there was collateral behind the receipts.

The swindle did not, however, occur in a vacuum. Both the exchanges and the Commodity Exchange Authority were aware of the massive purchases, often concentrated just before the day's close when they might be expected to exert a maximum effect on prices. But both felt unable or unwilling to take any action. Anthony (Tino) De Angelis, the builder of the bubble, clothed his activities in the legal habit of bona fide hedging operations.

The vegetable oil scandal pointed up weaknesses in self-regulation as practiced by the exchanges and deficiencies in the Commodity Exchange

Act and in its enforcement. Largely as a result, Congress in 1968 amended the act again.

Perhaps the most important change was a requirement that contract markets enforce their own trading rules. In addition, the Secretary of Agriculture was authorized to disapprove rules of the exchanges. For the first time futures commission merchants and floor brokers were required to meet minimum financial standards, and pass a fitness examination. Penalties for violations of the law, such as price manipulation and embezzlement, were increased. And the Commodity Exchange Authority was authorized to issue cease and desist orders against persons found guilty of violating the law. Previously, such orders could be issued only against contract markets.

The Department of Agriculture, which sought the changes, did not get all that it asked. It did not get the power to regulate margins—contract markets could still keep futures customers' required cash deposits at zero, if they chose—or the power of injunction, which meant that it could not move in on contract markets that failed to enforce their own and its rules. It could only recommend that they do so.

More important, neither the 1968 amendments to the Commodity Exchange Act or any other action of Congress have given the Commodity Exchange Authority any additional staff or appropriations. As a result, the authority is obliged to police its markets—doing an annual volume many times that of the several stock exchanges—with a staff of approximately 125 people, all but 30 or so of whom are clerical personnel.

Prodded by the CEA, the exchanges themselves have begun to organize internal policing operations, staffed with trained investigators. But the effort remains minimal, compared with that of the stock exchanges. Moreover, many traded commodities and commodity exchanges remain outside the ambit of Federal regulation, which applies only to agricultural commodities grown in the United States. This explains how some commodities and some markets escape regulation entirely. Some exchanges, such as the New York Mercantile Exchange, trade both regulated and unregulated commodities.

Historically, as it was noted earlier, commodity market regulation was undertaken to protect the farmer, not the speculator, but lately the balance has begun to shift. The Chicago Board of Trade, for instance, recently added the first public governors to its governing body. In time, self-regulation on the part of the industry and legislation affecting the commodity markets may come to reflect more fully the growth of the investing public both in numbers and political influence.

23. Foreign Trade and Foreign Exchange

International trade involves an enormous paradox. Transactions so commonplace that they are taken for granted when they are conducted within a country become arguable and suspect when they cut across national boundaries.

Consider the right of an individual to buy at the lowest and sell at the highest possible price. Trade becomes possible when two persons hold differing ideas of the worth of things they possess. Each gives up something he values less than the thing he gets back, the price representing their common agreement on the relative value of each item. In a free, open, and competitive situation, this meeting of minds is the only factor affecting price. Hence, the great reverence for competition in the United States.

Trade would not occur unless each of the two persons believed that the thing he was getting back was more valuable than his "exports." And yet, in the public mind, imports from foreign nations are viewed differently. They often are seen not as a boon, but as a threat, as a necessary evil permitting growth of a country's exports. The latter, by way of contrast, are held up as the goal of trade and one of the sources of a nation's wealth.

How can two such opposite views, one domestic and one international, exist side by side? The answer, of course, is that they cannot. If trade within a nation increases public satisfaction by giving people things more valuable than they give up, then trade across national boundaries must have the same result. Britain's slogan, "Export or Die," makes sense, but only as a way of obtaining imports she can get in no other way.

Robinson Crusoe was forced to do everything for himself, the things he did badly as well as the things he did well. Trade encourages specialization, the division of labor, which means simply that jobs get done by the people best able to do them. One man may be a better hunter, another a better farmer. Each is better off if the hunter produces meat only and the farmer products of the soil, and if each exchanges part of what he produces for what he wants. Multiply the number of specialists several hundred times and you have a village; many thousands of times, a city; and many millions, a nation. The broader a market, the less inhibited the movement of goods, men, and capital within it, the greater the level of well-being.

This isn't the whole story, though. A physician may be able to drive a nail better than the man he hires as a carpenter, and yet the community is better off—its gross product is increased—if the physician utilizes his scarcer and more highly valued skills and permits the carpenter to do his hammering. The same goes for nations. There are many reasons why one country may outperform another in the production of, say, oranges. The land may be more fertile and the availability of farm labor greater. It may have invested more in machinery and fertilizer, and the organization of its groves may permit greater efficiency. Its farm-to-market system may reduce risks and lower costs, and its agricultural research may produce better varieties of fruit and higher yields.

The country, however, may also be a maker of computers and peripheral equipment, items that command a far higher value in relation to their costs than oranges. The question is, would the country be better off to channel more of its manpower and capital into producing oranges—since no other nation can match the quality or cost of its product—or into computers? The answer should be apparent. It would be better off making computers.

The notion that countries, like individuals, should do their own thing, the thing they do best, wasn't always so obvious. As Europe emerged from the Middle Ages, the rulers of the new nation-states deluded themselves into thinking that they could grow rich if they could make beggars of their neighbors. Like their mariners, who had difficulty comprehending that the world might not be flat, they persisted in believing that one country somehow could sell more abroad than it purchased in return. The realization that all nations might grow and prosper together seemed completely beyond their ken.

This wasn't hard to understand. The mercantilists, as these early nationalists were known, were so intent on assuring that their own countries got ahead that they gave no attention whatsoever to the general welfare. The state, their own country, must be made strong at any cost. Navies must be built, armaments supplied, a fighting population sired. As much as possible must be produced at home. Production overseas, even at lower cost, was equated with national weakness.

The object was gold, the ultimate war treasure. It made little difference whether the gold was mined in colonies, pirated from enemy galleons, or paid for by foreign countries for the excess of what they purchased over what they sold. The fact that gold had little or no useful purpose made it no less sought; indeed, the fact that gold was nonproductive made it what it was, the supreme symbol of national power. Only a powerful ruler could keep his wealth in a nonproductive resource.

Remnants of the mercantilist philosophy persist to this day, according gold its unique place as a means of settling international claims. And yet, time and again, the mercantilist doctrine has been proven a false, if not a disastrous, course. The collapse of world trade in the years between the two world wars and the rise of Hitler can be laid in part at least to a revival of mercantilist thinking.

The opposite view, the idea that every country should produce the things for which it was best suited, came to be known as "the theory of comparative advantage." The United States was to become a living demonstration of the theory in action, a vast continent-wide market in which goods, manpower, and capital would flow unhampered by internal tariffs or restrictions. This huge common market was to prove so successful, creating a living standard for its people so far above that anywhere else, that it was to be emulated two centuries later by the nations of Europe, contrite after their latter-day intoxication with the wine of mercantilism.

Trade among nations is complicated by different laws and customs, different financial institutions, uncoordinated economic policies, but chiefly by the existence of more than a single currency. To understand how international trade gives rise to foreign exchange, it may be useful to trace a typical transaction.

International Business Machines Corporation, let's say, sells a computer to a company in England. When it delivers the machine to a shipping company, it gets back a bill of lading. This serves both as its receipt from the shipping company and as the British company's claim to the computer when it is landed in England.

IBM writes a draft, or check, directing the British company to pay a sum in British pounds to a third party in, say, ninety days. This is known as a "bill of exchange." The sum includes the pound equivalent of the American purchase price in dollars, and, in addition, the interest to be paid on the ninety-day extension of credit. The total might amount to $96,000. At the official rate of exchange of £1 to $2.40 that prevailed until August 1971*, this would come to £40,000.

* By ending the dollar's historic ties to gold and imposing a 10 percent surtax on imports, President Nixon encouraged other countries to raise the value of their currencies in terms of the dollar. Before new par values could be established, however, rules of the International Monetary Fund would have to be changed.

IBM takes its draft, plus the bill of lading and any other necessary papers, to a large New York bank. It sells the draft at discount—that is, at face value less the ninety-day interest charge—and receives dollars. If we assume an annual rate of 8 percent, the three-month interest cost would be 2 percent, or £800, the dollar equivalent of which would be $1,920. IBM thus gets $94,080, and for the firm, as the exporter, the transaction is completed.

The New York bank sends the draft and documents to its branch in London or to a British bank with which it enjoys correspondent relations. The London bank presents the bill of lading to the importing company after the company "accepts" the draft—that is, after it signs it, acknowledging its indebtedness. The importing company presents the bill of lading to the shipping company and claims its computer. When the bill of exchange matures, the company pays £40,000 to the London bank, and the pounds are put in the checking account of the New York bank in the London institution.

In terms of the American economy as a whole, the United States has supplied a computer to the rest of the world, exporting merchandise, and got back a checking account deposit in the London bank, importing a claim on British goods and services.

IBM might have written a dollar draft, directing the British importing company to pay for the computer in dollars, not pounds. In this case the draft would not have been discounted with a New York bank but sent directly to the British company, which would have been obliged to obtain dollars from its London bank. Thus, the export would be paid for, not by importing a claim on British goods and services, but by reducing existing British claims on American goods and services.

Either way, the export of American merchandise is paid for by the import of capital into the United States. Such capital movements are a necessary lubricant for international trade and investment, and only when some nations pile up continuing capital surpluses, and others continuing deficits, do problems arise. Of this, more later.

For the moment let's give a little closer attention to how exchange rates are determined. We said that the official exchange rate of sterling and dollars was £1 = $2.40 until August 1971. That is, if you had American currency, it would take $2.40 to obtain one British pound. But what if you were a Briton and wanted dollars? The same relationship can be expressed in another way, $1.00 = £.41667.

Let's suppose that the dollar is trading in the New York foreign exchange market at its former official rate. In London, however, it is trading at £1 = $2.39, or $1.00 = .41841. To a New Yorker the conclusion is that the New York price of the pound is too high, the London price too low, while to a Londoner the conclusion is that the London price of the dollar is too high, the New York price too low.

Either one realizes that he can profit by selling pounds and buying dollars in New York or by buying pounds and selling dollars in London. Foreign exchange dealers are quick to recognize when one currency gets out of line with another and, by buying one and selling the other, they quickly bring the rates together again, a practice known as "arbitrage."

Under rules of the International Monetary Fund that governed until August 1971, exchange rates could trade only within a range of 1 percent above or below their fixed par values, or official rates.) It was likely that this range would be widened in any restructuring of the international monetary mechanism resulting from President Nixon's cutting of the dollar's ties to gold.) When a currency reached its ceiling, $2.4240 in the case of the pound, the central bank had to sell its own currency in the open market. When the currency reached its floor, $2.3760 in the case of the pound, the central bank had to buy.

Funds aren't exchanged solely for dollars, of course. They are exchanged for marks, lire, guilder, yen, French, Belgian, and Swiss francs, Canadian dollars, and a host of other currencies. The pound isn't watched, then, solely in terms of its exchange rate with the dollar but in terms of its so-called cross rates with at least half a dozen other actively traded currencies. Arbitrage may involve simultaneous operations in three currencies or even more.

Foreign exchange users also have access to the forward markets, where they may insure against rate fluctuations by contracting now for foreign exchange needed one to six months or even a year hence. The behavior of forward rates, which central banks are under no obligation to control, is a further important influence on spot exchange, or exchange for immediate delivery.

General Electric, let's say, is considering submitting a bid to the British Central Electricity Generating Board for power plant equipment it will cost $2,400,000, including profit, to produce. General Electric knows that it will be paid in sterling, six months hence, when it delivers the equipment. What sterling price should it put on its bid?

Assuming sterling is worth $2.40, its old par, GE knows that the price should be around £1,000,000. Assuming also that the Bank of England stands ready to intervene at the old floor or ceiling, GE won't get less than $2,376,000 if it waits six months to take payment of the million pounds and sells them in the spot market, and it might get as much as $2,424,000. On the other hand, if the market rate should fall the full distance from ceiling to floor, it could lose $48,000. If there were a change in that official par value, it could lose even more.

Fortunately, GE doesn't have to take that risk. It can arrange to sell its sterling in the forward exchange market at the same time that it makes its contract to deliver the power equipment. It is quite possible that sterling six months forward might be selling at a discount from the spot rate and even below the floor. The difference between the forward rate now and the spot rate six months from now is GE's cost of insurance against exchange rate fluctuation. This is a cost it must consider in submitting its bid.

In the same way that exporters have to guard against the possibility of currency depreciation, importers have to concern themselves lest a currency appreciate in value between the time they buy goods overseas and the date they are required to pay for them. Instead of selling sterling for dollars forward, then, they buy, the risk borne by speculators, much as it is in commodity futures markets. In GE's case, a speculator will buy sterling forward when GE sells, betting that the spot rate will rise, not fall, and that he will be able to sell at a profit six months hence. If there are more sellers than buyers of forwards, the banks that operate as foreign exchange dealers will sell spot and buy forward to even up their long and short positions. In this way spot and forward markets are kept closely in line.

So far we have discussed how exchange rates adjust but have said nothing about why they move up and down. Like any other market item, a currency tends to move up in value when it is in demand and to move down when it is in excess supply. There are any number of temporary factors that may affect exchange rates: the seasonal rise and fall of exports, a strike affecting an important sector of the economy, a drought or an unusually cold winter, the timing of a large international payment, expectations of good things or bad things ahead. Apart from short-run influences, however, the principal factor tending to drive up the value of a currency is the persistence of a surplus in its international balance of payments, the principal factor tending to drive down the value of a currency being the persistence of a deficit.

A nation's international payments surplus or deficit is not unlike the figure one arrives at in balancing a checkbook. In one column, you add up all the checks you have written in a month, and in another you add your deposits. Then you subtract the sum of the checks written, or what you have spent, from the deposits, or what you have received. Assuming all transactions are made through the account, what's left at the end of the month is your balance of payments with the rest of the world.

There are notable differences, however, between a checking account and the balance of payments. The receipts and expenditures are not those due to or made by a single individual or concern. They reflect the ac-

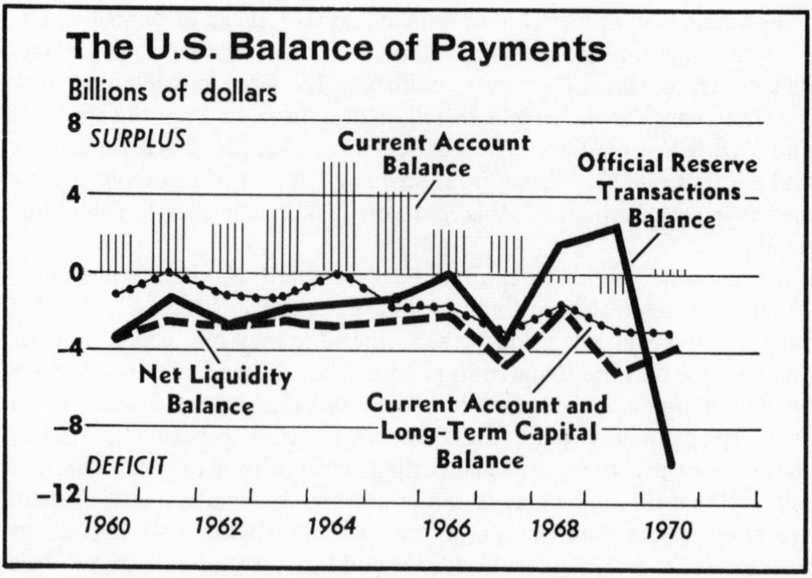

The balance of payments reflects the activities of anyone with dealings abroad plus the international transactions of the government. By all yardsticks, the balance of payments deteriorated badly in the late 1960's.

tivities of a myriad of people and businesses, anyone with dealings abroad, plus the international transactions of the government itself. Within the country payments are made in the same currency—the dollar in the United States, for instance, sterling in Britain, francs in France—while among countries settlements are made in gold, in an internationally acceptable currency like the United States dollar, or in Special Drawing Rights (SDRs) in the International Monetary Fund, so-called paper gold.

A country's balance of payments, moreover, is a double-entry system of accounts. Every transaction gives rise to a receipt or credit, which is recorded with a plus sign, and to a payment or debit, which is recorded with a minus sign. When IBM sold its computer to the British concern, the value of the export went down on the United States international payments books as a receipt in the merchandise account. At the same time the rise in the New York bank's checking account balance at its London correspondent was recorded as a payment under short-term capital.

The accounts are arranged in a series of six tiers with a separate balance at each level, the sum of all items above the level equaling the sum of all items below but with a minus sign if the other is plus or a plus sign if the other is minus. The balance on goods and services, for instance, measures exports less imports not only of goods but of such services as insurance and shipping, and in addition the income from American invest-

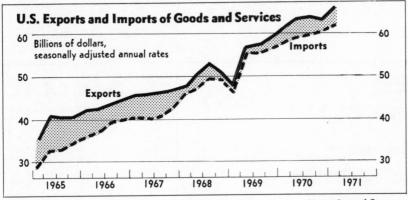

U.S. Exports and Imports of Goods and Services

Billions of dollars, seasonally adjusted annual rates

Exports

Imports

Source: Dept. of Commerce

The U.S. long has enjoyed a trade surplus. Because of inflation, imports have risen faster than exports in recent years, narrowing the surplus.

ments abroad less the income foreigners earn on their investments in the United States. The balance on goods and services indicates whether the United States is earning the foreign exchange needed to cover everything below, one-way transfers and gifts, both private and governmental, and international lending and investing.

The balance on goods, services and remittances takes into account additionally private transfers, the funds an immigrant might return to his family in the old country, for instance, or a charitable contribution for famine relief. The balance on current account adds in similarly United States government grants to foreigners.

The balance on current account and long-term capital, sometimes called the basic balance, is the current account balance plus additionally direct investment in overseas subsidiaries by business concerns, investment in the stock market and other securities, and bank term loans. It includes also flows of United States and foreign government capital except for changes in reserve assets. It is perhaps the best measure of long-term trends affecting the general health of the dollar.

The balance on current account and long-term capital, plus flows of short-term nonliquid private capital, new allocations of Special Drawing Rights in the International Monetary Fund, SDRs or so-called paper gold, and errors and omissions add up to the net liquidity balance. This is a broad indicator of potential pressures on the dollar resulting from changes in the liquidity position of the United States.

The official reserve transactions balance is the net liquidity balance plus changes in holdings of gold, SDRs (other than new allocations) or other official reserve assets and any increase in foreign official claims

(Credits +; debits −)	1965	1966	1967	1968	1969	1970
Merchandise trade balance [1]	4,942	3,927	3,859	624	660	2,110
Exports	26,438	29,390	30,680	33,588	36,490	41,980
Imports	−21,496	−25,463	−26,821	−32,964	−35,830	−39,870
Military transactions, net	−2,122	−2,935	−3,138	−3,140	−3,341	−3,371
Travel and transportation, net	−1,319	−1,382	−1,752	−1,558	−1,780	−1,979
Investment income, net [2]	5,294	5,375	5,888	6,220	5,975	6,242
U.S. direct investments abroad	5,162	5,374	5,956	6,519	7,340	7,906
Other U.S. investments abroad	1,930	2,207	2,355	2,714	3,199	3,503
Foreign investments in the United States	−1,798	−2,206	−2,423	−3,013	−4,564	−5,167
Other services, net	333	315	365	344	497	588
Balance on goods and services [3]	7,130	5,300	5,220	2,489	2,011	3,592
Remittances, pensions and other transfers	−1,028	−980	−1,278	−1,168	−1,266	−1,410
Balance on goods, services and remittances	6,102	4,320	3,942	1,321	745	2,182
U.S. Government grants (excluding military)	−1,808	−1,910	−1,802	−1,707	−1,644	−1,739
Balance on current account [4]	4,295	2,410	2,139	−386	−899	444
U.S. Government capital flows excluding nonscheduled repayments, net. [5]	−1,819	−1,963	−2,428	−2,538	−2,106	−1,837
Nonscheduled repayments of U.S. Government assets	221	429	6	269	−87	244
U.S. Government nonliquid liabilities to other than foreign official reserve agencies	66	65	−2	107	263	−436
Long-term private capital flows, net	−4,577	−2,555	−2,912	1,198	−50	−1,453
U.S. direct investments abroad	−3,468	−3,661	−3,137	−3,209	−3,254	−4,445
Foreign direct investments in the United States	57	86	258	319	832	969
Foreign securities	−759	−482	−1,266	−1,226	−1,494	−942
U.S. securities other than Treasury issues	−357	909	1,016	4,389	3,112	2,190
Other, reported by U.S. banks	9	525	413	430	477	199
Other, reported by U.S. nonbanking concerns	−59	68	−196	495	277	576
Balance on current account and long-term capital [5]	−1,814	−1,614	−3,196	−1,349	−2,879	−3,038
Nonliquid short-term private capital flows, net	−171	−102	−505	231	−602	−548
Claims reported by U.S. banks	−200	−220	−645	−44	−658	−1,015
Claims reported by U.S. nonbanking concerns	−120	−178	−359	−484	−35	−363
Liabilities reported by U.S. nonbanking concerns	149	296	499	759	91	830
Allocations of special drawing rights (SDR) [4]						867
Errors and omissions, net	−507	−431	−985	−493	−2,603	−1,132
Net liquidity balance	−2,493	−2,148	−4,685	−1,610	−6,084	−3,852
Liquid private capital flows, net	1,204	2,367	1,267	3,251	8,786	−5,969
Liquid claims	1,073	−17	−205	−559	124	273
Reported by U.S. banks	525	136	−85	−61	−209	−119
Reported by U.S. nonbanking concerns	548	−153	−120	−498	333	392
Liquid liabilities	131	2,384	1,472	3,810	8,662	−6,242
To foreign commercial banks	116	2,697	1,272	3,387	9,166	−6,507
To international and regional organizations	−291	−525	−214	48	−63	179
To other foreigners	306	212	414	375	−441	86
Official reserve transactions balance	−1,289	219	−3,418	1,641	2,702	−9,821
Financed by changes in:						
Nonliquid liabilities to foreign official reserve agencies reported by U.S. Government.	123	15	452	1,806	−162	535
Nonliquid liabilities to foreign official agencies reported by U.S. banks.	−38	793	894	534	−836	−810
Liquid liabilities to foreign official agencies	−18	−1,595	2,020	−3,101	−517	7,619
U.S. official reserve assets, net	1,222	568	52	−880	−1,187	2,477
Gold	1,665	571	1,170	1,173	−967	787
SDR						−851
Convertible currencies	−349	−540	−1,024	−1,183	814	2,152
Gold tranche position in IMF	−94	537	−94	−870	−1,034	389

against the dollar, both liquid and nonliquid. It is a measure of the deficit that must be financed or the surplus that must be accommodated.

We have considered so far how trade gives rise to foreign exchange, how an export of merchandise results in an import of capital, how exchange rates are adjusted, and why rates move up and down. We have emphasized the important influence of payments surpluses and deficits in exchange rate movements. It may be useful next to consider how payments deficits are financed.

Strictly speaking, what's left in an individual or business checking account at the end of a month is a payments surplus. Except in accounts which permit overdrafts, no bank would permit a depositor to run a deficit. If he thinks it likely that he may overdraw his account, an ordinary checking account holder has three choices: he can draw down past savings, obtain credit, or increase his income by working longer, harder, or more competitively.

When a country runs an international payments deficit, it faces similar alternatives. It can sell gold or other reserve assets. It can ask creditor countries to refrain from pressing their claims, to extend it, in effect, additional credit. And it can attempt to cut its outgo and improve its income.

In the years before and immediately after World War II, the United States was a creditor country. Its exports greatly exceeded its imports, and it was unable to export capital rapidly enough to offset the inflow of funds that came here, often in search of a safe haven. The gold stock swelled. Economists worried about a persistent shortage of dollars elsewhere in the world. But, beginning in the late 1950s, the situation changed. As Europe and Japan recovered from the war, their exports became more competitive, displacing American products from world markets. Discovering the profits to be made from overseas operations, United States capital moved abroad, and the balance of payments turned from surplus to deficit.

One result was a halving of the United States gold stock, from more than $22 billion in 1957 to $11 billion in 1968. Another was a rise in foreign official and private claims against the dollar, from $13 billion in 1957 to $41 billion in 1970. The United States was financing its deficits by drawing on past savings, but to a much greater extent it was obtaining credit from such surplus countries as Germany and Japan.

A somewhat accidental result was the development of the Eurodollar market. Eurodollars are dollars on deposit at foreign banks or at the overseas branches of American banks. Under its Regulation Q, the Federal Reserve set interest ceilings on time deposits in the United States, but it neglected to do so on time deposits at foreign branches of American banks. When domestic interest rates in the late 1960s rose above the

FOREIGN CLAIMS TO U.S. RESERVES

Billions of dollars

A series of U.S. payments deficits resulted in a decline in America's gold and other reserves plus a build-up of claims against those reserves.

Regulation Q ceilings, then, the banks were encouraged to bid actively for dollars at their overseas branches. Canny corporate treasurers moved funds from the United States to the Eurodollar market for a small interest rate advantage and no foreign exchange risk. Eventually the banks found themselves not only obtaining funds from but lending directly in the Eurodollar market and competing not only with other American banks but with European institutions as well. The latter, in much the same way that banks in the United States use their deposits at the Federal Reserve, pyramided new deposits atop the Eurodollars they held themselves, creating new money in the process. By the end of 1970 Eurodollar deposits were estimated at $50 billion.

The problem presented by the Eurodollar market arose from the fact that these short-term funds, which move in vast quantities from country to country in response to small changes in interest rates, are under the jurisdiction of no single nation. Because they move unimpeded across national boundaries, Eurodollars play havoc with domestic monetary policies, much more so for small nations than for large, and their rapid growth contributes to world inflation.

The huge quantity of dollars in foreign hands would not have accumulated if, beginning in the late 1950s, the dollar had been permitted to find its own level in the foreign exchange markets. A decline in the value of the dollar would have raised the price of imports and cut the price of exports, automatically eliminating the payments deficit.

Until August 1971, however, the possibility of dollar devaluation was ruled out. Under the Articles of Agreement of the International Monetary Fund, the United States committed itself to a fixed par value of thirty-five dollars equals one ounce of gold. Other signers of the agreement pledged themselves to establish fixed par values for their own currencies, but these could be defined in terms either of gold or the dollar. Thus, the value of other currencies could be changed upward or downward in relation to the dollar, but the value of the dollar remained fixed. As originally conceived, this commitment was less foolish than it might have appeared subsequently. It arose out of experience with the gold standard and with the beggar-thy-neighbor system of the 1930s.

One way a sovereign nation may attempt to cut its outgo and improve its income to finance a balance of payments deficit, as we noted, is to permit its currency to be devalued. Another is to permit, or deliberately induce a slowdown in domestic business activity. Because imports rise and fall sharply in response to home demand, a business slowdown should cut imports. At the same time—or at least it was so in the past—a recession should be able to be counted upon to exert downward pressure on costs, particularly wages, improving the competitiveness of a country's exports.

This was the theory behind the gold standard, the system of international payments that prevailed before World War I, when Britain was the world's foremost trading and investing nation, London its financial capital, and the pound sterling its most readily acceptable currency. Its cornerstone was the free movement of goods, manpower, and capital among nations. In popular belief the system worked automatically, but in actuality the governors of the Bank of England moved their lending rate up and down regularly—195 times between 1880 and 1913—to encourage inflows and outflows of capital. Maintaining the value of the pound was the prime objective, and economic stability was forced to take a back seat.

Another route open to a sovereign nation attempting to cut outgo and improve income is to push the sale of its own goods in world markets but to restrict the sale of imports in its own, to encourage investment from abroad but to limit the movement of capital by its own citizens overseas.

High tariffs, import quotas, export subsidies, and exchange controls are some of the devices employed. They are typical of the beggar-thy-neighbor system of the 1930s, the system that led to depression and to a disastrous decline in world trade and investment.

The representatives of many nations who met at Bretton Woods, New Hampshire, in the waning months of World War II to hammer out a postwar international monetary system rejected both the gold standard and the beggar-thy-neighbor system of the thirties. The latter was unthinkable, and the former required too high a price in unemployment and underutilization of economic resources.

The delegates focused, therefore, on a system that could provide adequate and growing international reserves, interim financing for periods of temporary payments difficulty, and machinery for effecting necessary changes in currency values. What they came up with involved the creation of a new kind of international money, to be used as a supplement to a country's gold and convertible currency reserves. Member nations were to be given drawing rights in an International Monetary Fund, based on their quotas or original contributions of gold or other reserves. A nation with a payments surplus would be required to sell its currency—under the circumstances in considerable demand—to the IMF as its reserves grew, while a nation with a deficit would be able to purchase needed currencies from the IMF as its reserves fell. The drawings were not credit, available only to countries which met proper standards for borrowers, but were to be money in the bank, available unconditionally to all IMF members. Growth in the supply of this international money was to be assured by regular quota increases. Devaluation would be permitted, but only after consultation with the IMF and only when it was agreed that there was "fundamental disequilibrium" in a country's balance of payments, which could mean a deficit that resisted other efforts at correction for three or four years. Large, competitive devaluations were ruled out.

The Bretton Woods delegates recognized that countries with continuing payments surpluses might be as guilty of upsetting the international payments mechanism as countries with regular deficits. To keep such countries from piling up gold and other reserves, therefore, the delegates wanted to encourage them to increase their imports of goods and exports of capital and to revalue their currencies upward if necessary. To achieve these aims, the delegates drafted the "scarce currency" provision, which branded a member country a poor world citizen if it failed to take appropriate action to reduce a long-standing payments surplus. The provisions also permitted other countries to discriminate against a declared reserve hoarder in world trade.

Unfortunately, the International Monetary Fund was not permitted to develop as it was intended. Countries were allowed to avoid regular use of the IMF mechanism. Drawings, conceived as the unconditional right of all member nations, were made subject to tortuous standards of credit worthiness. The "scarce currency" provision was allowed to wither on the vine. Deficit countries came to regard the IMF as a regrettable but often necessary source of bailout credit, and surplus countries tended to ignore it.

The Bretton Woods era came to an end in August 1971 when President Nixon cut the dollar's ties to gold and attempted to force other countries to revalue their currencies upward in relation to the dollar. The handwriting, however, had long been on the wall. It resulted from the failure to implement the original Bretton Woods design. Because of that failure, the world lacked a tried mechanism for regularly increasing monetary reserves, although the authorization of Special Drawing Rights in the IMF, the so-called paper gold, was a first step. More important, the world lacked a means of bringing continuing and effective pressure on both surplus and deficit countries, as well as machinery for avoiding the brief but intense payments crises that increasingly plagued the fixed exchange rate structure.

24. Tariffs and Quotas

Inflation and the long string of American payments deficits it produced—in the absence of an effective international mechanism for bringing undervalued and overvalued currencies back in line—has had at least one predictable effect. It has helped fan the fires of protectionism in the United States.

In the last half of the 1960s, five years of inflation-fueled demand produced a striking deterioration in the United States trade surplus. The dollar value of imports rose two-thirds, while the dollar value of exports rose only a little more than one-third. In the same years the prices of American exports rose 9 percent, while those of other developed nations held roughly stable. The rapid growth of imports—particularly in the textile, apparel, shoe, electronic, steel, and automobile industries—brought insistent demands, from unionized workers as well as company managements, that foreign competition be checked. At the same time the foes of more than thirty years of progress toward liberalizing world trade won strength in their attempts to reverse that policy.

Protectionist sentiment in the United States is not new. From its earliest days, the United States has shown a strange ambivalence toward the question of trade. Domestically it has learned well the lesson of the advantages to be derived from the free movement of goods, manpower, and capital, but externally the teaching has often been forgotten. What isn't always realized is that the American experiment, the success of which now is taken for granted, might never have begun, but might have died aborning. During the critical period when the colonies were governed by the Articles of Confederation, protectionism was rampant.

New York slapped import duties on New Jersey and Connecticut farm products. New Jersey retaliated by boosting the property tax on a Sandy

Hook lighthouse recently bought by New York for the safety of New York Harbor. Because Britain continued to discriminate against imports from the former colonies, retaliatory tariffs were put into effect. But each state acted on its own, the actions of one often canceling those of another.

It should come as no great surprise, then, that commercial interests were the chief supporters of a new constitution or that one of the first powers granted to Congress was the power to regulate commerce with foreign nations and among the several states. The Constitution showed that the sum could be greater than the parts. As new territory was added to the union, each state received the same status and recognition as the original thirteen, and, to prevent the erection of new barriers, a devastating civil war was fought.

At home, the United States was to become a living example of the theory of comparative advantage, of free trade in action. In its relations with other countries, however, it was to show an entirely different face. Tariffs were piled atop tariffs, culminating in the infamous Hawley-Smoot Tariff of 1932, which at its height brought duties paid to 59 percent of the value of the imports upon which they were levied. The devastation wrought by the Hawley-Smoot Tariff, and similar beggar-thy-neighbor efforts in other countries, speaks for itself. Between 1929 and 1933 world trade dropped two-thirds in value and one-third in volume. The United States share was particularly hurt, dropping, during the first half of the 1930s, from 16 to 11 percent of the total.

The long road back began in 1934, when Congress authorized the reciprocal trade agreements program. This permitted bilateral tariff cutting, or tariff cutting between the United States and other countries one at a time. Under these agreements the concessions granted were extended automatically to all other countries. By World War II, partly because of the program and partly because rising prices reduced the effectiveness of specific duties, United States tariffs on dutiable items were down almost 40 percent from their peak levels.

Bilateralism, however, had its limits. In large measure, the gains made under the reciprocal trade agreements program represented the pruning away of excess duties. To preserve bargaining power for later negotiations, tariff cutters tended to break up existing classifications into endless new ones, which effectively discriminated against third countries. At the same time they were powerless to do anything about quantitative limitations on imports, or quotas, a serious problem after World War II, having no power to take action against violators. A new approach was clearly called for.

The General Agreement on Tariffs and Trade was the answer. At Geneva in 1947, the United States negotiated trade agreements with each of twenty-two nations while they concluded agreements with each other. Quotas were prohibited except under unusual circumstances. No specific provision was made for enforcement, but machinery for fact-finding, hearings, and the opportunity to form a common judgment on violations was set up.

In principle, the GATT established that tariffs should be the only restrictions to international trade, that concessions granted by signers should be extended automatically to all other countries, and that signers were obliged to consult before taking action that might be harmful to the interests of others. There were hardship provisions. A signer could invoke quotas if it was experiencing severe international payments deficits, and it could withdraw tariff concessions if imports caused or threatened serious injury to domestic industries. Less developed countries could restrict imports to encourage infant industries.

Nevertheless, the GATT opened the way for a vast expansion of world trade. By 1968 world exports had risen to $213 billion from $53 billion twenty years earlier. The Kennedy Round, the biggest and possibly the last of the major tariff-cutting efforts under the GATT, brought together fifty nations accounting for 80 percent of world trade. The negotiations covered more than $40 billion worth of items, with 70 percent of the dutiable imports of the major participants affected. On some products, tariff reductions amounted to as much as 50 percent.

The Kennedy Round may have been the last major tariff-cutting effort because the barriers to trade that remained were no longer tariffs but quotas and other nontariff barriers, such things as European taxes on big American-made cars and United States health and safety standards, which made it difficult for all but the biggest foreign producers to enter the American market.

The protectionist arguments are familiar: that infant industries need nursing, that foreign competition endangers the jobs of American workers, that goods produced by low-wage foreign workers will flood the country, that the national interest requires self-sufficiency, and that to the United States, at least, foreign trade is unimportant.

The infant industry argument, expounded early in the nation's history by Alexander Hamilton, has some merit. There is no question that some companies that in time might become productive and efficient may be choked off in their infancy by foreign competition. The difficulty is knowing which ones to favor. By erecting barriers against the entrance of foreign widgets, all domestic widget manufacturers, inefficient as well as efficient, old as well as young, are aided. What is more, once granted protection, industries never seem to grow up. Like perennial students reluctant to take their chances in an adult world, protected industries seem to prolong infancy beyond maturity into middle and old age.

There is superficial truth also in the notion that foreign competition endangers the jobs of American workers. Industries heavily protected against import competition do employ more workers than others, and, by way of contrast, industries heavily oriented toward the production of exports employ fewer workers than the average. This says virtually the same thing. Manufacturers who enjoy protection are unwilling or unable to bring down the labor cost per unit of output—a gross of widgets, for instance—and therefore tend to be low-wage, low-profit industries. Exporters, on the other hand, find that investment in new machines, new products, and new techniques of production pays off. Because of their lower labor costs per unit of output, not only are they able to compete without protection in world markets, but they are better able to reward both their workers and their owners. It is no coincidence that America's research-based industries are also its export industries. This is as true of agriculture, where research and capital investment have produced a unique rise in productivity, as of more obvious products of American technology such as computers and jet aircraft.

Another way of looking at the situation is to recognize that industries compete not only for markets but for available resources—workers, materials, and capital. To the degree that tariffs and quotas insulate companies from competition, more resources are channeled into protected industries than would be otherwise, and there is less pressure on them to improve their efficiency, to bring down costs. Like sickly children, they not only have difficulty making their own way alone in the world unaided, but they are highly vulnerable to attack from outside.

The best way, then, for the American economy to ward off attack from low-wage foreign competition is to use its resources as productively as possible. This implies success in holding unit costs down, and profits and wages up. Without artificial barriers, capital will have little difficulty finding its way into industries providing the greatest profit potential, manpower into industries promising the highest potential wages.

It is sometimes argued that foreign trade is unimportant to the United States and that it should be able to afford protection for favored industries if it chooses. Imports, after all, amount to a little more than 3 percent of the total output of goods and services, or gross national product, compared with 20 percent or so in Germany and Britain. This argument, however, neglects the fact that because of its size the United States is the world's largest supplier. (As a group, however, the Common Market nations export more than the United States.) American exports in 1970 were a quarter again as large as those of Germany and more than double those of Britain, Japan and France. If the United States failed to trade abroad, other nations would be denied access to jet aircraft, computers, and other products of advanced American technology.

Equally important, Americans would have to go without, or pay substantially higher prices for, a host of things considered part of their every-day life: coffee, tea, cocoa, bananas, tin, copper and aluminum products, transistor radios, motorbikes, and automobiles. The list is lengthy.

The very presence of competition from small foreign imports helps to keep American automobile prices down and Detroit on its toes. But the absence of foreign trade would make car prices go up even more, because of the vast number of items from abroad that go into every domestically produced car: crude bauxite (from which aluminum is made), antimony, asbestos, beeswax (5 million pounds valued at more than $2 million was imported from twenty-seven countries in one recent year), bismuth, cadmium, chrome ore, cobalt, coconut oil, columbium, copper ore, cork, fluorspar, graphite, industrial diamonds (12 million carats valued at almost $50 million were imported in one recent year), iron ore, jute, lead, manganese, mercury, mica, petroleum, platinum, sisal, tin, tungsten, wool, zinc, and zirconium—plus others.

Low foreign wages are only a relative threat. In a competitive world, they may mean simply that foreign workers make items requiring large amounts of labor in relation to their value, freeing Americans for more productive and more pleasant tasks. This was true of Japan, for instance, when its exports were confined largely to low-value items—earthenware, toys, and cheap textiles—but it is true of Japan no longer. Its cameras, television sets, automobiles, ships, and steel compete not only in price but in quality with the best in the world.

The point here is that a country can keep raising its living standards only by remaining competitive. Freeing world trade is no guarantee that a country will increase its output in relation to the work contributed, or productivity. It must remain inventive, and it must continue to save and invest. But protection works in the wrong direction. It encourages lessened, rather than increased, production per hour of work. Pushed to extreme, protection would keep Americans performing the menial tasks, the rest of the world the more productive and interesting ones.

The notion that national interest requires self-sufficiency is invoked on behalf of almost every industry feeling the pain of import competition, among others in recent years textiles, steel, and chemicals. The idea, as we have seen, dates back to the days of Spanish galleons and British men-of-war, when kings were convinced that the only way for a nation to get ahead was by impoverishing others. The idea has found new life with every major revival of nationalism, particularly in the years between the two world wars, and came to full flower in the burst of protectionism that coincided with the Great Depression, led to a diastrous decline in world trade, and helped give rise to Hitler.

Two things have helped revive protectionism in the United States.

One is the declining importance of agricultural exports, particularly to the South, and the other is the changed attitude of much of American labor. For more than three decades southern agriculture and unionized northern labor were the chief supporters of trade expansion. In recent years, however, the South has moved increasingly out of cotton and tobacco farming into manufactures, chiefly textiles. At the same time not only textiles but such heavily unionized industries as steel and chemicals have come under heavy import competition.

The shifts are reflected in the changed composition of American exports. In 1965 farm products and raw materials accounted for 20.7 percent of the dollar value of exports, manufactures for 57.7 percent. Five years later farm products and raw materials had dropped to 16.9 percent, while manufactures had risen to 62.1 percent.

The new protectionists have ignored the tariff. They have campaigned unashamedly for import quotas, which, of all the barriers to trade, are particularly onerous. If the domestic supply of a commodity falls off unexpectedly—because of a long strike, for instance—tariffs can be paid and the need met. Quotas limit the supply absolutely. So much and no more, is what they determine. With only limited competition from imports, labor is free to press its demands and industry to raise its prices.

It was the growing demand for enactment of quota legislation by Congress that led directly to President Nixon's decision in August 1971 to cut the dollar's historic ties to gold and to impose a 10 percent surtax on imports not already subject to quantitative restrictions. The effect of the surtax, which the President described as temporary, was to wipe out in one stroke much of the progress toward lower tariffs accomplished in the postwar period. The key lay in labor's changing attitudes and the pivotal role of the automobile workers.

Several years earlier, under the threat of obtaining quota legislation, the steel industry had exacted a "voluntary" limitation of exports to the United States by European and Japanese producers. Early in 1971, Japanese textile manufacturers, because of similar pressure, offered the same kind of voluntary agreement, but the proposal was rejected as insufficient by the American industry which held out for legislated quotas. The danger was that the automobile workers, who had watched imports grow to claim one-sixth of the American market, would throw their weight behind the textile, steel, chemical and clothing workers in support of legislated quotas.

This explained the Nixon proposal to remove the 7 percent excise tax on automobiles that accompanied the surtax. Another result of removing the excise tax would be to make the Consumer Price Index look better, offsetting in part at least the higher prices consumers would have to pay for imports or import substitutes because of the surtax, and it would give a big prod to consumer spending. Importantly, however, the out-and-out protectionists would be fended off.*

President Nixon's actions were taken without international consultation, and they violated the treaties governing the General Agreement on Tariffs and Trade and the International Monetary Fund. Actually, however, they may have been the least onerous steps an American President could have taken. There was no question that an overvalued dollar, as the unions so readily agreed, was encouraging the export of investment and jobs from the United States, and despite continued importuning of its trading partners by the United States, there seemed no more likelihood that other countries would respond to entreaty than when the dollar first came under speculative attack more than ten years earlier. Under such circumstances, the imposition of the import surtax which forced open the door to international bargaining was clearly preferable to legislated quotas which slammed the door shut irrevocably.

If the stakes were high, the risks were equally great. The President promised that the surtax would be removed when countries like Japan raised the value of their currencies in terms of the dollar to end the special price advantage Japanese products had enjoyed over American products in the United States and world markets. There was danger that America's trading partners, faced with the loss of export markets, might retaliate against imports from the United States. An even greater danger was that workers and management in import-competitive industries would press for still more protection, particularly legislated quotas.

The problem of quotas has not been an American one alone. Europe, as it has been drawn more closely together in the European Economic Community, or Common Market, has continued quantitative restrictions on a number of products, including man-made textiles.

Quotas may actually damage the industries they were designed to protect. As a result of quotas on lead and zinc imports, for instance, a surplus of many years' standing turned unexpectedly to a shortage. Smelters found themselves unable to obtain enough ore to keep their plants operating.

Like wage and price controls, quotas must be administered. This means shifting the determination of supply and demand from the market to Washington. It means more mountains of paper work, more government officials to do the job. Because of the limited quantity of imports, a determination must be made betweeen those who get and those who are

---

* Still another nod in the direction of the protectionists was a proposal to revive the investment tax credit for business purchases of new machinery and equipment. Imported machinery would benefit but at a lower rate and only after the import surtax was removed.

denied. This means more lobbying, more opportunities for political favoritism.

Other nontariff barriers take a variety of forms: border taxes rebated to domestic producers; governmental purchasing policies that bar foreign competition; marking, labeling, and packaging requirements difficult for importers to meet; burdensome paperwork; excessive health and safety requirements; patent, trademark, and copyright regulations that fail to protect imports; restrictions on advertising.

One problem is that one country's environmental or safety requirements may be viewed by another as nontariff barriers, an example of which is the heavy European taxes on high-horsepower automobiles. Europeans view these taxes as essential to keep their narrow streets from becoming hopelessly clogged. American producers, on the other hand, view them as discrimination against the traditional Detroit product. In contrast, European and Japanese automobile makers have been described as viewing the increasingly severe United States automobile safety and antipollution requirements as a subtle form of discrimination against imports.

The growing campaign to clean up the American air and water has had another effect. It has put a cost burden on United States producers not shared by manufacturers in less fastidious nations. Steel, automobile, and chemical manufacturers, among others, have warned that the costs may encourage more imports and further price American products out of world markets. Indeed, a significant proportion of American investment has already been shifted overseas. How this has come about and what it may mean is the subject of the next chapter.

25. Foreign Investment

An overvalued dollar, the almost certain product of years of inflationary excesses and a creaking exchange adjustment mechanism, has had another predictable result, a larger outflow of investment funds from the United States.

The great increase in imports relative to exports was circumstantial evidence that it was becoming more profitable to produce abroad. So was the inflow of imported products that bore the labels of American manufacturers: General Motors' Opels from Germany, Fords from Britain, and Simcas, a Chrysler product, from France; SCM typewriters and Gillette razor blades from England; portable radios and television sets of all makes from Japan and Taiwan; and shirts, underwear, and fashions from Hong Kong.

Figures tended to offer confirmation. As capital export controls—in effect since the early 1960s—began to be dismantled, there was a renewed rise in direct investment by American concerns in overseas subsidiaries. After having held steady for three years at about $3 billion, such investment jumped to $4.4 billion in 1970.

The figures, however, were highly suspect. During the period of tight capital export controls, overseas subsidiaries of American concerns were forced to rely increasingly on locally borrowed funds and on retained earnings. It seemed quite possible that a relaxation of the barriers might not only produce a greater outflow of capital to these and other subsidiaries but a greater return flow of investment income.

What wasn't generally appreciated was that a basic change had occurred, not only in the United States, but in most other developed nations. The movement of private long-term investment had become bigger than exports and imports in the calculation of international payments deficits and surplus, and trade had become increasingly dependent on these investment flows.

In the United States much of the increase was in direct investment. By 1967, according to one estimate, United States investment in overseas subsidiaries amounted to $60 billion and accounted for $120 billion of world production, an output four times the value of American exports. Even more important, fully one fourth of the dollar value of American exports represented purchases by subsidiaries of United States concerns abroad.

There were confusing aspects to the situation, however. The capital outflow from the United States was under way before the inflation-fueled boom of the late 1960s. The big jump occurred in the first half of the decade, when prices were relatively stable. Also, there was some indication that inflation might be resulting in a greater pull of direct investment into the country than a push abroad. Foreign investment in American subsidiaries, after languishing at an annual rate of $100 million for the first half of the 1960s, jumped to $258 million in 1967, to $832 million in 1969, and to $969 million in 1970. And while the gap was still wide— United States investment in overseas subsidiaries was five times as great as foreign direct investment in America in 1970—a decade earlier it had been twenty times as great.

Any conclusions necessarily were tentative. Although investment flows had become an increasingly important part of the balance of payments of every developed nation, very little was known about them and even less was published.

One questionable verdict was that the United States was taking over Europe. The French journalist, J.-J. Servan-Schreiber, noted that in the years 1958–1967 American corporations had invested $10 billion in Europe, more than a third of their total investment abroad.* In one year alone, 1965, he said, American investment in Europe had increased $4 billion. Of this 90 percent represented credits and subsidies from European governments and borrowings in the Eurocapital market. Only 10 percent represented direct dollar transfers from the United States.

"In other words," M. Servan-Schreiber concluded, "we pay them to buy us."

There was more than one reason for the big bulge in American corporate investment in Europe: the rebirth of the continent after the ravages of World War II and the growth of its peoples' incomes; the efforts of governments to spur direct investments; and the determination of United States antitrust authorities to break up market-sharing arrangements, where they existed, between American companies and overseas cartels.

* *The American Challenge,* New York, Atheneum, 1968, p. 14.

Chiefly, however, the American interest in Europe grew out of the formation of the European Economic Community, or Common Market. After two world wars, in which their very survival was in doubt, six former belligerents—France, West Germany, Italy, the Netherlands, Belgium, and Luxembourg—elected to form the Common Market. The signing of the Treaty of Rome in 1957 marked its inception. Starting with the lowering and eventual removal of tariffs among members, the Six were to move steadily toward full economic integration. By cutting internal tariffs, the Common Market held out the prospect of greater intramural growth, and, by maintaining an external wall, it sought to prevent or at least delay foreigners from sharing in this growth. The result was somewhat unexpected. The external tariff wall encouraged foreign producers to leap over it by investing directly within the new economic community.

And leap they did. British, Swedish, Swiss, and American companies —particularly the American—stepped up their investments appreciably. French, German, and Italian companies talked about merger, but American companies were the first to set up area-wide marketing and production facilities, the first to make acquisitions in several European countries. For a time it seemed as if the Common Market might become an anachronism before it was fully functioning.

As an American arriving in almost any European city, it might seem to you that M. Servan-Schreiber's thesis that Europe was being taken over by American corporations needed little documentation. Arriving on a Pan American plane, you can rent a Ford from Hertz and fill it with Esso gasoline. At breakfast you can have Kellogg's cornflakes and Libby's tomato juice, and a maid will probably use a Hoover vacuum to clean your Hilton hotel room. If you fail to look about carefully, you might think you had never left home.

What M. Servan-Schreiber failed to perceive, however, was that the phenomenon was not purely American, that direct overseas investment by countries other than the United States was moving ahead in line with the size and growth rates of their economies. What was happening was that business, in Europe and Japan as well as the United States, was reaching out internationally, much as it had broken out from its local or regional orientation in the United States several generations before. The situation was not unlike the challenge to the neighborhood grocer posed by the A & P—and the emotional response was not dissimilar, either.

If the movement at first was largely American, it reflected the greater size of the American economy, its greater pool of funds for investment, and its earlier experimentation both with national and international corporate structures. One estimate for the mid-1960s gave the United

States 60 percent of all overseas direct investment, the rest of the world 40 percent. But this lopsided mix seemed unlikely to persist. The fact that Europe and Japan were growing more rapidly than the United States, plus the development of an international capital market, suggested that American corporations operating overseas would face increasing challenge from abroad.

Investment is like trade in helping to distribute the fruits of technological innovation and efficient production, but its effects are far more profound. The end of regionalism in American industry meant a leveling of wages and other costs. The new national corporations borrowed where they could do so most cheaply, usually in New York, and invested where costs were lowest and the prospect for profits were greatest. This probably did more to raise wages and lower interest costs in the South, it has been said, than either trade by local concerns or the limited movement of manpower or portfolio investment.

Similarly, direct international investment—the two-way interchange among the developed nations, at least—is moving in the direction of a closer-knit world in which all peoples enjoy a more nearly equal distribution of the fruits of production. Capital, past savings applied to current production, is extremely flexible. Invested in fertilizer, soil improvement, and better seed, it may be used to improve the return from land, and, invested in public health outlays and technical training, it may be used to upgrade the return from labor. Thought of another way, capital investment in a nuclear power plant may be considered a substitute for natural resources in a country deficient in coal or other fossil fuels. In the form of machinery, it may be considered a substitute for manpower in a labor-short economy.

The changed nature of capital and its increasing mobility are important influences bringing industrialized nations closer together and making them more alike. At one time, wealth in the ground and wealth in men's backs were the two principal sources of capital. Increasingly, however, wealth in men's minds—the ability to make new technological discoveries and to develop and manage them—has gained in importance. With this change, capital has been shifted more readily from place to place. Capital invested in a copper mine, for instance, is fixed in locale. It can't be moved from the site of the ore body. But capital invested in a research and development team is as mobile as those who staff it. Such people tend to migrate to areas where other professionals like themselves are situated, where the educational facilities are good, and where recreational and cultural opportunities abound. There is little, however, to prevent other areas from beckoning them away.

The increasing importance of wealth in the mind may even cause capital to flow upstream. Most investment still moves in the direction of areas with lower costs, particularly lower wages, and higher potential profits. Companies based in countries where technology has lagged may establish subsidiaries in higher-cost areas, however, if they perceive an opportunity to tap into a superior technology or to utilize improved management techniques—which can result in whittling down the advantage one nation may have over others as the result of technological superiority. European and Japanese steel mills got the jump on the American industry because of their early adoption of the basic oxygen process, but it should not be impossible to overcome their lead. On the other hand, although the United States is ahead in the manufacture of jet aircraft and computers, it should not regard its position with complacency.

The free movement of capital across national boundaries, like the unrestricted movement of goods, is a step in the direction of one world—but not necessarily so. It may simply be a step toward larger regional trading blocs. Just as modern nations emerged first from duchies and then from federations of smaller nation-states, so the world today is moving toward larger economic units. The pace, however, is by no means steady, nor is the outcome inevitable. Logic may dictate the removal of barriers to the movement of goods and investment; reason may argue for the harmonization of transport, tax, labor, antitrust, and farm policies; and common sense may prescribe a unified currency. But the force of nationalism may prevail over logic, reason, and common sense.

Nationalists sometimes find themselves on the horns of a dilemma, as their reponse to the formation of the Common Market shows. For nationalists, the Common Market held out the happy prospect that the nations of Europe would be strengthened in their ability to confront the rest of the world, particularly the United States. It held out the appalling possibility also, however, that member countries might be submerged in the new union. French foot-dragging, then, slowed realization of the original vision. It also invited a defensive response from Great Britain and six smaller European nations denied charter membership in the Common Market. The so-called Outer Seven—Sweden, Norway, Denmark, Switzerland, Austria, and Portugal, in addition to the United Kingdom—banded together to form the European Free Trade Association. This was a limited partnership founded for the purpose of reducing trade barriers and thus of protecting the smaller countries against the new giant on the Continent.

In October 1971, after French opposition had been withdrawn, parliament approved British entry, paving the way eventually for most of the EFTA countries to join as well.

There is no inevitability to the free movement of capital across national borders any more than there is inevitability to the free movement of goods. The French, for instance, could have prohibited American companies from establishing subsidiaries in France. Indeed, there was much fulmination against attempts of several large American companies to take over French concerns. In the end, however, there was no ban, since prohibition would have denied France access to American technology and management techniques and might also have slowed the movement of goods. The Communist nations of eastern Europe do not discourage trade with the West. But their prohibition against foreign investment—Yugoslavia is an exception—limits the transfer of manufactured products between subsidiaries of foreign concerns and the parent country.

No country, of course, is obliged to accept foreign investment. Do-it-yourself development, however, is difficult, costly, and not often successful. Without violent social upheaval and subsequent authoritarian control, such as that which emerged from the Russian and Chinese revolutions, or a unique exercise of national willpower, such as that of postwar Japan, it is difficult for a country to divert enough resources from current consumption to capital investment to spur rapid and sustained economic growth.

A chronic shortage of capital is a crucial problem of the less-developed countries. It is not the only problem, or even the most critical one. The latter is the pressure of an exploding population on a limited food supply, for the population of the less-developed countries is growing about 2.5 percent a year, compared with 1.1 percent for the developed nations. In some developing lands the rate of population growth may be as high as 3.8 percent a year, which means that the less-developed countries could double their population in as little as twenty or thirty years. And since even now, it is estimated that 10 to 15 percent of the world population is undernourished and that up to 50 percent suffers some degree of hunger or malnutrition, food supplies would have to more than double to meet requirements.

Investment is no substitute for controlling population growth and hunger and the associated misery of poor housing, inadequate medical care, and insufficient education. A reduction of only 0.1 percent in population growth in the less-developed countries, it has been estimated, would be the equivalent of $600 million in capital investment. Nevertheless, investment—properly channeled and efficiently utilized—can go far toward advancing a country from less developed to developed status.

The less-developed countries suffer from the fact that they are raw-material suppliers, while the developed lands are producers of manufactured goods. Seven commodities—cocoa, coffee, copper, cotton, rubber, tin, and wool—account for one-quarter of the export earnings of the less-developed countries outside Europe if petroleum is excluded.

These are products in which no nation enjoys a monopoly, and they are products subject to severe price competition, both from other supplier nations and from synthetics.

The prices of manufactured goods, by way of contrast, reflect the high values placed on scarce new products, on items in close step with current fashion, and on monopoly production. It is significant that, of fifteen countries accounting for three-quarters of world trade in 1968, all but one—a major oil producer—were industrial countries. Two decades earlier the same fifteen nations had accounted for only two-thirds of world trade.

Far from narrowing, the gap between the developed and the less-developed world has been widening. What is needed is investment—capital for roads, telephones, power systems, schools, irrigation, and drainage from public sources, capital for manufacturing from private. The Development Assistance Committee of the Organization for Economic Cooperation and Development has proposed that the sixteen developed nations that comprise its membership direct 1 percent of their national incomes into investment—both public and private—in the less-developed countries.

The goal has not been met. Official aid has been trimmed, and private investment has failed to reach hoped-for levels. One reason is the cool reception investment sometimes receives in the less-developed countries, and another is the conditions sometimes placed on private investment. A country may insist, for instance, that a manufacturing company produce all parts locally instead of importing some, even when it is uneconomic to do so. It may compel the subsidiary of a foreign company to divide its ownership and profits with its own nationals, which may seem only fair, but such an insistence may cause an international company to favor subsidiaries in other countries where the condition does not apply. Thus, it may deny the country the wages for its workers, market for suppliers, and demand for financial and other services that such an enterprise might bring.

The problem won't go away. By 1975, it is estimated, the needs of the less-developed countries will involve an international payments cost of $20 billion a year or more.

26. The International Monetary Structure

For the international monetary structure, the postwar era came to an end when President Nixon went before television cameras on a Sunday night in August 1971 to announce that the United States was cutting the dollar's ties to gold and imposing a 10 percent surtax on imports to improve the competitive capacity of American industry in world markets and stanch a hemorrhage in the United States balance of payments. What would follow was far from clear. A prolonged period of international negotiation seemed likely before some new machinery would be found, but there seemed little doubt that the monetary mechanism that had evolved from a conference at Bretton Woods, New Hampshire, in the waning days of World War II was being superseded.

The international monetary system that evolved after Bretton Woods, in contrast to the grand design laid down there, was frequently rocked by crises. It is not too much to say that it invited them.

Both overvalued and undervalued currencies came under pressure, the latter more often than the former. The dollar drew fire not only because of American policies that shook its value in foreign exchange markets but because of its position as the principal reserve and trading currency.

A devaluation crisis, such as sterling weathered in 1964 but was unable to survive in 1967 and the one to which the franc succumbed two years later, developed in fairly typical fashion. First, over a period of a year or two there were a string of payments deficits that failed to respond to the conventional remedies. Then, the currency weakened and frequent government intervention was needed to keep it above the exchange floor. Often an untoward event occurred, such as the dock strike in Britain or the student riots in France, which brought in the speculators. Their selling in the forward market caused commercial exchange users who did not ordinarily do so to cover their positions, adding to the downward pressures and forcing the government to intervene almost continuously. As reserves poured out, the government was forced to ask itself whether defense of the old fixed par value was worth the price. The answer was often reluctant devaluation.

Speculators play the same role in foreign exchange markets as they do in commodity futures trading. They help to absorb the risks of day-to-day and seasonal price fluctuations and give the market added breadth, depth, and resiliency. Under the Bretton Woods system of rigid exchange rates, however, betting on a valuation change was a favored kind of risk-taking. It was low cost, low risk, and encouraged by interest rate differences among nations that often couldn't be readily eliminated. Speculation wasn't limited to the forward exchange market. Someone expecting the value of sterling, for instance, to rise might buy spot sterling for dollars now, expecting to resell it later at a higher rate of exchange. Someone expecting sterling to decline might borrow sterling and sell it in the spot market, expecting to buy it back at a lower exchange rate before his loan became due. The bull had an immediate dollar outlay, the bear an interest cost—each in addition to the exchange risk.

By way of contrast, speculation in the forward exchange market involved no immediate outlay of dollars, unless margin or earnest money was required, and it incurred no interest cost. A bull bought sterling for forward delivery hoping that he would be able to resell it in the spot market at a higher price when the contract matured. A bear sold sterling forward hoping that he would be able to buy sterling in the spot market below his contract price in time to make delivery. The risk was limited by the government's pledge to intervene in the spot market 1 percent either side of the fixed par value.

Pressure on the forward market, which was quickly translated to the spot market, was exacerbated by widening gaps between key short-term interest rates that could not always be closed quickly. Take the case of liquid funds that might as readily be invested in United States or British Treasury bills. When the discount rate on British Treasury bills rose above that on United States Treasury bills, it became advantageous to shift funds from New York to London. Investors who did this, however, wanted to be sure that they could transfer their funds back into dollars at maturity without incurring an exchange risk. So they sold sterling forward. At some point the decline in the forward rate would wipe out the interest rate advantage of British Treasury bills, so the transfer of funds halted before that point was reached. Funds usually would flow as long as a half-point and sometimes a quarter-point advantage remained.

A dollar crisis was a bit different from other currency crises. Since other currencies were pegged to the dollar and the dollar alone was pegged to gold, it might be experienced in one of two ways or both: the appreciation of other currencies, notably those of countries with surplus payments positions, or a rise in the free market price of gold. Often the paternity of a speculative buildup like the one that preceded the 1969 revaluation of the German mark was a matter of semantics. If the Germans were to blame for not abandoning the old valuation sooner, it was a mark crisis. If the United States was to blame for not doing a better job of controlling inflation, it was a dollar crisis.

A rise in the free market price of gold reflected the betting of speculators that the United States would be forced to abandon its fixed price of thirty-five dollars an ounce in favor of a higher price for monetary gold.

At one time gold was not only a medium of international settlement but coin of the realm. Its characteristics—high value, durability, and divisibility—caused it to be accepted as a monetary medium without equal. But the very fact that made gold valuable, its limited supply, led to its gradual replacement as money.

The California gold rush of 1849 and the Klondike gold rush of 1898 demonstrated that such finds could touch off vast internal economic expansions, but there was no way of assuring that the supply of money would increase at a proper pace, neither too slow nor too fast. To assure a more manageable money supply, the Federal Reserve system was created. Gold has gradually been dethroned internationally in much the same way, first by supplementing it as a reserve medium with dollars and SDRs, then by restricting the existing monetary gold supply to use by central banks, and finally by withdrawal of the United States pledge to buy or sell at a fixed price.

The acceptance of the dollar as a reserve medium arose in part from the fact that the United States is by far the world's biggest overseas trader and investor. It arose also from its role as banker to the world. This was a role the United States did not choose but had thrust upon it as a result of the flight of capital from Europe during the 1930s and the devastation of World War II. The United States entered the war with the biggest of all economies and emerged with its resources intact and and its productive capacity unscathed. Is it any wonder that the dollar became a universally accepted international reserve currency?

If the United States did not opt to become central banker to the world, it did little to eschew the role—except, of course, to treat its position irresponsibly. The continuing string of United States balance of payments deficits, as we have noted, threatened to break the world into trading blocs, accelerated the trend toward multinational organization of business, and produced frequent currency crises.

Early in the 1960s, when the question of whether the dollar was overvalued was still debatable, the United States took a number of emergency measures. These included the erection outside the IMF of a network of currency swap arrangements with European central banks, "tying" foreign aid to purchases of goods made in America, an unsuccessful attempt to restrict overseas travel, and a "temporary" restriction on lending and investing abroad that was proving difficult to dismantle a decade later.

If these were hardly the marks of a nation moving toward one world economically, they were understandable as the desperation moves of an international banker trying to halt a run. The emergency measures of the early 1960s did not halt the speculative attacks. Under United States prodding, and after four years of difficult negotiation, a plan for the creation of Special Drawing Rights (SDRs) was approved by the International Monetary Fund at Rio de Janeiro in 1967. SDRs were addressed to the problem of providing international liquidity, but it was soon apparent that they did nothing to oil the sticky balance-of-payments adjustment mechanism.

The Rio meeting was hardly out of the way when the pound and the dollar came under attack again. For the pound, late in the year, the result was sterling's second postwar devaluation. For the dollar the result was a huge outflow of gold. By March 1968 the United States was forced to announce that it, and the other leading nations from whom it obtained agreement, would no longer feed gold to the private market. A two-tier gold price was thus born, the free market price for private transactions, the thirty-five-dollar-an-ounce fixed price for monetary transactions.

With the United States gold stock protected from direct speculative assault, the pressure grew upon Germany, the chief nation with a continuing payments surplus, to adjust the value of the mark upward. In September 1969, after the French devalued the franc, Germany permitted the mark to float. This was a temporary device, not a commitment to flexible exchange rates, but it produced none of the havoc predicted by advocates of rigidly fixed rates and greatly strengthened the case for more frequent exchange rate adjustment. The mark moved upward promptly, and when it had found a new level official parity was re-established.

The siege of the dollar was not over yet, however. The big pull of Eurodollars into the United States by American banks, the flow of European funds into the American stock market, and the transfer of certain official foreign claims from short term to long term—the kind of now-you-see-it, now-you-don't accounting that would have caused the Securities and Exchange Commission to pounce on a securities issuer —helped for several years to paper over the huge underlying deficits in the balance of payments. By 1971 these could no longer be concealed, and one result was renewed demands for formal dollar devaluation.

Until it cut the dollar's ties to gold, the United States had never seriously considered devaluation. Even then, President Nixon insisted the dollar wasn't being devalued. Other countries, notably Japan, were being encouraged to raise the value of their currencies in terms of the dollar. It was thought unlikely that other nations would permit the world's largest trading nation to devalue without retaliating, and, more important, devaluation by the United States—in the sense that it meant a rise in the dollar price of gold—would reward gold-holding and producing countries, including South Africa and the Soviet Union, and would penalize those nations, mostly less-developed lands, that held their reserves in dollars.

The chief point was that devaluation would not make the United States less irresponsible as banker to the world and might make it more so. Increasingly, however, it was recognized that the matter of responsibility was not America's burden alone. In retrospect, the sixties might have been less difficult if Germany and other surplus nations had been less export oriented and had made more frequent upward exchange adjustments, if France had been less single-minded in its pursuit of solely national objectives, and if Japan had been more receptive to capital imports. A common failing was that no nation seemed fully ready to accept the fact that every country can't enjoy a payments surplus at the same time. Countries that chided the United States for its deficits pursued policies that collectively made it difficult for any reduction to be achieved.

One thing that was needed, if the system was not to collapse, was a steady increase in world money, roughly in line with the expected increase in world trade and investment. SDRs were an answer, unfortunately not the whole one. In the first three years of their use, 1970–72, $9.5 billion of SDRs were to be allocated, a third roughly each year. This compared with total monetary gold holdings of slightly more than $41 billion. In time it was expected that SDRs would gradually supplant dollars in the reserve holdings of governments and central banks. Even among official holders, however, the dollar seemed likely to remain in some demand, if only because such dollar obligations as United States Treasury bills earned the going market interest rates— close to 7 percent at their peak in 1970—while gold earned no return and SDRs a nominal 1.5 percent.

Gold and SDRs, moreover, could not be used for commercial transactions. As long as dollars remained the preferred currency for international trade and investment, continued private demand from abroad could be expected, which meant United States payments deficits—deficits large enough to facilitate the growth of world trade and investment but not so large as to keep the dollar permanently overvalued or to subvert domestic monetary management in other countries.

Easier said than done, perhaps, for even if the United States were once again to achieve sustainable price stability and economic growth, the surplus countries were under no compulsion to step up the pace of their own economic expansion or to revalue their currencies upward. Nor were they under any obligation to behave in a gentlemanly way or even consistently in their acceptance of claims against the dollar. If they disliked the purpose for which the American deficit was being used —the Vietnam war, for example—they could cash in their chips. If they were pleased with the way things were going, they could extend credit to the United States indefinitely.

It was possible that the issue of reserve adequacy—as distinct from the need for a growing currency to serve as a vehicle for international trade and investment—was fictitious. If exchange rates could be kept in adjustment, reserve transfers might be obviated.

Three approaches to greater flexibility were widely debated. One, floating rates, would permit market forces alone to determine currency values. Another, wider bands, would permit the value of a currency to fluctuate to a greater degree either side of its fixed value before its government or central bank was obliged to intervene in the market. A third, the so-called sliding peg, would permit currency values to respond to changed market conditions, but only at regular intervals and after some period of time.

The differences among the proposals centered around the questions of how rapidly the market should be permitted to adjust, how much official intervention should remain, and what role, if any, speculators might be expected to play. Fears were expressed that swift changes in rates might make trade and investment more precarious, especially if intervention were removed, and that export industries and those that compete with imports might suffer disruption as manpower and capital were shifted toward more efficient uses. An unfettered exchange market, on the other hand, seemed likely not only to increase the speculative risk of betting on changes in currency valuations but to work in the direction of lower barriers to trade and investment. As for business risk, the freedom from large, sudden shifts in currency values seemed to outweigh the uncertainty that might increase from day-to-day or seasonal variations.

Without changing its rules, the International Monetary Fund agreed, smaller and more frequent exchange rate adjustments could be accommodated.

A major experiment with floating rates by Canada, from 1950 to 1961, produced none of the dire consequences predicted by advocates of rigidly fixed rates. In the face of huge capital imports, Canada in September 1950 abandoned an attempt to hold the Canadian dollar at its existing value of 90.91 cents (U.S.). The value of the Canadian dollar immediately moved upward until, by February 1952, it had risen to a premium over the United States dollar. Then, over a period of a little more than eight years, it floated at a premium that never rose above 6 percent and was usually between 2 and 4 percent. Under prodding from the IMF, which seemed to regard Canada as a misbehaving child, the experiment was abandoned in fact in 1961 and officially a year later, when a new par value was established.

Various explanations were offered for the embarrassing Canadian success, most of them relating to the United States dollar's fixed par value and Canada's close economic ties to the United States. Few who studied the question were willing to credit the market process, and in an essay reviewing the episode, A. F. W. Plumptre, Canada's assistant deputy director of finance at the time and her executive director on the board of the International Monetary Fund, wondered why. He wrote:

> Our beliefs about the normal behavior of exchange markets are perhaps perverted by the fact that there have been relatively few occasions when an exchange market has actually been left alone to look after itself, without even the anticipation of official direction. Further, floating rates have so often been associated with unstable economic conditions, as they were during the aftermath of World War I and during the Great Depression, that they have acquired for themselves an aura of inevitable instability.*

Another occasion was to present itself at the end of May 1970 when, in the face of a strong payments position and domestic inflation, the Canadian government again withdrew its defense of an existing par value and permitted the Candian dollar to float upward.

The problems involved in greater exchange flexibility were dramatized a year later when, after a brief, intense pounding, the mark and several currencies closely tied to it were permitted to float upward again. The episode was described as a dollar crisis, and certainly, in light of the symptoms, that was what it appeared to be. The price of gold rose in London and Zurich. The dollar was at the floor against all major European currencies.

The proximate cause of the crisis was a huge outpouring of short-

---

* *Essays in Honor of Thorkil Kristensen,* Paris, Organization for Economic Co-operation and Development, 1970, p. 160.

term funds from the United States to Europe. This could be viewed as a hangover from the United States inflationary binge, for the Eurodollars that had been pulled here in 1968–69 were returning, in a rush.

A rise in the value of the mark was seen by informed Germans as the quickest, most practical way of checking excess demand, particularly from export industries. But it was not universally welcomed. It seemed likely to delay, at least until the continental currencies had settled at new par values, negotiations leading toward a common currency for the Common Market. A common currency, of course, meant no exchange variations among the mark, the lira, the guilder, and the French and Belgian francs. To get there, the negotiations were attempting steadily to narrow the range of fluctuations. And France was in no mood for revaluation. On the other hand, the mark revaluation might help shoehorn Britain into the economic community, for one of the principal misgivings on the continent about British entry concerned the value of sterling and the role it might be expected to play in a widened union.

The episode held several lessons. One was that all leading nations could be given credit for good behavior, or at least good intentions, and that a crisis could still occur. The whole thing could be put down to differences in the business cycle in Europe and in the United States. Germany, which was determined to beat down inflation, had permitted interest rates to rise, and the United States, which had gone through its chastening, had permitted interest rates to fall to encourage recovery. It was as simple as that.

Another lesson was that crises no longer need months, or even weeks, to develop. In a time of instant communications and instant money flows, they can occur in days. Under such circumstances the coordinated management of interest rates by central banks, seen by some as a remedy, becomes more difficult than ever.

Early in 1971, it seemed possible that the United States international payments position might be beginning to improve. The figures for the previous year, when they were published, indicated gains in both the current account and net liquidity balances, although capital outflows showed a big rise. By midsummer, however, it was apparent that any appearance of improvement had been an illusion. In the second quarter, the surplus of exports over imports reversed and the United States was threatened with its first full-year trade deficit of the century. As the information became known, the dollar came under attack once again in foreign exchange markets, the price of gold rose, and governments were forced to intervene in the market to keep the value of their currencies from rising in relation to the dollar. By mid-August the pressures had become intense.

This was the situation when President Nixon went before the television cameras to announce his new three-part economic plan. Although he described the plan as a trinity of equal parts, to combat unemployment, inflation and the troubles of the dollar, concern for the dollar clearly dominated. The key items were the 10 percent surtax on imports and the severing of the dollar's ties to gold. The surtax meant that foreign producers would have to increase their prices in the American market by up to 10 percent or trim their profits to absorb the added cost. Cutting the dollar's ties to gold meant that foreign nations might continue to finance a United States payments deficit but they could no longer expect to redeem the dollars they received in gold. If countries revalued their currencies upward in relation to the dollar as the United States hoped, the surtax would be removed but their producers would have to increase their prices worldwide or trim their profits to absorb the added costs.

The domestic aspects of the Nixon program followed from the international ones. The wage-price freeze was inevitable if industries that benefited from the new-found protection of the import surtax weren't to embark on a spree of price-gouging. The budgetary aspects of the program were window dressing to make it appear to the world that the President meant what he said about restraining inflation.

At home, the reaction to the President's plan was generally favorable. Overseas, however, it produced consternation and anger. The United States was not the first country to violate the rules of the General Agreement on Tariffs and Trades by imposing an added tax on imports. Britain had done much the same thing when faced with its 1964 payments crisis. Nor was the United States the only country to flout the rules of the International Monetary Fund by attempting to break its currency away from a fixed par value. Canada, West Germany and the Netherlands did much the same thing when they decided to let their currencies float. The American moves were made, however, without consultation. They hit the world with much the effect of a nuclear explosion. No one questioned America's power as the world's largest trading nation, but few expected it to use this power to bludgeon a realignment of world currency values.

If there was no immediate retaliation, it was because America's trading partners stood to lose far more than the United States, with its vast internal market, from any contraction of commerce. Unless agreement was reached quickly, however, there was little doubt that there would be repercussions. Because of the 1969 revaluation of the West German mark, earnings of the big German automobile producer, Volkswagen, had come under severe pressure and the West German offspring of Zeiss, the camera concern,* had closed its doors. It was likely that such major Japanese export concerns as Toyota, Nissan and Sony would survive a major revaluation of the yen, but there almost certainly would be casualties among smaller companies.

This was simply another way of saying that in every country trading with the United States, there were internal political pressures no less compelling than those in the United States that caused Mr. Nixon to act. One result, in all probability would be the fall of some governments. Another, unless agreement was reached quickly and the import surtax was removed, was a proliferation of counter measures. The spectre of the spiraling downturn of the years between the two world wars was raised anew.

What the United States wanted was a $13 billion turnaround in its trade account, from a projected $5 billion deficit in 1971 to an $8 billion surplus in 1972. This would permit it to finance $4 billion of government aid plus a $2 billion private capital outflow, and give it a $2 billion margin of safety. This meant a much bigger revaluaton of other currencies, particularly the Japanese yen, in terms of the dollar.† In addition, the United States asked that Europe and Japan open their doors further to United States trade and investment and that they absórb a bigger share of defense costs.

Europe and Japan, for their part, demanded that the United States bear some of the political burden of dollar devaluation. They refused to accept the American contention that the responsibility for realignment of currency values was theirs alone, to be obtained by revaluing their currencies upward in terms of the dollar, and insisted that the United States also formally devalue by increasing the price of gold. One suggestion was a 10 percent increase to $38.50 an ounce. Foreign products would be equally disadvantaged in world markets whether the devaluation of the dollar occurred one way or the other, but a formal devaluation in terms of the price of gold might make it easier for a French politician, or a Japanese, to sell the settlement to his constituents. "See," he would be able to say, "we gave, but we forced the Americans to give, too." The negotiations centered in the Group of Ten, an informal grouping of the leading monetary and industrial nations: the United States, Belgium, Canada, France, West Germany, Italy, Japan, the Netherlands, Sweden, and the United Kingdom.‡

* The East German concern of the same name was a wholly separate enterprise.

† All major currencies were permitted to float after President Nixon imposed the import surtax and cut the dollar's ties to gold, but tight exchange controls in Japan and France limited the upward revaluation.

‡ On December 18, 1971, President Nixon said he would ask Congress to raise the price of gold from $35 an ounce to $38 an ounce, or 8.57%, the equivalent of

It was becoming apparent, then, that gold might still have usefulness—as a magnificent fiction. The irony of the situation was that only a few months earlier it had seemed on its way to monetary oblivion.

For all the seemingly intractable differences between the United States and its trading partners, there was considerable agreement on the essentials of a new monetary structure. The system of fixed par values should be restored. The bands of permissible fluctuation around parity should be widened. The role of the dollar as a reserve currency should be reduced. And international reserves should be denominated in some common unit of account, such as SDRs.

Beyond these areas of agreement, however, there was still need for a mechanism to permit regular adjustment of par values, for as long as one nation remained more inflationary or less productive than another, the likelihood of payments deficits, speculative attacks on its currency and devaluation remained. And there was still no compulsion on surplus countries to revalue their currencies upward.

---

a 7.89% devaluation of the dollar. New central exchange rates were established for other major currencies looking toward an overall dollar devaluation of about 12%. In giving temporary approval to the move the IMF said it would permit currencies to fluctuate in wider bands, 2¼% either side of the new central rates. Subsequently, the president removed the 10% import surtax.

Index